MIND AT EASE

MIND AT EASE

SELF-LIBERATION THROUGH MAHAMUDRA MEDITATION

TRALEG KYABGON
Foreword by Khenchen Thrangu

SHAMBHALA
Boston & London
2004

Shambhala Publications, Inc.
Horticultural Hall
300 Massachusetts Avenue
Boston, Massachusetts 02115
www.shambhala.com

9 8 7 6 5 4 3 2 1

First Shambhala Edition
Printed in the United States of America

Designed by Ruth Kolbert

♾ This edition is printed on acid-free paper that meets
the American National Standards Institute Z39.48 Standard.
Distributed in the United States by Random House, Inc.,
and in Canada by Random House of Canada Ltd

Library of Congress Cataloging-in-Publication Data
Kyabgon, Traleg, 1955−
Mind at ease: self-liberation through Mahamudra meditation/
Traleg Kyabgon.—1st Shambhala Ed.
p.   cm.
Includes bibliographical references and index.
ISBN 1-59030-156-0 (Pbk. : alk. paper)
1. Mahāmudrā (Tantric rite)   2. Spiritual life—Bka'-rgyud-pa
(Sect) I. Title
BQ7699.M34 K93 2004
294.3'4435—dc22
2003026572

I would like to dedicate this book to the continuity and the propagation of the great Dagpo Kagyu lineage.

CONTENTS

———

PART THREE
PATH MAHAMUDRA

PART FOUR
FRUITION MAHAMUDRA

THRANGU TASHI CHOELING

༄༅། །གསང་སྔགས་རྡོ་རྗེ་ཐེག་པའི་ ཉམས་ལེན་སྐོར་ ཐུན་མོང་གི་སྟོན་འགྲོ་དང་ ཚོད་མེད་བཞི་ ཞི་
གནས་ ལྷག་མཐོང་བཅས་ཀྱི་བཀའ་ཁྲིད་དང་ ལྷག་པར་ལྷའི་སྐོར་ཤིན་ཏུ་གལ་ཆེ་ཚུལ་གྱི་དགོས་པ་དང་
རྒྱུ་མཚན་བཅས་གསལ་བའི་ ཕྱག་དཔེའི་འདི་ཉིད་མཛད་པ་པོ་སྐུབས་རྗེ་ཁྲ་ལེགས་རིན་པོ་ཆེ་ནི་ བཀའ་བརྒྱུད་
ཡོངས་ཀྱི་སྐྱེ་མེས་མཐམ་མེད་དགས་པོ་ལྷ་རྗེའི་ཞལ་སློབ་ཀྱི་གཙོ་བོ་གྲུབ་ཐོབ་ཁམས་པ་མི་གསུམ་ཀྱི་ཡ་གྱལ་
གསལ་སྟོང་ཕོ་སྐྱ་བ་ཆེན་པོའི་སྤྱལ་བརྒྱུད་ཉི་མའི་མཚན་ཅན་རིམ་པར་ཕྱིན་པ་ལས་སྐུ་ཕྲེང་དགུ་པ་ཀརྨ་བསྟན་
པའི་ཉི་མ་ཕྱིན་ལས་ཀུན་ཁྱབ་དཔལ་བཟང་པོ་སྟེ་འདི་ཉིད་རྒྱལ་བའི་དབང་པོ་སྐྱེ་དགུ་པ་ཀརྨ་བསྟན་
པའི་རྡོ་རྗེས་མ་འོངས་མཚན་གཟིགས་ཀྱི་ལུང་སྲུ་མ་ལུགས་པའི་ལོ་གཅིག་གི་གོང་རྒྱོ་སྐྱལ་གྱི་ལོར་ཆོས་
འཇིན་བརྒྱགས་ཡིག་གནང་སྟེ་ ལོ་གཅིག་གི་རིང་བཀའ་གྲོག་དམ་རྒྱ་དགོས་པ་དང་ ཤིན་མོ་ཁྱག་གི་ལྭ་བ་དང་
པོའི་ཆེས་བཅུ་ཉིན་བཀའ་གྲོག་ཞལ་དྲེ་དགོས་པའི་གསུང་ཐིས་དུས་ནས་ ཁམས་ཁྲ་ལེགས་རིན་པོ་ཆེའི་གདན་
ས་ཁྲ་འགུ་དགོན་དུ་བཅལ་བ་བཞིན་ དུས་ཚོད་དེའི་ཐོག་བརྒྱགས་ཡིག་གསུང་གོག་ཞལ་དྲེ་སྐབས་ དགོན་
ནས་སློ་ཐུབ་ཕྱོགས་ཏུ་པའི་ཉིན་ལམ་གསུམ་ཀྱི་སར་ ཕ་འགྱུར་མེད་རྡོ་གྲོས་མ་པདྲ་རྱང་གི་ ཇིའུ་ལུག་ལོ་ལ་ཞེས་
དེ་སྐབས་སྐུ་འགྱུངས་མ་ཐག་ཡིན་པར་བརྟེན་ཀུན་ཀྱི་ཏོ་མཆར་སྐྱེ་དགོས་པའི་ཏོང་འཇིན་གནང་བས་རིན་པོ་ཆེ
མཆོག་ལ་ཐུན་མོང་མ་ཡིན་པའི་ཡོན་ཏན་མངའ་བ་དང་ ཕྱིན་ལས་འབྱུང་བར་ཚམ་མས་གྲུབ་པར་མ་ཟད་ དམ་
པའི་ཆོས་དང་ རིག་གསར་སེམས་ཀྱི་ཚན་རིག་གཉིས་ཀར་བསླབ་སྦྱང་དང་ཉམས་སྦྱོང་ལྷན་ལས་རྩུལ་ཕྱོགས་
པའི་ཞལ་སློབ་རྣམས་ཀྱིས་ཆེས་རིས་ཤེས་སྟེ་སྨྲ་ཞིང་གོ་བའི་བ་དང་ ཕན་ཐོག་ཆེ་བས་ ཁྱད་ཆོས་མང་པོ་དང་
ཕྱིན་པ་ཕྱགས་རེས་ཞུ། །ཁ་འགྱ་སྒྱལ་མེད་བས་KTD གདན་ས་ནས་ཕུལ།། ||

FOREWORD

———

In this book the author explains spiritual cultivation from the Vajrayana perspective on the common preliminaries, the four immeasurables, tranquillity meditation, and insight meditation. In particular, he elucidates the need to develop the correct view.

The author of this text is Kyabje Traleg Rinpoche, the emanation of Saltong Shogam, one of the three principal disciples of the physician Gampopa, who is the common lineage forefather of the Kagyu tradition. This line of *tulku*s successively reincarnated, with each bearing the name Nyima. The ninth one, whose name is Karma Tenpa Rabgye Thinley Nyima Gocha Pal Zangpo, was recognized by the glorious sixteenth Karmapa, Rangjung Rigpe Dorje. Through his vision and faculty of foreknowledge, one year prior to conception, in the year of the Snake, a prediction letter was given with the instruction that this letter should remained sealed for a period of one year and opened only on the tenth day of the first month of the Wood Sheep year. From the central part of Tibet a search was launched to eastern Tibet, where the Traleg tulkus had their seat at Thrangu Monastery. Upon opening the letter at the appointed time, the search party was led to the home of his parents: his father, Gyurme Lodrö, and his mother, Pema Zung. The house was located west of Thrangu Monastery, three days' journey by horse, where Traleg Rinpoche had just taken birth in the year of the Sheep, thus confirming the prediction letter to the amazement of all.

Rinpoche is exceptionally learned and demonstrates marked and genuine spiritual activity. He has undergone extensive study and experience in the traditional Buddhist training as well as having studied the contemporary mind sciences. His book is bound to generate both certainty and ease of understanding and will, with its many outstanding qualities, bring tremendous benefit to all spiritual seekers in the West. Please, students of the Dharma, take this to heart.

KHENCHEN THRANGU RINPOCHE,
tutor to His Holiness the seventeenth Gyalwa Karmapa,
Urgyen Thinley Dorje, at Karma Triyana Dharmachakra,
Woodstock, New York, 2 August 2003.

PREFACE

Although this book is aimed at a general readership, and I have done my best to keep it as simple and accessible as possible, it necessarily employs some basic Buddhist concepts, particularly concepts belonging to the Mahamudra tradition. This was required in order to provide the reader with a real introduction to Mahamudra and to properly flesh out the context of this practice. Meditation is best practiced within a particular spiritual framework—be it Buddhism or any other tradition—if one is to gain the maximum benefit.

I have not referred to many of my own experiences in giving meditation instruction, spiritual counsel, or assistance to people over the years, nor have I included any personal stories of spiritual practice, because I do not feel these reminiscences are particularly relevant to the Buddhist teachings. This may be a reflection of the Eastern cultural baggage that I still carry around. I often feel that including too many personal stories in Dharma discourse only degrades the Dharma into a self-serving, self-indulgent exercise. As an author, I cannot improve upon the veracity and profundity of the Buddhist teachings.

Nonetheless, as a human being, my own experience has doubtless filtered into this book to some extent, even if not explicitly stated, and any errors or defects herein are a result of my own inadequacies. Unless otherwise indicated, all foreign terms are in Sanskrit and all translations from Tibetan texts are mine.

I am, as always, forever indebted to all of my teachers, who unfortunately are now no longer present in their physical forms. Without their kindness, I would not have been so fortunate as to devote all of my life to spiritual practice. If and when I have failed to do just that, it has never been due to any lack of opportunity or external circumstances. I learned so much from my teachers while they were alive, and I continue to learn from them as I attempt to expand and deepen my knowledge of the Dharma. Even to this day I devote a lot of my time to reading and contemplating Tibetan Buddhist texts. This interest in the Dharma is also a gift from my own teachers, seeds sown by them early in my life.

I would especially like to thank Khenchen Thrangu Rinpoche for writing the foreword to this book. I would also like to thank all of the wonderful people I have met over the years while living in the West, where I have come to know and share the Dharma with many people. I particularly want to thank my own students from Kagyu E-Vam Buddhist Institute in Australia and E-Vam Institute in New York for their continued support, dedication, and sincere interest in the Dharma. I would like to thank Deirdre Collings yet again for helping me put this book together.

INTRODUCTION

There seems to have been a revival in spirituality in the modern West. People are showing a genuine, sincere interest in things spiritual. Moreover, they no longer think of themselves as deeply flawed or morally corrupt individuals in need of punishment before they can be worthy of spiritual counsel and training. The practices of self-torture and self-flagellation, if not completely a thing of the past, are at least not in vogue any longer. There is a need for a balanced, practical, and at the same time liberating kind of spiritual practice.

The subject of this book is the Mahamudra approach to meditation, a form of Buddhist meditation that is unique to the Tibetan Kagyu tradition. By this I do not mean to imply that the Kagyu tradition is superior to the other major traditions of Tibetan Buddhism or that the Kagyu forms of Mahamudra meditation have not been incorporated into the practices of particular masters of other Tibetan lineages. There is, for example, a Kagyu-Gelug Mahamudra lineage and so on. It should also be briefly mentioned that the unique practice of Kagyu Mahamudra has also sometimes been criticized by masters from other Tibetan traditions, particularly for its emphasis on the notion of nonmentation (*amanasikara*). Certain Sakya masters have even been vociferous in their objections. Since I am more interested in presenting a practice manual for Mahamudra meditation here, I will not go into the intricacies of these exchanges between the Kagyu and other Sarma traditions, namely the Sakya and Gelug. I believe that Mahamudra meditation is a most congenial match for the contemporary world. This type of meditation is not founded on the moralistic, judgmental, punitive approaches modern people often associate with religion, nor does it emphasize a spiritual path involving extensive periods of discipline, self-denial, and self-abnegation.

The notions of detachment and renunciation are all too often the things that most religions emphasize, sometimes to an extreme. This has been at the expense of cultivating our potential for psychological and physical well-being, of learning to be at ease with ourselves, our environment, and our fellow creatures. I hope that this book will go some way toward helping people have a spiritual outlook based upon a positive view of things. Instead of highlighting the negatives in our lives and seeing evil lurking in every corner, the Mahamudra approach to spirituality allows us to see things in a positive and open light. Even things that we might normally regard as bad and undesirable can be interpreted in a more uplifting way due to the expansiveness of the Mahamudra vision, allowing us to benefit from them spiritually.

PART ONE

—

FUNDAMENTALS

1

WHAT IS
MAHAMUDRA?

THE MAHAMUDRA TRADITION ENCOMPASSES MANY KEY BUD-
dhist terms and presents them in a unique light. The Sanskrit word *mahamudra* literally translates as "great seal," or "great symbol," which
suggests that all that exists in the conditioned world is stamped with the
same seal—the seal of ultimate reality. Ultimate reality is synonymous
with the quintessential Buddhist term *emptiness* (*shunyata*), which describes the insubstantiality of all things—the underlying groundless-
ness, spaciousness, and indeterminacy that imbues all of our experiences
of the subjective and objective world. In the Kagyu tradition of Tibetan Buddhism, the word *mahamudra* is also used to refer to the nature
of the mind. The nature of the mind is a pivotal concept in this tradition. The essential quality of the mind is emptiness, but it is described
as a luminous emptiness, for the mind has the inherent capacity to
know, or to cognize. When spiritual fulfillment is attained, this luminous emptiness is experienced as pervasively and profoundly blissful,
and enlightenment is characterized as luminous bliss.

The Tibetan term for Mahamudra is *chag gya chen po*. The word
chag denotes wisdom; *gya* implies that this wisdom transcends mental
defilement; and *chen po* verifies that together they express a sense of
unity. At a more profound level of interpretation, *chag gya* suggests that

our natural state of being has no origin, because we cannot posit a particular time when it came into being, nor can we say what caused it to come into existence or what it is dependent upon. Our natural state of being is self-sustaining, self-existing, and not dependent upon anything. It was Gampopa Sonam Rinchen (1079–1153), the founder of the Tibetan Kagyu school, who coined this expression for the meditative approach of Mahamudra. He defined it in these words:

> *Chag* is the intuitive understanding that all that appears and is possible, Samsara and Nirvana, do not go beyond the sphere of the ultimate which is unoriginated. *rGya* means that all that appears as something and can become something does not go beyond that which alone is genuine. *Chen po* means that this happens because of the intuitive understanding that the ultimate is free in itself.[1]

Mahamudra is also associated with the concept of nonduality, which refers to the possibility that samsara and nirvana can be experienced in a nondual way without denying the relative existence of either. As Saraha, the eighth-century Indian master who is credited with being the actual originator of the Mahamudra tradition, states in his *Song to the People*, "As is Nirvana, so is Samsara. Do not think there is any distinction. Yet it possesses no single nature, For I know it as quite pure."[2] This is because samsara and nirvana emerge together from emptiness. When the term *nonduality* is used in the context of Mahamudra experience, it does not suggest that two things come together as one; it implies that two seemingly opposite things have the same underlying nature—the nature of emptiness. Mahamudra is therefore a "seal" in the sense that it transcends all dualistic concepts and encompasses both samsara and nirvana. As such, it cannot be limited to any philosophical view.

Mahamudra, then, refers to reality itself and encompasses all opposites, because within it everything exists in its own perfection. Whatever experiences we have in terms of virtue and vice, happiness and unhappiness, good and bad, beautiful and ugly, subject and object, being and nonbeing are inseparable within the realm of emptiness. Emptiness can be compared with space, because space does not discriminate between things that are repellent and things that are enticing; space accommodates everything. This is also the nature of the mind. Again Saraha explains:

Space is designated as empty,
Yet its exact nature cannot be verbalized.
Similarly the mind is designated as luminously clear,
Yet its exact nature is empty, with no ground for definition.
Thus the self-nature of mind is and has been
From the very beginning like that of space.[3]

THE ORIGINS OF THE
KAGYU MAHAMUDRA TRADITION

Mahamudra is a specific practice of Tibetan Buddhism, a practice inherited from its forebears, the *mahasiddhas* (*maha* denotes "great" and *siddha* denotes "saint" or "adept") of India, such as Saraha, Savaripa (eighth century), Tilopa (988–1069), and Maitripa (1010–1087). Although other Tibetan Buddhist schools always practice Mahamudra in conjunction with Tantrism, in the Kagyu tradition it is treated as a separate path to enlightenment, one that in fact transcends tantric methods and techniques, emphasizing the concept of self-liberation as opposed to the tantric idea of self-transformation. This tradition is unique to the Kagyu school.

The distinction between the Mahamudra of the Kagyu school and the tantric practices of the other Tibetan schools is not well understood by Western Buddhists. It may be useful to provide a brief overview of the historical context of Tantrism in Buddhist thought. The Buddha lived and taught in the fourth century BCE, and his doctrine of individual salvation predominated in Indian Buddhist spiritual life until the first century CE, when the doctrines of the Mahayana began to supersede them. Tantrism was not yet on the scene, arriving later in northeast and northwest India from around the fifth century onward.

The Mahayana movement was fueled by an altruistic ideal that transformed the Buddhist goal of individual salvation into a spiritual vision that embraced the welfare of all beings. It began somewhere around 200 BCE in India and emphasized the two related virtues of compassion (*karuna*) and wisdom (*prajna*). The Mahayana vision was innovative on a number of fronts: its inclusion of the laity; its expanded concept of enlightenment into something that transcends both samsara and nirvana (rather than positing it *as* nirvana, in opposition to samsara); its emphasis on the notions of emptiness, compassion, and skillful means; and its detailed exposition of the paths and stages of the bodhisattva. The bodhisattva is a being (*sattva*) who develops greater and greater enlightened qualities (*bodhi*) as a result of his or her increasingly selfless ability to benefit all beings.

Mahayana ideas were based upon a number of newly emerging texts, some of which are collectively known as the *Prajnaparamita* (transcendental actions of wisdom) sutras, along with other key sutras such as the *Gandhavyuha-sutra, Samadhiraja-sutra*, and *Lankavatara-sutra*. These in turn gave rise to the philosophical schools of Madhyamaka and Yogachara (the Yogachara also drawing on sutras related to the subject of *tathagatagarbha*, or buddha-nature, of which more will be said in chapter 7). These philosophical schools were founded by Mahayana masters such as Nagarjuna (ca. 150–250 CE), Aryadeva (ca. third century). Asanga (ca. fourth century), Vasubandhu (ca. 330–400), and Chandrakirti (ca. seventh century). These developments took place within a predominantly monastic culture, eventually giving rise to a Buddhist orthodoxy increasingly intent on maintaining and defending the established doctrine. Huge monastic universities were established for devotional practices and the study and dissemination of Buddhist ideas.

A lay movement, largely meditative in focus, was quietly emerging alongside the monastic culture. It combined a unique system of yogic techniques with Buddhist ideas in order to effect the transformation of the practitioner's body, speech, and mind from those of an ordinary being to those of a buddha. The texts of this movement were known as tantras, a term that expresses the idea of a continuity of enlightened qualities as somewhat present in beings already, in potential form, rather than being brought about through linear causal development.

There was in fact a tantric tradition in both Buddhism and Hinduism in the first millennium of the common era. Tantra was controversial for its claim that adherents could attain enlightenment in a single lifetime, rather than the three measureless eons espoused by Mahayanists. It retained the Mahayana ideal of the bodhisattva, however, and assimilated ideas from Madhyamaka and Yogachara as well as the idea of tathagatagarbha. In tantric Buddhism, adherents used their esoteric practices (*sadhana*) as an aid for acquiring enlightenment, not just to acquire supernatural abilities (*siddhi*). They used tantric practices to clear psychophysical blockages within the psychophysical energy system of the body. The ultimate goal, or culmination of their practice, was to realize the luminous bliss of the awakened mind.

The term *mahamudra* was used to describe the highest teachings of the Buddhist tantras that predominated in northwest India during the Pala period (750–1150). The practitioners of Tantra at the time, the mahasiddhas, were not monks and nuns but serious lay practitioners of both sexes and all castes (in open defiance of India's rigid caste system). Comprising some ex-monks, this lay tradition was easily distinguished by its unconventional methods of spiritual instruction, bohemian lifestyle, and critical dissension from the social conventions of its time. In the tantric system of Buddhism, the practitioner is known as a *sadhaka*, who then engages in the tantric practices known as *sadhana* in order to attain the tantric realizations known as supernatural abilities or *siddhi*s. When these siddhis are attained, one becomes a siddha, and eventually a great siddha, or Mahasiddha. A detailed description of the great Indian *tantrika*s (practitioners of Tantra) can be found in the work of the renowned scholar Jonangpa Taranatha, who had a special connection to the Mahasiddha lineage. His work *The Seven Instruction Lineages* (*Kabab dunden*) has been masterfully translated and edited by David Templeman, who accounts for their lives with scholarly finesse, and Keith Dowman, who presents a condensed but colorful version of their period. The original *Lives of the Eighty-Four Mahasiddhas* by Indian scholar Abhayadatta (ca. twelfth century), which has also been translated by James B. Robinson, depicts the siddhas, yogis, and yoginis as members of a nonmonastic, noncelibate movement. Abhayadatta lived some two hundred years after many of the figures portrayed in his book and, while modern scholars doubt the historical accuracy of his record, there is no doubt that such mahasiddhas did live in India and lived the kinds of lives that Abhayadatta describes.[4]

It seems that Tantra developed in India alongside orthodox monastic culture for many centuries before emerging as a popular form of Buddhism in the eighth century. Some modern historians surmise that Tantra became part of the Buddhist tradition just prior to the sixth century, because it was already established in some of the Hindu sects of India by that time. Tibet's renowned seventeenth-century historian, Jonang Taranatha, claims the tantras appeared shortly after the spread of the Mahayana teachings in India, becoming quite prevalent by the fifth century.[5] In any case, most of the major tantras had been revealed by the eight and ninth centuries.

From about the eighth century onward, we start to see numerous examples of Indian mahasiddhas repudiating traditional tantric methods and advocating instead a direct perception of the nature of the mind as the quintessential method for realizing enlightenment. According to the well-known Tibetan author and translator Go Lotsawa (ca. 1392–1481), "the great brahmana Saraha was the first to introduce the Mahamudra as the chief of all paths" Takpo Tashi Namgyal (ca. 1512–1587), another prolific Tibetan master from the Kagyu tradition, records that siddhas such as Saraha, Savaripa, Tilopa, and Maitripa did not follow conventional tantric practices. Discussing Maitripa, he states:

> Maitrīpa, also, having been dissatisfied with his proficient knowledge of the sutras and tantras followed [the mystic teacher] Śavarīśvara and received the illuminating instructions on the quintessential great seal, which was not based on the tantric teachings. Maitrīpa then achieved spiritual liberation.[6]

The situation arose where some mahasiddhas continued to promote Mahamudra as the apex of tantric practices and conventions, while others, such as Saraha and Maitripa, began to disassociate themselves and their Mahamudra teachings from Tantrism. Saraha decisively criticizes the tantric path in his *doha*s (songs) claiming, "Mantra and Tantra, meditation and concentration, they are all a cause of self-deception." He criticizes monastic Buddhism for perpetuating endless doctrinal disputes, and tantric practitioners for further binding themselves to subtle fixations and dualistic concepts with their methods. He maintained that enlightenment can be more readily obtained by simply resting in the nature of the mind. In another doha, Saraha says this of Mahamudra:

> *It is empty of any mandala.*
> *Empty of devotees who make burned offerings,*
> *Detached from any mantras, mudras, and the visualization of deities.*
> *It cannot be realized through tantras and shastras.*
> *This indestructible awareness, which is our own*
> *   natural state of being, is perfect in its natural state.*

A synopsis of this historical evolution of Mahamudra in relation to the Kagyu tradition may be more useful here. The Kagyu tradition was founded by Marpa the Translator (ca. 1012–1097), a student of the Indian tantric mahasiddha Naropa (ca. 1016–1100), who had attained enlightenment with his guru Tilopa. The Mahamudra tradition that Marpa inherited was systematized and made popular by Gampopa, a student of the famous Tibetan yogi–poet Milarepa (ca. 1040–1123).

It was not until the eleventh and twelfth centuries that Mahamudra doctrine attained a distinct position within the Kagyu school, after Gampopa formally introduced the approach into the mainstream Buddhist practices of his lineage. For even though Marpa had received the Mahamudra teachings on the nature of the mind from his gurus Naropa and Maitripa, he also received and transmitted all the tantric teachings from the Indian mahasiddha tradition and passed them on in turn to his student Milarepa. Milarepa too taught Mahamudra mainly in relation to tantric practices. It was only Gampopa, toward the end of his life, who began to emphasize a practice of Mahamudra independent of tantric practices and empowerments that became a separate practice unto itself. As Takpo Tashi Namgyal explains in his famous Mahamudra manual:

> The teachers of this meditational lineage up to Milarepa meditated mainly on the key instructions of the Mantrayāna mysticism [Tantra] while at various times incorporating vital instructions on mahāmudrā from the discourses on the yogas of inner heat and lucid awareness [tantric practices]. Yet, the great master Gampopa, having been moved by immeasurable compassion, expounded mainly on the quintessential instructions on mahāmudrā. As a result it became widely known as the single path for all predestined seekers.

Go Lotsawa also mentions that, prior to Gampopa, the Mahamudra teachings were exclusively given as a highly secret instruction to practitioners who had received tantric initiation. Gampopa was revolutionary in this matter as well. Not only did he extract the Mahamudra practice as a self-sufficient doctrine; he also significantly liberalized its dispersion by giving instructions outside of the tantric environment. While Milarepa did not teach Mahamudra separate from the tantric teachings, Gampopa began to give tantric initiations to select students and Mahamudra teachings to all the rest without giving them tantric initiations. He thus initiated a widespread practice of separating the Mahamudra cycle of teachings from their tantric origins.

Gampopa preferred to teach this simple, direct insight into the nature of the mind. At one point in the record of his teachings, he commented on his decision to give these normally secret teachings of

Mahamudra so freely. In a dialogue with his student Dusum Khyenpa, the first Karmapa (1110–1193), Gampopa remarks:

> "I have broken the command of my master by teaching Mahamudra freely."
> "In what way?" inquired Dusum Khyenpa.
> "By expounding the teachings of Mahamudra to people."
> Then, on another occasion he remarked to the same student, "I have obeyed the command of my master Milarepa."
> "In what way is that?" inquired Dusum Khyenpa. "By devoting my entire life to practice," came the response.[7]

Here Gampopa is acknowledging his teaching style to be very different from Milarepa's, for Milarepa was deeply steeped in tantric teachings and practices. It is thanks to Milarepa's perseverance that the advanced tantric practices of the Kagyu tradition are still preserved. At the same time, Gampopa felt people could learn to realize their true nature directly, through the use of the more simple methods of the Mahamudra teachings.

DIFFERENT VEHICLES
FOR THE PATH TO ENLIGHTENMENT

Mahamudra meditation is a particular type of Buddhist practice, so it is important to know where it stands in relation to Buddhist teachings generally. The fundamental aim of Buddhist practice is to achieve enlightenment, to emulate the Buddha, who became known as "the awakened one," or "the enlightened one." Through our spiritual practice we aim to become more aware, conscious, and integrated. By so doing we are able to eradicate ignorance (*avidya*) and replace it with wisdom (prajna). Buddhist practice is about learning how to perceive ourselves in a genuine and authentic fashion so that we are no longer in conflict, with dark subconscious corners of the mind constantly acting on our conscious awareness and disturbing its peace. Everything that is going on in the mind has the potential to become conscious, so that nothing is hidden any more. Overcoming ignorance, then, is being able to perceive ourselves in a completely authentic fashion by removing the conflicting emotions of the mind. Buddhism offers a multitude of approaches to achieving this kind of liberation. Even the Buddha himself frequently

said that his teachings varied in order to benefit people of different predispositions, interests, and needs. Consequently, it is impossible to derive
any kind of fixed dogma from what the Buddha taught.

The Tibetan tradition usually divides the different historical and
philosophical approaches to Buddhist practice into three vehicles
(*yana*s). These are the Hinayana (small vehicle), the Mahayana (great
vehicle), and the Vajrayana (indestructible vehicle). Sometimes a fourth
vehicle is also included in Tibetan literature, as noted by some
twentieth-century Indian historians. This is the Sahajayana (the vehicle
of coemergence). In Tibetan this is called *lhen chig kye pa (lhen chig* is
equivalent to *saha* and *kye* is the same as *ja*). *Sahaja* literally denotes
"being born (*ja*) together with (*saha*)" and was applied to the teachings
and dohas of many of the Indian mahasiddhas who are associated with
the Indian Mahamudra lineage. Therefore the Mahamudra approach
can also be described as the Sahajayana (the vehicle of sahaja) as opposed to Tantrayana (the vehicle of Tantra). It might be useful to use
the notion of the Sahajayana here to emphasize that the Mahamudra
teachings are a unique and separate vehicle in their own right.

The Kagyu tradition extends this classification further by identify-
ing four fundamental approaches to enlightenment: renunciation,
purification, transformation, and self-liberation. Each approach corresponds to one of the four vehicles. The Hinayana corresponds to the
approach of renunciation, the Mahayana to the approach of purification, the Vajrayana to the approach of transformation, and the Sahajayana (or Mahamudra) to the approach of self-liberation.

We shall add one further overarching typology to those above. All
the Buddhist teachings can be divided into exoteric, esoteric, and mystical categories. In general terms, these three could be said to correspond respectively to codified orthodoxies, secret teachings given only
to initiates, and mystical teachings that transcend the reference points of
most worldly activities. The Hinayana and Mahayana fall into the general category of an exoteric approach, the Vajrayana (tantric) is the esoteric approach, and the Mahamudra tradition is the mystical approach.
This schema of exoteric, esoteric, and mystical will be used throughout
this book. The following descriptions provide a brief overview of this
classification system.

Renunciation (Exoteric)

The approach of renunciation is taken by the Hinayana teachings. It is important to bear in mind that while Hinayana denotes "small vehicle," it does not refer to the Theravada tradition of early Buddhism. *Hinayana* is a term coined by Mahayana practitioners to refer to Buddhist schools that no longer survive in India or elsewhere. For the purposes of understanding the yana system, however, we can safely understand Hinayana to include the fundamental doctrines of the Buddha, including the Four Noble Truths, selflessness, dependent origination, karma and rebirth, and individual salvation within nirvana. When we are on this spiritual path, there are many things that we might notice within ourselves that we do not like, want, or need—excessive anger, excessive jealousy, extreme forms of selfishness, self-centeredness, violence, hatred, and so forth. In order to rid ourselves of these things, to displace them from our consciousness, we renounce them in favor of a more caring attitude.

Purification (Exoteric)

The Mahayana teachings relate to negative mental states and emotions in a more open and accommodating manner, aiming to reconcile and purify these emotions rather than attempting the more aggressive eradication of the Hinayana approach. The main methods employed here are the practices of wisdom and compassion, two complementary qualities developed through cultivating the six transcendental actions (*paramitas*) of generosity, patience, ethical conduct, perseverance, meditation, and wisdom. These actions help propel us along the bodhisattva paths and stages toward the ultimate goal of complete enlightenment.

In this approach, we start by recognizing that we are subject to conflicting emotions. We then make an effort to deepen our insight into the nature of these emotions themselves. Instead of trying to escape from them, we begin to see that the nature of negative mental states is ultimately the same as the nature of the positive mental states we are trying to develop. In other words, we no longer think about things in a strictly dualistic fashion, regarding negative thoughts and emotions as intrinsically bad and positive thoughts and emotions as intrinsically good. From the point of view of ultimate reality, there is no difference between the two states, because both are imbued with the same reality—the reality of emptiness. There is a difference between these two realities on the relative level; ignorance is not wisdom, and defilement is not liberating. Nonetheless, on a deeper level, ignorance and wisdom have the same underlying reality. It is this reality that we are trying to realize directly through the practices of compassionate action and through gaining meditative insight into emptiness.

Transformation (Esoteric)

Transformation describes the Vajrayana or tantric approach that is the signal inheritance of the Tibetan Buddhist traditions. The main techniques and methods of this system are the visualization of deities, recitation of mantras, chanting, and various other rituals and physical gestures. What is emphasized here is the transformation of our defiling mental states and emotional conflicts. According to the tantric teachings, transformation occurs through learning to associate our psychic tendencies and states, like confusion for instance, with the visualization of peaceful deities, wrathful deities, and deities in sexual union. Through associating these negative habits with their enlightened counterparts, we are able to employ active imaginative processes to transform them into their opposite qualities. In this way, what was once disturbing to our minds becomes a source of liberation. As the *Hevajra Tantra* states, "The things that bind us can actually be the source of liberation when we have the necessary skills."

Instead of thinking that liberation must come from a source other than our defiled minds, we come to recognize that the very things that afflict and torment us can be the source of our emancipation. Although strong emotions have the unmistakable and harmful effect of clouding our judgment and compelling us to act irrationally, it is not the emotions themselves that are the source of our mental anguish and pain. This pain itself has to be attributed to our lack of clear and distinct insight into the true nature of these emotions. To attain such insight, practitioners of Tantra will typically engage in visualization practices, psychophysical yogas, special breathing exercises, and so forth, all of which are designed to transform the very emotions that harm us into transcendental wisdoms that can free and transform us.

Self-Liberation (Mystical)

True Mahamudra practice is the approach of self-liberation. With this approach, we are not attempting to renounce, purify, or transform anything at all. Instead, the idea is to allow our negativities and conflicting emotions to become self-liberated. As long as we are trying to renounce, purify, or transform, we are trying to *do* or contrive something. This involves seeing ourselves as fundamentally flawed, because we have no control over our strong emotions. We feel if we are ever going to become a better human being and be spiritually redeemed, we must do everything in our power to dispose of these undesirable states of mind. In the Mahamudra view, by deliberately trying to eradicate conflicting emotions, the source of our conflicting emotions, we are perpetuating a negative view of these things. Ultimately these emotions and conflicting emotions have no intrinsic nature, and the Mahamudra method incorporates this premise from the outset. In so doing, it is designed to cut through conflicting emotions rather than wear them out, eliminate them, or transform them.

Rather than going through this long process of elimination, purification, and transformation, we simply enter immediately into our own spiritual being or rest in our natural state, as it is said. If we can do this, liberation is automatic. Mahamudra is sometimes described as the sudden approach to enlightenment. This does not necessarily indicate that we can become enlightened instantly but rather that the conflicting emotions that obstruct our enlightenment can become self-liberated naturally. Self-liberation is called *rangdrol* in Tibetan—*rang* is "self" and *drol* is "liberation." Self-liberation is achieved through recognizing our innate state of being, or the nature of the mind, according to the Mahamudra teachings. Self-liberation comes through resisting the temptation to deliberately try to create a particular state of mind. Instead we allow ourselves to be with whatever arises in the mind. When we allow things to come and go without fixating on them and without trying to solidify, correct, or react to them, everything can become self-liberated. It is simply a matter of maintaining our awareness (*sampajanya*).

GROUND MAHAMUDRA

The Mahamudra view is based on the underlying metaphysical concept of the nature of the mind, a term used interchangeably with the terms *ground Mahamudra* and *ground of being*. It is said that this ground has been pure right from the beginning because it has not been caused to come into existence but is spontaneously established. It is also atemporal, because we cannot talk about it in relation to the past, present, or future. We cannot attribute any form of action to it by saying it has come into being or has gone out of existence, and so on. We cannot speak about using our normal reifying concepts of existence or nonexistence, permanence or impermanence, good or evil, sublime or degraded, and so forth. It is even completely devoid of notions of samsara, nirvana, or a spiritual path. While it is the source from which all samsaric and nirvanic experiences arise, it is not subject to causes and conditions, nor is it something that can be affirmed or negated. It is free from all the limitations of our ordinary empirical consciousness. This aspect of Mahamudra reality is called ground Mahamudra because it is the innate existential condition in which we all find ourselves. In his *Mahamudra Song*, the great Kagyu master Jamgön Kongtrül Lodrö Thaye (1813–1899) describes the ground Mahamudra in these terms:

> As for ground *mahāmudrā*:
> There are both things as they are and the way of confusion.
> It does not incline toward either *saṃsāra* or *nirvāṇa*,
> And is free from the extremes of exaggeration and denigration.
> Not produced by causes, not changed by conditions,
> It is not spoiled by confusion
> Nor exalted by realization.
> It does not know either confusion or liberation.[8]

Ground Mahamudra is an open state of being that is identical to our authentic condition. It is the ground from which all our experiences originate. Our liberating experiences arise from it, as do our experiences of imprisonment, constriction, and constraint. It is completely impartial in terms of both samsaric and nirvanic experiences—pain, pleasure, happiness, unhappiness, and so on. Our authentic condition is totally open and undifferentiated. As soon as we speak of our own authentic condition as being this or that, as inclining toward nirvana and away from samsara, we introduce a dualism that simply does not exist in reality.

This authentic condition is present in ordinary sentient beings as well as enlightened beings. In other words, there is ultimately no real difference between the two. The only difference is that enlightened beings have recognized their authentic condition, whereas ordinary sentient beings have not. This nonrecognition of our true condition is called ignorance, which is the reason we wander about in the cyclic existence of birth, death, and rebirth.

Mental fabrications of every conceivable kind have to be put to rest when we contemplate our natural state of being. If we try to conceptualize about it, we will think things like: "Does it exist or not exist? Does it favor our effort to realize nirvana and disfavor our samsaric tendencies? Is it permanent or impermanent?" One should resist forming ideas entirely. The point is not to develop ideas but to learn to rest in the natural state of being through the practice of Mahamudra, which we will discuss in the following chapters.

In Buddhist logic, it is said that all concepts are based upon exclusion. As soon as we affirm something by saying, "It is this," we automatically exclude so many other things it might have been. By imposing a conceptual limitation we fabricate an idea. The suggestion here is that it is just an idea—it is not an open experience. The thrust of Mahamudra meditation is to allow our mind to be open so that we can ease into a more natural state of perceiving and being. This does not imply that we should not have ideas at all but that we really need to be skeptical and careful about getting overly fixated on any descriptions of the qualities of our original state of being.

A great Mahamudra master known as Jowo Gotsangpa said that we need three things in order to stay with the correct view—the correct view here being "the view of no view," because it is a view that subverts or undercuts all views. The first thing we need is a decisive understanding of our original being. The second is nonbias toward samsara and nirvana. The third is conviction, because once we have attained conviction, we cannot change our minds back again. Gotsangpa claims that this view is like a spear that shoots through open space.

Mahamudra uses the expression *ordinary mind (thamal gyi shepa* in Tibetan) to describe the nature of the mind as the mind we already have. The nature of the mind is not lurking somewhere underneath our normal empirical consciousness. Rather, we gain insight into the nature of the mind by gaining insight into this ordinary mind. If we avoid judgment of our thoughts, we will be able to attain the luminous bliss of the nature of the mind, which is the ordinary mind itself. Making this point, Jamgön Kongtrül says in his *Mahamudra Song*:

Like the center of a cloudless sky,
This self-luminous mind is impossible to express.
It is wisdom of nonthought beyond analogy,
Naked ordinary mind.[9]

PATH MAHAMUDRA

Ground Mahamudra is referred to as the basis of purification. The ground itself does not require any form of purification. However, even though the ground, the nature of the mind, is unsullied and pure, adventitious mental conflicting emotions have arisen. This is precisely the reason we need a path, a method to alleviate our condition. The objects of purification, then, are the adventitious mental conflicting emotions; the means of purification is the practice of Mahamudra meditation; and the fruit of purification is the realization of the ground of being—the luminous bliss of the inherent nature of the mind. In other words, the nature of the mind does not need to be purified. The ground Mahamudra and fruition Mahamudra are in actuality one and the same thing. Once the adventitious mental conflicting emotions have been purified, there is nothing to stand in the way of our realizing our own true nature.

Tranquillity Meditation

Path Mahamudra consists of the practices of tranquillity meditation (*shamatha*) and insight meditation (*vipashyana*). First, tranquillity meditation is used to still the mind. We do not—as is done in more conventional forms of Buddhist meditation—attempt to tame the mind. In other meditative traditions, the mind is compared to a wild elephant, and meditation techniques are compared to the implements an elephant tamer uses to tame an elephant. That image is not applicable here. Rather, in tranquillity meditation, the mind is allowed to subside naturally of its own accord, using the method of self-liberation (which will be explained in later chapters). Mindfulness is present, but there is no artifice or contrivance at all. In Mahamudra, the thoughts themselves are allowed to settle of their own accord; there is no need to force them into submission. The third Karmapa, Rangjung Dorje, had this to say about tranquillity meditation in his *Prayer of Mahamudra*:

Not adulterating meditation with conceptual striving,
Unmoved by the wind of worldly bustle,
Knowing how to rest in the spontaneous, uncontrived flow,
Being skilled in the practice, may I now continue it.

Insight Meditation

Insight meditation involves an intimate and methodical examination of what the mind is. During this form of meditation, we ask ourselves questions like: "What is the mind? What is a thought? Where is a thought? What is the nature of thought? What is the nature of emotion?" Persistent analysis of this sort will reveal that the mind is not an entity or a substance. In the Mahamudra tradition, this is viewed as a supreme realization. As Savaripa, the eighth-century Indian mahasiddha stated:

> *In the process of searching for all that manifests as mind and matter*
> *There is neither anything to be found nor is there any seeker,*
> *For to be unreal is to be unborn and unceasing*
> *In the three periods of time.*
> *That which is immutable*
> *Is the state of great bliss.*[10]

By analyzing every experience that we have in this fashion, we come to realize that even our own confused thoughts—those we normally see as the very source of our mental disturbances—have the same nature as the mind itself. In this way we realize the ground Mahamudra. In Mahamudra insight meditation, everything that we experience is regarded as having the potential to reveal our true nature. Our disturbing thoughts and negative emotions are not something we try to abandon; we simply need to develop an understanding of their nature. Through the methods of the Mahamudra teachings, we can learn to use our thoughts to attain a meditative state.

FRUITION MAHAMUDRA

Mahamudra practice culminates in the four yogas of Mahamudra: the yoga of one-pointedness, the yoga of nonconceptuality, the yoga of one flavor, and the yoga of nonmeditation. Each yoga represent the fruition of a certain level of meditative practice. Je Gomchung, an important Kagyu Mahamudra master, explains:

> To rest in tranquillity is the stage of one-pointedness;
> To terminate confused thoughts is the stage of nonconceptuality;
> To transcend the duality of accepting and rejecting is the stage of one flavor;
> To perfect experiences is the stage of nonmeditation.

The yoga of one-pointedness essentially denotes recognizing the nature of the mind. One has attained this stage with the first taste of luminous bliss while in a state of deep, undisturbed meditative equipoise. The fruition is the ability to maintain meditative luminosity (*prabhasvara*). The yoga of nonconceptuality is attained by realizing that the mind has no root and is devoid of enduring essence. Not only is the nature of the mind devoid of essence, but everything that occurs in the mind is also devoid of essence, including the confused thoughts and disturbing emotions. If we look for where these thoughts and emotions arise, persist, and dissipate, we will find nothing. Therefore, while the first yoga is concerned with gaining insight into the luminous quality of the mind, the second yoga is concerned with insight into emptiness. The yoga of one flavor refers to the experience of nonduality. The division between the mind and the external world, subject and object, and all other dualistic notions are overcome at this level. Everything, including the liberation of nirvana and the bondage of samsara, is equalized in this state of one flavor. The yoga of nonmeditation signifies the genuine, ultimate fruition of path Mahamudra. It is inseparable from the ground Mahamudra, the departure point of the spiritual journey. The yoga of nonmeditation has nothing to do with not meditating per se; it simply means that the meditation state has become the natural state to be in, rather than something that we need to pursue. Therefore, there is no division between the meditation and postmeditation states.

OVERVIEW OF THE PATH

The next five chapters of this book will discuss the importance of developing a correct view as the basis for making the spiritual journey. The notion of undeluded states of mind will also be introduced as part of an overview of the spiritual path, including important preparatory practices known as the four preliminaries and the four immeasurables.

These chapters appear to focus on practices of self-transformation rather than the self-liberation method of Mahamudra, but this is done only to demonstrate that the esoteric Buddhist techniques of self-transformation are complementary to the mystical technique of self-liberation. The two approaches are not incompatible in essence.

This manual should be used as a supplement to the instructions of a qualified meditation instructor. If you genuinely wish to follow this meditative tradition you should first find a qualified instructor, as a book can never be a substitute for oral instructions. Begin each meditation session by chanting the Kagyu lineage prayers or whatever prayers your teacher has given you. The prayer by Padma Karpo included at the end of this book would also be beneficial.

Although they are not directly related to the practice of Mahamudra, these other methods are regarded as essential aids for our development of tranquillity and insight meditation. The general approach of the Kagyu Mahamudra tradition is to begin each meditation session by contemplating the subjects of the four preliminaries, which reinforces our desire to be vigilant in our practice. Contemplation of the four immeasurables of love, compassion, joy, and equanimity is also necessary because it encourages us to stay connected to our world and to develop the kind of wholesome emotional states that will empower us to express our full potential as human beings.

The meditation exercises in this book are structured so that contemplation of the four preliminaries should take five minutes, the four immeasurables five minutes, tranquillity meditation twenty minutes, and insight meditation five minutes. That is why each session in the chapter on insight meditation begins with the preliminaries, immeasurables, and tranquillity meditation. This is a fairly new innovation in the context of traditional practice, but as time is scarce it is necessary to approach our practice in this way unless you are undertaking weekly or monthly retreats.

Chapters 7 through 11 follow the outline of ground Mahamudra, path Mahamudra, and fruition Mahamudra. Ground Mahamudra is discussed in terms of our own true condition, or buddha-nature. Path Mahamudra uses the meditation practices of tranquillity and insight in order to realize the nature of the mind directly. Fruition Mahamudra is the ultimate realization of the nature of mind as having three qualities: it is empty, it is luminous, and it is the experience of bliss. When the emptiness of physical and mental phenomena is directly experienced as a subjective reality and the mind is stable and able to maintain awareness, the luminous clarity of the mind gives rise to a sense of well-being that transcends both happiness and unhappiness. This is the experience of all-pervasive bliss, the goal of Mahamudra practice. When we no longer fixate on our thoughts and emotions but let them arise without interference and without hope and fear, our minds will become blissfully clear.

2

THE IMPORTANCE OF
CORRECT VIEW

I BELIEVE THAT BUDDHISM NEEDS TO ADAPT AND CHANGE AS IT travels to different Western countries. Cultural appropriations of Buddhism are inevitable and have occurred numerous times in the past, but we must be very attentive to this process. When I came to Australia in 1980, there were very few Buddhists and very few books on Buddhism. Things have changed a great deal since then, but Buddhist ideas are still very new in the West. Buddhism has a lot to offer the West, and it is important for it to take root here in a way that will enrich modern cultures. That requires time, so we should not take to harshly pruning Buddhism according to what we think is relevant to this modern world.

The issue is not whether Buddhism need or should change—in fact, Buddhism more than any other religion stresses the need to contemplate change and impermanence—but *how* it is to change without losing its essential elements. If we try to transform Buddhism into something that fits neatly into modern Western thought, very little of the original Buddhadharma would remain. It would simply be absorbed into prevalent secular thinking or have bits and pieces appropriated by popular spiritual revivalism such as that found in various New Age philosophies.

We should not always try to make religion palatable by mixing it with popular secular ideas and repackaging it. Many people say things like "You can be a Buddhist without believing in rebirth" or "You can be a Buddhist and not believe in karma." This is a very dangerous approach. Before we decide how we are going to assimilate Buddhism into Western culture, we must first understand the meaning of what the uniquely Buddhist concepts are trying to convey. As with many new ideas, it will take time for them to be integrated and make their meaning apparent.

THE NEED FOR A
MEANINGFUL BELIEF SYSTEM

While many people want to learn Buddhist meditation, often they are skeptical and uneasy about the philosophical and religious elements of Buddhism. Consequently, it is quite common for people to think Buddhist meditative experiences can and should be separated from the belief systems within which they are embedded. That notion, however widespread, is highly questionable and bears examining. It is very important to recognize that we have to make use of certain Buddhist concepts in order to make sense of meditation practice. For example, proper meditation practice requires us to believe many things: that there is such a thing as liberation, that ignorance is the cause of samsaric bondage, and that the conflicting emotions of the mind restrict our ability to realize our goal.

Many modern educated people view all belief systems—especially religious ones—as harmful. They regard anyone who is a "believer" as a dogmatic person or a conservative, someone whose mind is closed to new ideas. Naturally, such people are often afraid of being "converted" when introduced to Buddhism, which they assume would be a terrible outcome. There is some merit to this reservation, in that there is some truth to the perception that people can be dogmatic and sometimes express their cherished beliefs in opinionated and fundamentalist ways. But we should not then conclude that we could embark on a spiritual path without explicitly believing in anything. With no philosophical orientation, we would have no idea of what we are trying to achieve or what our spiritual vision is. Furthermore, we would be blind to how we are supposed to travel on the spiritual path; we would also not know how to understand our personal predicament and our existential condition, not to mention the potential psychological and spiritual conflicts that we might encounter along the way. Therefore, while it is sometimes said that we should learn to dispense with our beliefs at a later point on the Buddhist path, we cannot approach spiritual practices without having any viewpoints or making use of belief systems.

Buddhist meditation practices and experiences are always discussed from a particular viewpoint that is taken to be valid and true—this cannot be otherwise. From this, of course, we should not draw the dubious conclusion that the Buddhist way is the *only* way or that its view is superior to all other religious or spiritual traditions. It is just that the Buddhist approach to realizing the ultimate truth and discovering the sacredness of spiritual reality can only be attained through adopting the Buddhist view and following the Buddhist path. We as Buddhists do not have to regard ourselves as the sole custodians of the ultimate truth, but we have to approach our meditation practice from a Buddhist point of view. This may apply to people of other faiths who, for whatever reason, may want to practice Buddhist meditation. We cannot say, "I'm doing insight meditation, and worldviews do not matter." They do matter, and that is why developing the "correct view" comes before starting our meditation practice in Buddhism.

The correct view (*drsti*) is also called the "noble view," and the incorrect view is called the "ignoble view." This noble view should act as a guideline for the beliefs we need to hold and those we need to discard. Through this process of refining our views, we learn how to reorient ourselves on the spiritual path and realize how appropriate belief systems and liberation are intimately related.

CORRECT VIEW: LIBERATION

Correct views have the ability to lead us to liberation, while incorrect views increase the delusions of our mind by fanning the flames of anger and increasing our sense of superiority and pride. That is why we need a proper orientation or correct view when we embark on the path. Correct view is in fact our spiritual vehicle, the transport we use to journey from the bondage of samsara to the liberation of nirvana. Conversely, incorrect views have the potential to lead us off course and, like a poorly constructed raft, will cast us adrift and deposit us on the shores of misery. There is no separation between the vehicle that transports us to our spiritual destination and the views that we hold in our mind.

We have to think about views and viewpoints quite carefully. Buddhism states that our normal views inhibit us and chain us to the limited condition of samsara, whereas the correct view can lead us to our ultimate spiritual destination. We should not conclude from this—although modern Western Buddhists often do—that meditation is all about getting rid of views or that all views will hinder us from attaining our spiritual goal. This assumption is based on the legitimate premise that Buddhist teachings emphatically identify the need to develop a nonconceptual wisdom mind in order to attain liberation and enlightenment. However, many people mistakenly think that this implies that we do not need to believe in anything and that all forms of conceptuality must be dispensed with right from the beginning. It is only incorrect views that we need to overcome. The correct and noble view is to be cultivated with great diligence.

In the Buddha's early discourses on the Four Noble Truths, the Noble Eightfold Path begins with the cultivation of the correct view. For example, even if we have no intention of becoming a Buddhist, a desire to practice meditation indicates that we already think of our lives as incomplete and are seeking ultimate fulfillment in something "spiritual." This kind of thinking actually requires a lot of conceptual categories, schemas, and preexisting beliefs. This is why it is not possible to simply jettison the things we believe in. We may not be conscious of their machinations but they are there, which is why it is difficult to jettison the things that we believe in.

Our meditative experiences may be independent of our particular viewpoints, but we need those viewpoints to guide us toward an appropriate understanding of those experiences. Without a conceptual framework, meditative experiences would be totally incomprehensible. What we experience in meditation has to be properly interpreted, and its significance—or lack thereof—has to be understood. This interpretive act requires appropriate conceptual categories and the correct use of those categories.

That is not to say conceptual categories will render our meditative experiences fully comprehensible or that they will produce the liberated state. It is rather that we would not be able to make any sense of our experiences without them. While we are often told that meditation is about emptying the mind, that it is the discursive, agitated thoughts of our mind that keeps us trapped in false appearances, meditative experiences in fact are impossible without the use of conceptual formulations.

It is therefore extremely important to try to understand meditative experiences by consulting the historical literature that describes them. We should endeavor to know which sorts of mind states are conducive to meditative experiences and which are detrimental. We would also gain insight into the type of meditative experiences we should regard as confirmation of spiritual progress and providing of reassurance and, conversely, the sort to regard as signs of having gone astray, or as pure indulgence in egotistical fantasy.

Some meditative experiences may have the appearance of being genuine but in reality are false or misleading. Such experiences can be deceptive, giving us the false conviction that we have attained a particular meditative state when in reality we have simply gone astray or fallen victim to fanciful thinking. To separate the wheat from the chaff, so to speak, and to endeavor to find out whether anything genuine has occurred, we must make use of conceptual tools that steer us in the right direction. That way, we can purposefully continue with our spiritual practice by critically examining and refining our views.

Correct views are also connected to liberation because of their potential to lead us to a proper understanding of our human condition. Genuine, authentic understanding leads to insight, or transcendental knowledge, prajna, which in turn gives birth to wisdom, or gnosis (jnana).[1] According to traditional Mahayana Buddhist literature, we are first instructed to cultivate transcendental knowledge by developing the correct view, and then gnosis issues forth from transcendental knowledge. In order to cultivate transcendental knowledge, we need first to hear and study the teachings, then to contemplate their deeper meaning, and finally to follow up by meditating on their inner mental and spiritual significance. Conceptual understanding and transcendental knowledge are inseparable in this context and are always a precondition for the dawning of wisdom.

CORRECT VIEW: MEDITATION

In the Mahamudra tradition, we have to acquire a correct conceptual understanding of emptiness, or the nature of the mind. We cannot simply practice meditation and hope for the best; we need a conceptual framework that is based on a correct view. To use a secular analogy, scientists do not just perform experiments or collect data haphazardly;

they have to be guided by scientific hypotheses, which they are seeking to verify or falsify. Similarly, if we are going to practice Buddhist meditation we need to have a comprehensive view of our human nature, our place in the scheme of things, and our relationship to the world in which we live and to our fellow sentient beings. Instead of thinking that all concepts are defiling in their nature and thus need to be overcome, we have to realize that it is only by developing an understanding of certain truths that we can gain insight. All of these considerations have to be taken into account when we do meditation, and our practice has to be informed by them. Otherwise, our worldview may become increasingly fragmented and incommensurate with our own experience; developing "nonconceptuality" then becomes an additional conceptual burden that leads inevitably to confusion.

This correct view comes from having a proper understanding, and proper understanding is the result of becoming familiar with the teachings. Basically, we cannot separate Buddhist doctrine from Buddhist meditative experiences, simply because the doctrine *is* the path to enlightenment. As the Kagyu master Jamgön Kongtrül Lodrö Thaye sang:

> *The one who meditates without the view*
> *Is like a blind man wandering the plains.*
> *There is no reference point for where the true path is.*
> *The one who does not meditate, but merely holds the view*
> *Is like a rich man tethered by stinginess.*
> *He is unable to bring appropriate fruition to himself and others.*
> *Joining the view and meditation is the holy tradition.*[2]

FOUR CHARACTERISTICS
OF THE BUDDHIST TEACHINGS

According to the *Mahayanuttaratantra*, a fifth-century Indian Mahayana text by Maitreya, the Buddhist teachings are supposed to have four characteristics. The first characteristic is that they have the quality of leading sentient beings to enlightenment. The second characteristic is that the words that express their meaning are devoid of any linguistic imperfections. The third characteristic is that their function is to eliminate mental afflictions. The fourth characteristic is that their purpose is the pacification of the suffering of sentient beings. Any teaching that fails to meet these requirements would be considered the cause of engendering wrong views in people. We develop correct understanding by familiarizing ourselves with teachings that have these four characteristics. Through study and familiarization, we absorb their content into the continuum of our own experience, whereby a fusion of the external teachings and internal comprehension takes place. This is known in the teachings as the fusion of *lung* (written texts) and *tog* (internal understanding). In that way, the teachings and our own inner experiences become inseparable and intermingled. Indeed, that is why the *Mahayanuttaratantra* states that the teachings themselves represent liberation.

It is sometimes said there are outer expressions and inner of the teachings. Outer expressions are the teachings in written or spoken form, and inner expressions are our own experiences. This is called *lung dang tog pa* in Tibetan. The written and oral traditions are contained in the Buddhist Kangyur and Tengyur. The Kangyur represents the Indian Buddhist canon, or Tripitaka in Sanskrit.[3] *Ka* means "the Buddha's teachings" and *gyur* means " 'translation," so the Kangyur holds all the translated material of the Buddha's discourses from Sanskrit into Tibetan. The Kangyur also contains texts that Buddha Shakyamuni did not actually expound, but which were compiled later and indirectly attributed to him. These are the more esoteric or tantric teachings of Buddhism and they are also enshrined in the Tibetan Kangyur, making the Tibetan canon more expansive than the Buddhist canons of India, China, and Japan. The Tibetan Kangyur comprises 103 volumes from which all Buddhist teachings and practices are drawn.

Tibetan Buddhists do not rely solely on the Kangyur, however. Commentarial material is also contained and enshrined in yet another revered collection of Buddhist texts known as the Tengyur. *Ten* is short for *tencho*, which denotes "commentarial materials" and *gyur* again means "translation." This collection consists mainly of translations from Sanskrit texts, although there are some from Chinese and other sources. The Tengyur was compiled as a supplement to the original teachings of the Buddha as contained in the Kangyur. Altogether, the Buddhist canon is enormous, spanning many subjects; it is pitched at many levels of understanding and presented in a wide variety of forms. For instance, some discourses can be pedagogic and strictly logical, while others are more like stories or parables.

The commentarial literature was logically conceived as a way of systematizing the various discourses and ordering their themes. Sometimes the Buddha explained things in a certain way in one context and then quite differently in another, perhaps even giving different answers to the same questions, depending upon his assessment of the most effective teaching for a particular time and place. The commentarial literature was committed to writing in order to help clarify such issues, but it has more than a supplementary role. It is a rich and varied source of instruction in its own right, authored by renowned scholars and highly realized masters. The specialists of esoteric Buddhism—the tantric siddhas and the masters of the mystical path of Mahamudra—are to be found in the Tengyur, as are treatises on logic, metaphysics, epistemology, and various other fields such as composition, grammar, and literature.

It is very useful to understand where the Buddhist teachings and instructions come from, for this has a real influence on their character and emphasis. Some teachings approach the Dharma on an abstract, philosophical, or theological level; others address it in a more practical, spiritual, inspirational way. It is the so-called essential instructions (*upadesha* in Sanskrit, *men ngag* in Tibetan) of the Buddha's teachings that we must rely on principally, and they have been extracted from the commentarial materials of the Tengyur, which in turn were drawn from the Buddha's original discourses in the Kangyur. The essential instructions are not philosophical or metaphysical discourses but practical instructions on how to cultivate ourselves on the spiritual path, particularly in relation to our meditation practice. The inner expressions of the teachings (*tog pa*) that have developed from the continuum of experience of a Buddhist practitioner are part of an oral tradition that forms these essential pith instructions.

A Buddhist seeks to develop correct view through familiarity with the three modes of accumulated knowledge. The first mode is reading and learning, the second is contemplation, and the third is meditation. As Buddhists, we are really required to reflect upon and digest what we read and hear and to determine for ourselves whether it makes any sense. This type of reflection, and its application to meditation, is in essence the avenue for gaining knowledge on the Buddhist path. It is always paramount that all knowledge and learning be joined with meditation, otherwise it will have very little importance.

Thus, we have to appreciate the importance of developing a correct view in relation to our meditation practice. While Buddhism offers many analogies about the utilitarian nature of the teachings, these have to be understood in the context of the path. For example, the Buddha said that the teachings are like a raft for crossing a river and that once we have reached the other shore, we will not need to carry the raft any longer. There is also a well-known Zen story that suggests the teachings are like a finger pointing to the moon and that once we see the moon we no longer need to gaze at the finger. People unfortunately misconstrue these metaphors when they understand them too literally and take them to mean that Buddhist meditation practitioners should reject all belief systems. The point of both of these analogies is that the raft and the finger are necessary initially, because they provide the spiritual vehicle that we desperately need. Without them we will drown in the turbulent and murky waters of samsara. It is only once the content and the significance of the teachings have been thoroughly assimilated into our being, so that the external and internal teachings have intermingled, that we can let go of our conceptual understanding. When there is no separation between the teachings and ourselves, we no longer have any need for the conceptual tools that the Buddhist teachings provide.

Some people contend that it is only through meditation that we gain enlightenment and that intellectual understanding is of no help—they even perceive it as the main hindrance on the path. Such people even go so far as to actively discourage others from studying the Dharma. This strikes me as intellectual laziness. There is absolutely no support in the Buddhist tradition for this spurious contention, not in Theravada, Zen, Tibetan Buddhism, or Mahayana Buddhism. It is in fact belied by the voluminous Buddhist texts and teachings in each of these traditions. It does not matter what level of realization we may have attained—until we reach enlightenment, it is definitely necessary to rely on the useful conceptual tools that are provided in the teachings.

These conceptual tools—the worldviews and belief systems—are indispensable, just as it is indispensable to have a boat in order to cross a river. They are our means of transport. As with any type of transport, we have already embarked on a journey as soon as we have boarded that vehicle. Likewise, upon the assimilation of a particular spiritual worldview, the effect of that change in view has already taken place. This is why we have to practice Buddhist meditation by trying to understand the teachings as thoroughly as we can and by placing our own experiences in the context of those teachings that we have so fortunately received. The understanding that we develop through assimilating the teachings into our being is liberating in itself. It is not true that we first have to understand the teachings, then do certain practices, and only then find liberation. The assimilation of the teachings in itself is the same as liberation, because when they are fully understood, they do not simply remain on a conceptual level but become converted into deep spiritual realizations. They have become part of our being, inseparable from us. That is the luminous bliss of enlightenment; that is the goal of the spiritual path.

3

THE
SPIRITUAL PATH

I HAVE DISCUSSED THE NEED TO CULTIVATE THE CORRECT VIEW
through studying the teachings and applying them to meditation. Before we try to make sense of the mystical approach of the Mahamudra
tradition, it is important to continue with these more general themes of
the exoteric Buddhist teachings. The Mahamudra tradition itself is
often considered a "path without a path," and the mystical approach has
been described as "sudden enlightenment," in contrast to the exoteric
methods. It takes a long time to embody the reality of Mahamudra in
our lives. Just because we are practicing Mahamudra, we should not automatically assume that "sudden" equals easy. It may in fact indicate the
opposite, in the sense that so much has to be done and compressed
within a very short time frame, so we cannot devalue the notion of a
spiritual journey even within the practice of Mahamudra meditation.
While it is true that the Mahamudra path places great emphasis on the
idea of returning home to find our true self or true nature, it still requires a great deal of determination, time, and energy to accomplish
this. Consequently, this chapter is devoted to a general overview of the
Buddhist spiritual path and its practices.

Buddhist teachings often refer to the path (*marga* in Sanskrit; *lam* in
Tibetan), but we need to reflect carefully upon what it actually means

to travel this spiritual path.[1] Essentially it entails undergoing a journey of change and transformation, discovering things that were previously outside our experience. A spiritual practitioner can be compared to a traveler or a pilgrim. When you become a traveler, you leave behind your familiar world and venture forth into unknown territory. You may have read something about the places that you want to visit or heard stories about them, but you have never actually been there yourself. Likewise, on a spiritual journey you can never really know where you are going or what to expect, no matter how much you have read or heard. Until you actually undertake the journey yourself, you will always remain substantially rooted in your own environment.

A spiritual journey contains many different kinds of experiences—unpleasant, challenging, and uncomfortable ones, as well as very positive and pleasant ones. It is through dealing with this variety of experience that we grow and mature and transform ourselves spiritually.

THE LIFE STORY OF MILAREPA

All of the elements of a genuine spiritual journey are exemplified in this life of one of Tibet's greatest spiritual masters, the eleventh-century saint and yogi Milarepa. The Kagyu school and the Mahamudra tradition follow his lineage. Milarepa's early life was very difficult, and he did some terrible things as a result, including bringing death to a number of people. Overcome by remorse and shame, he set out on a spiritual quest, leaving behind everything he owned. At this early stage, all Milarepa wanted was expiation or redemption, and perhaps forgiveness.

He encountered many difficulties on his journey. He initially met teachers who introduced him to advanced esoteric practices, but he was unable to relate to them—he needed more vigorous practices that would make him feel purified. He wanted to redeem himself in his own mind and in the opinion of others.

Fortunately, he met Marpa, who was both an astute judge of his students' needs and quite a hard taskmaster. Their encounter and Milarepa's subsequent hardships should be understood within the context of the teacher's unexcelled expertise in being able to read people accurately. Milarepa did not have to put himself through difficult circumstances and situations—Marpa did that for him! Marpa set harsh physical tasks for Milarepa without any acknowledgment or reward and refused to give him formal teachings. Milarepa began to fear he would never receive any teachings or guidance from Marpa. What he did not understand was that Marpa was already teaching him every day. Teachings do not emanate solely from texts and formal instruction; indeed some of the most profound teachings come through the interactions between a teacher and student.

Marpa knew very well that Milarepa needed to feel that he had purified his negative karma, so he set about assigning Milarepa various difficult tasks, including the construction of a number of buildings— a square house, a round house, a triangular house, and so forth—but Marpa was always unhappy with them and would order Milarepa to tear them down immediately. Eventually he built a nine-story tower that finally satisfied his guru, and at this point Marpa decided that Milarepa had purified his mind sufficiently and was ready to receive formal teachings.

Milarepa applied himself with great fortitude to the meditation practices that accompanied these teachings. He was determined to spend the rest of his life in solitude; he was deeply disaffected with people and vowed to waste no more time with them. In human affairs, wherever he looked, Milarepa saw superficiality and dishonesty. This was the incentive he needed to go into retreat for a long time, practicing meditation in mountain solitude. After many years of struggling with himself in this way, he was able to come to terms with the predilections of his own mind.

A significant turning point came in Milarepa's spiritual journey once he began to come to terms with himself. All the while in retreat, Mila had been starving himself by living solely on nettle soup. He had actually turned green and was emaciated, like a walking skeleton. One day some hunters stumbled upon him in the mountains, initially thinking he was a ghost. After realizing he was a renunciate, they offered to bring him decent food and beer to support his meditation practice. Thereafter Milarepa started to spend more time with other human beings and established an inner circle of friends and students. In response to their pleading, he started to teach. Milarepa, in fairly unorthodox fashion, emulated the earlier Indian mahasiddhas' predilection for teaching in the form of dohas, or spiritual songs. These are recorded in *The Hundred Thousand Songs of Milarepa*.

This story is an important point for spiritual aspirants because it provides an example of a single-minded ascetic returning to the world with a completely new perspective. It is possible to renounce the world, realizing that it cannot offer any enduring satisfaction, and yet return to the world without being constantly swayed this way and that, pulled and pushed by everything that we encounter.

BEGINNING THE JOURNEY

An element of uncertainty characterizes any journey. Buddhism teaches that we are already traveling around in uncertainty. It is just that we have become familiar with it—this familiar world is regarded as cyclic existence, samsara. Therefore, the impulse to embark on a spiritual journey arises from the fact that we do not feel at home in this world. We feel that there must be another kind of world to explore. We have begun to see through the facade, the inauthenticity of everything we experience.

Almost all of the world's literature concerned with the individual spiritual journey begins with protagonists who are overwhelmed by a sense of having squandered their opportunities and having been duped by the world. They recognize that their thoughts and actions have been less than good, and they feel mortified. These experiences and feelings propel the individual to embark on the spiritual path and leave behind the corrupting influences of the world. This is important, because if there were no sense of seeing through what is illusory, we would not embark on a journey true to ourselves and others. It is the idea of being able to live life in an authentic way that propels the spiritually inclined individual forward.

Once thrust into the unknown, we are bound to experience a sense of uncertainty and to feel trepidation and anxiety. Even on an ordinary journey, when we travel to a foreign country where the language is different from our own and the people have different customs and a different way of life, it is a shocking and disorienting experience. Similarly, the spiritual journey will not necessarily be smooth and easy to adapt to right away.

When beginning such a journey, it is necessary to try to detach ourselves from everything that is familiar. Resistance to our usual activities is necessary so that we do not fall back into old ways of being. This in itself is difficult, because even if our old way of life is full of self-deception, we may still be tempted to return to it due to sheer force of habit. We therefore need to dissociate from them by renouncing the concerns and affairs of the world. In a real sense, it is necessary to become a recluse, but this does not have to be understood altogether literally. It is possible to be a recluse in a metaphorical sense as well—that is, one can detach oneself on a mental level from everything that is worldly. Cutting attachment to things, in other words, is a form of renunciation.

THE NEED FOR AN
ADEQUATE SPIRITUAL VISION

Even though steady progress on the path may be made initially, this does not imply that things will work out exactly as we expect. Initially our perspective is limited—it is tainted by habitual ways of viewing and experiencing things. Wishes, desires, and expectations are all projected outward, and all sorts of preconceived ideas are hatched about what our spiritual life and goals should be.

We should note right from the beginning that our views are distorted and heavily biased. This will protect from having absolute conviction in your opinions about what a spiritual life should be and how it should proceed. This is not the kind of knowledge that we can possess yet, but something that we accumulate in the course of the journey. We do not begin the spiritual journey with clarity, and as we proceed we find many of our expectations are unmet or frustrated. Other expectations may be exceeded. Nothing about the spiritual journey is predetermined.

A traveler in the physical world who is so meticulous that everything has to be done precisely often ends up being obstructed by circumstances. This applies to the traveler on the spiritual path as well. We need an overall vision of what it is we want to achieve and how we intend to go about realizing our objectives. We also need some idea of how to avoid unnecessary obstacles and how to stay on course. Apart from that, we have to leave much of it to the vicissitudes of life and avoid getting caught up in egotistic willfulness. We will make more progress if we can keep egotism from interfering with our practice. Spiritual experiences cannot be coerced into being.

We fear the highs and lows that we might experience on the spiritual path. We fear the heights, the ecstatic, awe-inspiring experiences just as much as the terrifying ones that bring depression, frustration, and despair. According to the writings of various spiritual masters, none of these experiences should be feared. We fear them only because of the defensive posturing of our ego. The ego is timid and vulnerable by nature and fears that these things will overwhelm it.

SELF-PERCEPTION
AND SELF-TRANSFORMATION

Trying to renounce familiar ways and worldly things is not in itself sufficient for a real spiritual journey. We also require what are known as purification practices, which involve rigorous ascetic disciplines such as periods of isolation in meditation retreat or spending time living in the wilderness fasting. Such practices are undertaken in the spiritual traditions of both East and West.

These practices are necessary because simply saying, "I am a transformed person and a worthy spiritual traveler" does not have any power to effect real change. Putting our mind and body through a rigorous process of discipline will produce all kinds of new and transformative experiences. As we advance on the path, such disciplines will bring about mind-altering experiences, unfolding in ways totally different from our everyday experiences. We call such experiences mind-altering because they are completely unfamiliar; we do not know how to assimilate them into our normal view of self (*atman*) or the world. We might think we are experiencing a visitation of angels or evil spirits or gods and goddesses and so forth—all of which can be quite unsettling for the ego.

Our perception of our normal, conventional self is based upon what is familiar to us. When this self is put to the test, the ego has an overwhelming response, which in some cases can be quite terrifying or awe-inspiring. The normal ego is not equipped to deal with these things and can experience them as very threatening, as something that engulfs the conventional idea of the self completely. At other times, experiences may bring about ecstasy and bliss (*sukha*). It is not all that uncommon for even nonpractitioners who go into the wilderness to have such experiences, as has been attested to by mountaineers and outback adventurers.

According to spiritual literature, we will not deal well with these expressions by focusing on the self, thinking, "This is me, I am going mad, I am losing my mind." If we think, "I am having this or that experience," our anxiety will be heightened. Indeed, in some cases individuals have had breakdowns, and this comes entirely from being overly concerned with the self.

We have to be turned outward, toward something other than the self. Our attention has to be on the reality of things in order to realize that everything we experience arises *from* that reality. This is part of the dissociating process, the loosening of ourselves from fixation on worldly things and moving toward a more open and accommodating view of how things are. If we can do this, we will transform ourselves.

Self-transformation is actually the key to the spiritual journey. As we travel the path, we are transformed by encountering new experiences and exploring new things. Even an ordinary traveler in a foreign country can experience an identity crisis. One who persists with the journey and develops more curiosity about things instead of trying to shut one's mind to all the stimuli will be automatically transformed by the experience.

Spiritual practice is similar: Transformation is achieved by embracing our experiences, even if they appear overwhelming and threatening at the time. The key is how we approach these new experiences. If we focus solely upon the self and its well-being, feelings of vulnerability and weakness will only increase, and we could become completely overwhelmed. If we focus instead on where these experiences are originating from, the self will become rejuvenated and strengthened.

THE IMPORTANCE OF A HEALTHY EGO

According to the Buddhist teachings, a mental breakdown or psychotic episode is not the result of an altered state of consciousness or an experience of seeing and hearing things. It is the result of how these experiences are processed by that person's ego. The health of the ego is important here. An ego that is unhealthy—even in the context of spiritual practice—only produces unhealthy results and experiences. This can lead to psychological distress. *The Cloud of Unknowing*, a Christian mystical text by an unknown author, warns against treating spiritual matters in a materialistic way, a mistake that is easily made by beginners who arrogantly confuse intellectual understanding with spiritual insight.[2] The author describes what happens when egotism gets in the way and people think that they know better than everyone else. They think they no longer need their spiritual mentor or guru and set themselves up as an authority before they have really learned how to detach from their normal passions. They may even believe that they are directly in touch with God or have realized their true nature.

We will have less difficulty on the spiritual path if we do not focus on the ego. The Buddhist teachings say certain unusual experiences might be very disquieting the first time, but as we become acquainted with them they will become easier to handle—as long as we do not focus on ourselves.

Self-obsession can be an acute problem in spiritual practice. For instance, we might experience depression or a sense of despondency and frustration with our lack of spiritual progress, but if we do not pay attention to the ego, all these experiences can be profoundly helpful. The same advice applies to the edifying or uplifting spiritual experiences of joy, delight, rapture, or even ecstasy. Obsessing over these will only boost the ego and start to produce thoughts of greatness and superiority.

For the spiritual path to work, you have to be "reality-centered" rather than "self-centered." In both Buddhism and Christianity, the idea of love is of paramount importance, albeit in Buddhism love is directed toward other beings rather than God. Love and compassion are central to both traditions because they work as an antidote to self-obsession. Reality-centeredness and other-centeredness allow us to progress on the spiritual path more easily and with fewer obstacles. We learn how to have a general sense of happiness no matter what occurs. This is not to say that we will never again experience pain or suffering or that there will be an end to periods of doubt. These things will still afflict us from time to time, but an overall sense of happiness will underlie it all. This is expressed well by Milarepa in these verses from a song sung at Tiger Cave of Senge Tsön:

> Oh, happy are the myriad manifestations!
> The more ups-and-downs, the more joy I feel.
> Happy is the body with no sinful Karma.
> Happy indeed are the countless confusions!

The greater the fear, the greater the happiness I feel.
Oh, happy is the death of sensations and passions!

The greater the distress and passions,
The more can one be blithe and gay!
What happiness to feel no ailment or illness;
What happiness to feel that joy and suffering are one;
What happiness to play in bodily movement
With the power aroused by Yoga.
To jump and run, to dance and leap, is more joyful still.[3]

As this song eloquently implies, while the spiritual journey is a difficult one, it is extremely rewarding. It is not a luxury cruise! It is enriching precisely because we are experiencing everything in its rawness. Milarepa is saying that as we begin to learn to handle these things without being egotistical, our self-power increases.

This is very important to realize, for it is widely misunderstood. Not focusing on our own egotistic well-being does not mean we neglect the well-being of the ego. On the contrary, the health of the ego improves when we focus on the vicissitudes of life within the context of spiritual practice. We actually become more self-empowered, and our capacity to deal with various things increases. This is perhaps the irony of the spiritual journey. The health of the ego improves when we are not fussing over its well-being, always thinking we have to protect and nurture it. When we are always building and bolstering our ego, it is because we feel it to be so fragile that any discomfort will make it fall to pieces. When we protect our ego in this way, we are afraid to venture out and explore. As a consequence, the ego is contracted. When we approach the spiritual path without being egotistical, there is an expansion of the self in a healthy and uplifting way.

ELIMINATION AND ASSIMILATION

The beginning is always the most difficult part of any journey. However, the more time that one spends away from home, the easier it becomes. It is similar with spiritual practice. After we have moved through the difficult early period, there is another level of experiencing things that is less turbulent and more directed.

This next level of practice consists of the elimination and assimilation of various negative and positive mental states. It is concerned with learning how to overcome certain ingrained thoughts and emotions and assimilating others.

Once we learn to assimilate wholesome experiences and eliminate negative ones, the quality of our experiences grows more subtle and intense. People often have the notion that the experiences of a spiritual person are simplified or even neutralized. This is the complete opposite of what occurs. Spiritual experiences actually expand the parameters of human existence in many ways, because the spiritual journey opens up our mind to whole new dimensions of experience and whole new ways of being. It improves the quality of our lives exponentially.

Normally, our experiences do not enrich us much at all—even our good experiences are not particularly illuminating in the long run. A spiritual journey enriches *everything* we experience and aids us in our growth. Through the elimination and assimilation of bad and good experiences respectively, we can begin to develop the wholesome attributes of courage, strength, wisdom, and mental focus and overcome the unwholesome states of weakness, cowardice, ignorance, and distraction—and in the process deepen and enhance our experience of the world.

RENOUNCING THE SPIRITUAL

Eventually we come to a point where we realize that there is a need for another form of renunciation. This is actually the renunciation of spiritual things themselves. Turning the mind away from worldly things and instead focusing on spiritual things can simply lead to attachment to those spiritual things instead. In his *Dark Night of the Soul*, Saint John of the Cross says spiritual people can be just as contemptuous as worldly people. They may not be selfish about material things, but they are about spiritual things, squabbling and fighting over their spirituality, becoming envious of the spiritual attainments of others and proud of their own realizations. In this way, spiritual experiences themselves become a source of anguish, something one can well do without.[4] Buddhist teachings continually alert the unwary to such dangers of becoming overly attached to spiritual things. Even spiritual things can turn demonic when they become embroiled in our egoistic one-upmanship and competitiveness. It is not possible to carry around spiritual things as a possession—

they have to become part of oneself. Instead of thinking, "I have more wisdom than someone else," you have to assimilate whatever spiritual experiences you have, no matter how insignificant. Any spiritual attribute or quality worthy of the name that you experience must become a genuine feature of your own makeup, your own personality. It must be totally assimilated.

As we attain a degree of understanding on the path, we also begin to realize that the spiritual journey has many destinations. There are things that we know that may be useful for some parts of the journey, but not much help later on. A spiritual journey is not like climbing a mountain where we set out from the beginning to reach the peak. It consists of many peaks and valleys, with alternating high points and low points. Nonetheless, steady progress can be made, and it is the sum total of all our experiences that contribute toward our reaching the goal.

As we accumulate more and more knowledge and experience on the spiritual path, many things learned at the beginning become something to renounce, so that they do not themselves become a burden. Fixation on anything that we have learned will only become an obstacle to new experiences. This is another reason renunciation of spiritual things is emphasized.

HUMILITY

Another significant mistake on the path is to lack humility. We must aspire to *mo gu*, which is Tibetan for "interested humility." A sense of humility is emphasized over and over in many traditions' spiritual teachings and storytelling, such as this Judaic story: A much-loved old rabbi was lying on his deathbed surrounded by a number of his close disciples, who were extolling his virtues in subdued tones. "There has been no one as wise as him since Solomon," said one. "His faith is equal to that of Abraham," said another. "His patience was equal to that of Job," said a third. The rabbi seemed restless when his disciples left, and his wife asked him gently, "Didn't you hear the wonderful things your disciples were saying just now?" "I did," said the rabbi. "Then why are you so fretful?" she asked. "My modesty," he complained. "No one mentioned my modesty."

According to many of these spiritual teachings, humility is the gateway to all kinds of spiritual boons. Humility does not suggest that we regard ourselves as "nothing"; that approach is merely the other extreme of blatant egotism. In a sense, it is our destiny to realize our true nature, but this is prevented by our ignorance, confusion, conflicting emotions, conceptual complexity, and so on. If we regard ourselves as nothing, we may feel too inadequate even to undertake the journey in the first place. In spiritual terms, humility is based on strength and courage and resolve. This kind of humility is of the utmost importance.

Let us return to the life story of Milarepa for clarification. Milarepa had two primary students, of whom the best known was Gampopa Sonam Rinchen and the lesser known was Rechungpa (ca. 1083–1156). Gampopa was to become famous for founding the Kagyu school by blending the yogic and monastic traditions. Rechungpa remained a yogi for the duration of his life.

According to traditional sources, Rechungpa and Milarepa had a very difficult teacher–student relationship. This was mainly due to Rechungpa's extreme egotism and willfulness. In one story, Milarepa had tried to impress Rechungpa with magic tricks, but he was not impressed. In response, Milarepa sang the following song known as *Rechungpa's Repentance*:

> *Rechungpa, listen to me for a moment!*
> *Hard horn, and solid wood,*
> *Can be bent if one tries;*
> *But a harsh mind is hard to "bend."*
> *Rechungpa, try to subdue your mind within!*
>
> *Fierce tigers in the South,*
> *And wild yaks in the North*
> *Can be tamed if one tries;*
> *But pride and egotism are hard to tame.*
> *Rechungpa, try to subdue conceit within!*
>
> *Mice under the ground,*
> *And birds in the sky*
> *Can be caught if one tries;*
> *But a lost mind is hard to catch.*
> *Rechungpa, try your own faults to see!*
>
> *The Dharma of words*
> *And speculation*

Can be learned if one tries;
But the void Self-mind is hard to learn.
Rechungpa, try to meditate on the uncreated mind!

. . . .

My son, try to correct your wrong ideas,
Abandon your bad actions,
Discipline your unruly mind,
Your impious thoughts restrain,
Avoid the demon of egotism.
When I come to die this shall I will for you;
No profounder teaching can I give you in my life.
Rechungpa, my son, bear my words in mind![5]

This is a teaching on the obstacles presented by egotism. Milarepa is saying that even if you focus your mind totally on spiritual practices so that everything else has ceased to matter, it will all come to naught if you have not overcome egotism. Milarepa points out that it is easier to leave worldly things behind than it is to leave a mind that is dominated by selfishness and egotism. It is this mind that is the fundamental obstacle to spiritual practice and the most prevalent reason spiritual aspirants will stray from the path.

RENOUNCING CONCEPTUAL UNDERSTANDING

The next step on the journey is to renounce conceptual understanding. This directive might be puzzling, given my insistence in the previous chapter on the necessity of having certain conceptual frameworks and beliefs in order to make sense of experience. However, as I pointed out, whereas conceptual understanding that we develop is a crucial part of the spiritual path, once it has served its purpose it can be relinquished. We need not hang on to our conceptual frameworks forever, but they are absolutely essential at the beginning of our journey. Once our understanding increases, we can let them go.

To return to the analogies of the finger pointing at the moon and the raft that crosses the turbulent waters of samsaric suffering, they encapsulate just this—the enormous usefulness of conceptual tools and also the end of their usefulness. One can still make use of concepts, even at more advanced stages of the spiritual journey. This may be a helpful distinction to maintain as you read. It might also be useful to reflect on the fact that any use of language inevitably entails the use of concepts.

As we advance on the spiritual path, renunciation of reified concepts will come to mean not getting swayed by thoughts of good versus bad, spiritual versus material, worldly versus otherworldly, samsara versus nirvana, spiritual attainment versus nonspiritual attainment, and so on. We can let go of the chronic habit of clinging to these concepts because as we progress along the path we will experience a transcendental realm where there is no need to conceptualize about either the finite world or ultimate reality.

Ultimate reality and the spiritual experiences that allow us to go from the "unknowing of ignorance" to the "knowing of wisdom" are based upon direct experience. Conceptual understanding, on the other hand, is based on inference. For a good part of the journey, we can have only an inferential understanding of ultimate reality, not a direct experience of it. When we have a direct experience of ultimate reality, it is actually not possible to conceptualize it or express it through words and ideas. It is said, "Seeing that which cannot be seen is the ultimate seeing." In other words, "to know" is only to know something in terms of intellectual understanding; it is nothing compared to the wisdom that comes from really grasping something with our whole being.

Conceptual understanding has to lead to realization, which is going beyond understanding. Realization is about seeing the ultimate reality in all things and seeing all things in ultimate reality. We no longer distinguish between the world that we had to renounce and the transcendental realm that we have been trying to enter.

SPIRITUAL EXPERIENCES AND REALIZATIONS

There will be all sorts of experiences on the spiritual path. Positive periods of development, those that are reassuring and comforting, are also an important part of the process. It is important to realize however, that even these positive experiences will fluctuate. We will rarely if ever perceive a steady development of them, precisely because experiences are fickle by nature. Enjoying a series of good experiences does not ensure they will continue indefinitely; they may stop suddenly. Even so, they remain an important part of spiritual practice, not least because they help to maintain our motivation to continue practicing.

The way in which these positive experiences arise also varies enormously. You may have some amazingly moving experiences, something like a spiritual awakening that appears to arise out of the blue. In fact, such experiences do not really come from nowhere; there will always have been prior psychic conditions preceding them, although they appear to our conscious experience as instantaneous. They can also vanish just as quickly as they appear. At other times certain experiences will grow over a period of time, peak, and then gradually fade away again.

As spiritual practitioners, we are instructed not to attach too much significance to these experiences. The advice is to resist the temptation to become fixated on the experiences themselves. Experiences will come and go. Each experience has to be let go, or the mind will simply close down in its fixation on that experience, leaving little or no room for new experiences to arise. This is because your fixation will encourage worries and doubts to arise in the mind and interfere with the development process.

If something does not last, you should assume that it had no reality, because if something is real it has to last. All the same, just because something did not last and is no longer evident in your life does not mean that it was not important. Whether an experience lasts for a long time or was merely a flash in your consciousness does not in itself indicate its significance. A brief experience may be more significant than one that endured over a longer period. Trying to evaluate our spiritual experiences like this is definitely discouraged, because it will only lead to more endless worries and elaborations. If there is no fixation involved in the process, positive spiritual experiences (*nyam* in Tibetan) will start to lead you to having spiritual realizations (*togpa* in Tibetan).

In Buddhism we distinguish between spiritual experiences and spiritual realizations (about which more will be said in later chapters). Spiritual experiences are usually more vivid and intense than realizations, because they generally are accompanied by physiological and psychological changes. Realizations, on the other hand, may be felt, but their feeling tone is less pronounced. Realization is about acquiring insight. Therefore, while realizations arise out of our spiritual experiences, they are not identical to them. Spiritual realizations are considered vastly more important, because they cannot fluctuate.

The distinction between spiritual experiences and realizations is continually emphasized in Buddhist thought. If we avoid excessively fixating on our experiences, we will be under less stress and strain in our practice. Without that stress and strain, we will be better able to cope with whatever arises; the possibility of suffering from psychic disturbances will be greatly reduced, and we will notice a significant shift in the fundamental texture of our experience. There are many accounts in Tibetan Buddhist literature of how spiritual disturbances may arise, but all point to fixation on experiences as the cause. Fixation on our experiences is seen as another variation of fixation on the self.

In the overall context of the spiritual journey, it is important to remember that self-transformation is a continuous process, not a onetime event. One cannot say, "I used to be a non-spiritual person, but now I have been transformed into a spiritual person. My old self is dead." We are constantly being transformed when we travel on the path. While the same individual on one level, on another level we are different. There is always continuity, and yet at each major turning point in the journey, we have become transformed, because certain habits have dropped away. It is a dynamic process, which is why spiritual insights have to be continuous as well. Therefore we should not fixate on the notion of spiritual states, because that implies some kind of place where one arrives. The spiritual journey is dynamic and always tends forward, because we are not fixating on things.

LETTING GO

The spiritual journey, then, is a journey of detachment, a process of learning how to let go of things. All of our problems, miseries, and unhappiness are caused by fixation—latching on to things and not being able to let them go. First we have to let go of fixation on material things. This does not mean jettisoning all our material possessions necessarily, but it implies that we should not look to material things for lasting happiness. Normally, our position in life, our family, our standing in the community, and so forth are perceived to be the source of our happiness. This perspective has to be reversed, according to spiritual teachings, by relinquishing our fixation on material things.

Letting go of fixation is effectively a process of learning to be free, because every time we let go of something, we become free of it. Whatever we fixate upon limits us, because fixation makes us dependent upon something other than ourselves. Each time we let go of something, we experience another level of freedom.

Eventually, in order to be totally free, we learn to let go of concepts.

Ultimately we need to relinquish our fixation on the reification of concepts of things being "this" or "that." Thinking of this and that binds us to a particular way of experiencing things. Even spiritual experiences will not be given complete, spontaneous, unmediated expression when even the subtlest kind of conceptual distinction is present. Experience will still be mediated, adulterated, and tainted by all kinds of psychic content when we discriminate. Therefore, it will remain impossible to ever be truly free.

The final step in the process of letting go is relinquishing the idea that material corruption and spiritual freedom are unequivocally opposed to one another and that we have to give up the former to attain the latter. While this is an important distinction to observe at the beginning of the spiritual journey, we have to overcome that duality. We have to transcend both the seduction of samsaric pleasure that turns out to be so illusory and the seduction of our spiritual goal that appears to be offering eternal happiness. Once the pull between these two poles is harmonized and transcended, we are ready to return home.

THE FRUITION OF THE SPIRITUAL PATH

The ultimate goal of the spiritual journey is to realize the union of your mind and ultimate reality. You discover eventually that not only are you in reality, but that you embody that reality. Your ordinary body becomes the body of a buddha, your ordinary speech becomes the speech of a buddha and your ordinary mind becomes the mind of a buddha. This is the great transition that you have to make, relinquishing your fixation on the separation of samsaric beings and buddhas. When we can talk about them as ultimately the same, when this actual transformation occurs within an individual, it is a truly great occurrence. It is remarkable because an ordinary, confused being becomes fully transformed into a realized being. Even so, there still remains that preexisting continuity between an ordinary being and an enlightened being, in the sense that what you become is what you have always been. At the end of the journey, you are simply returning home.

Yet the journey itself was absolutely necessary. It was necessary to leave your familiar environment and venture through various trials and tribulations. It was necessary to deal with the many unexpected things, to grapple with your inner demonic forces. It was necessary to go through the spiritual struggle and engage in vigorous disciplines. Spiritual struggle is valuable for the purification of the mind. Your mind has to be cleansed of the delusions and conflicting emotions that are the product of your karma, the product of the negative thoughts and actions that have accumulated in your mind-stream over a long period of time.

After a point, however, you have to ease off with that struggle. As progress is made on the path, the positive qualities required for further advancement will become part of you, and you will gradually learn how to assimilate and become these positive qualities, rather than regarding them as something to be attained and possessed. So after the initial focus on learning how to replace vices with virtues, we must learn to let go of our fixation with virtues. We have to stop thinking about accumulating virtues, spiritual qualities, experiences, and realizations as if they were a form of wealth. This is simply a way of substituting our previous obsession with material wealth with an obsession for accumulating spiritual wealth. We do not require spiritual wealth; moreover, spiritual wealth can only be accumulated by not fixating on it. All fixations lead only to all manner of trouble—envy, possessiveness, and egotism, for example. It is then that we really go astray and wander from the spiritual path.

As our virtuous qualities of love, compassion, joy, courage, determination, resolve, mindfulness, awareness, and wisdom develop, we progress further along the path. At some point, we have to accomplish one final act of detachment, which is to let go of reifying concepts altogether. Even the concepts of virtue and vice, redemption, karma, and liberation have to be relinquished. By way of illustration, I will finish this chapter with a story from the Zen tradition.

It is not uncommon for Zen meditation students to keep in regular contact with their teachers concerning their spiritual progress. In this particular story, a Zen student had a penchant for writing to his teacher monthly with an account of his development. His letters began to take a mystical turn when he wrote, "I am experiencing a oneness with the universe." When his teacher received this letter, he merely glanced at it and threw it away. The next month the student wrote, "I have discovered that the divine is present in everything." His teacher used this letter to start his fire. A month later, the student had become even more ecstatic and wrote, "The mystery of the one and many has revealed itself to my wonderment," at which his teacher yawned. The following month, another letter arrived, which simply said, "There is no self, no one is born, and no one dies." At this his teacher threw his hands up in despair. After this fourth letter, the student stopped writing to his teacher, and after a year had passed, the teacher began to feel concerned and wrote to his student, asking to be kept informed of his spiritual progress. The student wrote back with the words, "Who cares?" When the teacher read this, he smiled and said, "At last! He's finally got it!" At the end of the journey you will be able to engage in everything on both the material and the spiritual planes without being tainted by them, because a spiritually realized being is no longer affected by the world in the same way an ordinary person is. Without going through the trials and tribulations of this journey, however, you will never find your home. You cannot simply stay at home and say, "I am already where I want to be." It is only the journey that makes you realize your true potential. It is only at the end of the journey that you understand that the goal is not separate from the starting point. That is the attainment of buddhahood, the natural state of your own mind.

4

DELUDED MIND, ENLIGHTENED MIND

THE BUDDHIST SPIRITUAL QUEST BEGINS WITH OUR OWN MIND. Being a nontheistic religion—that is, neither theistic nor atheistic—Buddhism does not begin with a belief in God or some other kind of supernatural power. Buddhism does not necessarily deny the existence of God; it just has a different frame of reference. It says we can only ever understand ourselves and our world through the kind of mind that we have. The structure of our mind and the functions, states, and processes of our consciousness determine the range of what we experience. This is true from the basic level of our sensory consciousness to the higher functionings of our cognitive activities. It follows from this that we must develop an understanding of our consciousness before we can even think of developing as spiritual beings. If we do not pay attention to our mind, we cannot really speak about Buddhist spirituality at all.

As Buddhists, we try to emulate the example of Gautama Shakyamuni Buddha, who lived in India roughly 2,500 years ago. Far from being a divine incarnation of some sort, the Buddha started his spiritual journey as an ordinary human being, just like you and me. It was precisely his humanness that drove Shakyamuni Buddha to seek enlightenment. He had no special link to a greater spiritual reality. The enlightened state that the Buddha was able to connect with and realize is something we all can attain.

In order to develop the spiritual qualities that the Buddha embodied, we need to utilize the mind that we have. Buddhism teaches that the mind functions on two different levels. At one level is the deluded mind (*namshe* in Tibetan), which is the cause of all of our misery, frustration, and pain. The other level is the enlightened mind (*yeshe* in Tibetan), which has the capacity to free us from that suffering and pain. This will not make a lot of sense, though, until we appreciate that the Buddhist understanding of the mind is not the same as our normal, empirical understanding and experience of mind. That is only one level of consciousness. There is another level that we currently are totally unfamiliar with. Buddhism speaks of these two levels of mind as the deluded and undeluded mind. This distinction is something we need to understand. The topic of the nature of the mind resurfaces regularly in the Mahamudra teachings, which state there is no real difference between the deluded and undeluded states of mind. However, this Mahamudra perspective must be understood from the ultimate point of view, whereby the deluded mind and the undeluded mind are considered to have the same nature. From the relative perspective, though, they invariably appear as two radically different mental phenomena.

WHAT IS ENLIGHTENMENT?

When we speak about the attainment of enlightenment, we are not referring to an altered psychological state. Buddhists seeking enlightenment are not looking for altered states of consciousness or psychological insight into the workings of our so-called ordinary consciousness.

We are not concerned with notions of psychological health here, so Buddhist mind training should not be understood as a form of ancient psychotherapy. Buddhist meditation is not really therapy at all. Its primary concern is not to address our psychological neuroses or emotional disorders. We should not expect to find out why we eat so much, why we feel so anxious, or where all our self-loathing comes from. Certainly this kind of understanding may come about as an incidental by-product of meditation—becoming more conscious of our mental states will likely enable us to realize certain things about ourselves along the way.

If we follow the spiritual path advisedly, putting the requisite effort into our mental cultivation, we will definitely experience some relief from our neurosis and confusion. However, an improved sense of psycho-physical well-being cannot be equated with the spiritual transformation of enlightenment.

ORDINARY CONSCIOUSNESS
AND WISDOM CONSCIOUSNESS

It would be a serious misunderstanding to think that spiritual transformation is obtained through cultivating the mind that we experience on a daily basis, the mind that anticipates, remembers, worries, and has all manner of confused, agitated states. The mind that we are counseled to cultivate in Buddhist teachings is not the empirical mind we normally experience, even though our mental training is dependent upon that mind. It is the undeluded mind that we have to cultivate in order to transcend the limitations of our normal states of consciousness.

Undeluded mind is called "wisdom consciousness," or yeshe, in Buddhism and the empirical consciousness is called "ordinary deluded consciousness," or namshe. This distinction is difficult to convey in words. In Buddhism *namshe* and *yeshe* are different concepts. *Yeshe* is actually Tibetan for the Sanskrit word *jnana*, which was translated as "gnosis" in chapter 2. As we begin to access wisdom consciousness, we will be able to generate a genuine, penetrating spiritual insight—transcendental knowledge, or prajna. To briefly reiterate what was said in chapter 2, transcendental knowledge gives rise to gnosis. Transcendental knowledge is more akin to a conceptual form of understanding and is always a precondition for the dawning of genuine gnosis. It is important to understand this distinction between the two types of spiritual insight, transcendental knowledge and gnosis, that become manifest from the cultivation of our undeluded state of consciousness.

Our deluded, samsaric mind—the ordinary states of consciousness that we experience from moment to moment in everyday life—is not the same as our undeluded mind. According to Buddhism, the samsaric mind is seriously affected by the inflammation of various forms of spurious illusory states. Our minds have been driven into a state of confusion through the relentless arousal of conflicting emotions (*klesha*): excessive anger, overwhelming desire, inflated pride, unforgiving

resentment, and so forth. Our samsaric mind, then, is in a state of constant, unremitting restlessness. That being the case, this state of consciousness can hardly be said to be conscious at all.

When Buddhism stresses cultivating the mind, our primary concern is learning how to deal with our ordinary deluded consciousness
in such a skillful way that we can go beyond it and realize our wisdom
consciousness. We do not attain wisdom as something new, via the
overcoming of our ordinary deluded mind. Our delusions have to be
overcome so that our innate wisdom mind is allowed to arise naturally,
because the capacity to attain wisdom consciousness is already present
as the innate quality of our mind.

MIND TRAINING

Mental cultivation, or mind training, is the essence of the Buddhist path
of practice. All the meditative techniques and various other disciplines
of body, speech, and mind are all forms of mental cultivation. We
should, however, be clear about what is meant by mind training and
mind cultivation. We are not talking about manipulating our everyday
experiences of consciousness in some purposeful fashion. In a way, we
are trying to bypass that mind and access a state of consciousness that is
undeluded precisely because there is a sense of perspicacity or clarity
within it already. According to Buddhist thinking, such deliberate ma-
neuvers would still stem from everyday consciousness that is not all that
conscious, due to the delusions that we constantly carry around and reinforce, producing diminished awareness and a dull, incapacitated mind.

There is another way of being ourselves. We are not at all familiar
with this other way in our normal states of consciousness, because we
perceive and experience things from a limited, myopic, egotistic perspective. In fact, this is the only way the deluded consciousness will ever
be able to perceive things. Through mental cultivation, we can rise
above deluded, egotistic perception. This is the attainment of wisdom
consciousness, a level of consciousness that is literally lit up or illuminated so that our ability to perceive things increases exponentially.

Mind training develops wisdom consciousness and allows us to
gradually extricate our being from the influence of our ordinary deluded consciousness, which is so habituated that it can only bring more
misery and pain to ourselves and others. As such, mind cultivation is the

very essence of Buddhist spiritual practice. There is no separation between the two. Buddhist spirituality would not exist if it were not for
the cultivation of the mind. Part of this training includes inculcating
the correct view.

As we train our mind, the influence of our deluded consciousness
gradually decreases, and as a result the greater powers of our wisdom
consciousness begin to develop. Eventually the ordinary deluded consciousness ceases to operate completely, leaving only the undeluded
wisdom consciousness.

Hence a buddha's mind is completely different from our own
mind. This seems obvious in some ways, but it is not generally well understood in the West because we try to psychologize spiritual realities.
It is important to resist that temptation. We can still appreciate the importance of psychological techniques and psychotherapies, but we
should not confuse them with the Buddhist view of mind and mind
training. They are quite different and distinct conceptions of mind.

It is extremely important to understand that in the Buddhist view
there has to be a complete transformation in our individual mental continuum. In the West, many people say that Buddhist practice involves
nothing more than simply being aware; if you can stay in the present
moment you will be less likely to be overwhelmed by negative states of
mind. They equate this lack of disturbance with enlightenment and
claim there is no difference between a mind that is aware and a mind that
is enlightened. That is not entirely true. Of course, we have to start with
a state of awareness in terms of our psychological states, but true awareness stems from the wisdom consciousness, not from the deluded state of
mind. Simply training your ordinary deluded consciousness to be aware
and in the present will not lead to liberation so easily. If that were the
case, every professional athlete would be enlightened by now, because
they have to focus and be in the present; their livelihood depends upon
it. The distinction between these two different types of awareness—the
psychological and the spiritual—is exceptionally important from a spiritual point of view. Psychological awareness is still a deluded state and
should never be confused with wisdom consciousness.

Spiritual realization occurs over an extended period of time. There can
be no quick transition from deluded states of mind to wisdom consciousness. We must learn gradually to operate from the level of the wisdom mind
through methods of cultivation and endeavor to extricate ourselves from

delusory, habituated states of consciousness. This is regarded as an option in Buddhist spiritual practice, for it is firmly believed that we are not and never can be free in our normal states of consciousness.

Ordinarily, even when we think we are making choices about our lives, we are not choosing in any genuine sense. It is more the case that we are following our habitual tendencies and deluded understandings. We will never be free as long as our habits are continuously reinforced, and according to Buddhist teachings, this karmic reinforcement is going on twenty-four hours a day. Every experience leaves an imprint on our consciousness, which contributes to the many distorted ways in which we perceive the world. Whatever we perceive, we perceive according to the structured functioning of the mind. As we have seen, this is a mistaken structure formed of distorted thoughts and conflicting emotions. The sorts of things we think about and the sorts of emotions we experience all go toward perpetuating delusory states of mind. We have to understand that our perception of normal consciousness is illusory, predicated on and animated by distorted views and emotional turbulence. This is the state of samsaric bondage described in the teachings, and this is what we need to extricate ourselves from.

If we are honest with ourselves, we know from our own experience that the more we try to find solutions to our problems through thinking about them, the more we start going around in circles, sometimes interminably. Buddhism counsels us to resist being abused by our conflicting emotions and to let go of excessive thinking. Emotions can be expressed in an unhealthy, self-destructive manner or in a healthy and constructive fashion. Similarly, we can think in a self-destructive, confused way, which reinforces our negative habits, or we can think in a constructive way. Buddhism emphasizes that overindulgence in conflicting emotions and distorted forms of thinking only reinforces our old habits, which solidifies our karmic tendencies even further.

This is not to say that we are trying to eradicate our feelings and emotions altogether. It is not the emotions or the feelings themselves that contribute to our spiritual ignorance. Many people have a notion of the spiritual state as something extremely rarefied and lofty because we have left behind all our normal mental states and attained some pure state of consciousness. According to Buddhism, this is not true. Once ignorance has been purified, all the capacities and functionings of normal consciousness are in fact enhanced. None of the features of our functioning consciousness need be renounced. We simply have to train our minds to renounce the ignorance that is behind our deluded states of mind.

The Importance of Meditative Practices

There are many kinds of Buddhist meditation, but all practices will partake to a greater or lesser extent in three fundamental techniques. The first meditation technique is designed to enable us to deal with our conflicting emotions. This is called shamatha, or tranquillity meditation. The second technique is designed to aid us in our effort to overcome the proliferation of thoughts that we have spoken about. This is called vipashyana, or insight meditation. The third technique is designed to assist our feelings and emotions and is called meditation on the four immeasurables (*brahmaviharas*). It includes the contemplation of love, compassion, joy, and equanimity. (These three techniques will be discussed later—the four immeasurables in chapter 6 and tranquillity and insight meditation in chapters 8 and 9.) Each specific practice addresses certain aspects of our consciousness and deals with a particular source of our delusions.

Tranquillity meditation and insight meditation are both concerned with giving rise to our wisdom consciousness. Tranquillity meditation deals with our emotions and with the disturbed mind in general. Its main technique is the development of mindfulness and awareness. We must ask ourselves this fundamental question: How do our habits become entrenched? They become entrenched through our lack of awareness, through going about our business in a mindless, inattentive fashion without being fully conscious of what we are doing, what we are thinking and feeling. We have to learn to master our distracted mind, which has become scattered by the conflicting emotions and discursive thoughts that run rampant.

To understand how these emotions and distorted forms of thinking arise, we have to first calm the mind through tranquillity meditation. From this we train ourselves to recognize the experience of our thinking and of our emotions through insight meditation. According to Buddhism, emotions are not in themselves evil, base, or defiling. There are emotions that perpetuate delusions and conflicting emotions, and there are emotions that aid the development of wisdom. Therefore, we supplement tranquillity and insight meditation with meditation on the four immeasurables, for they teach us how to generate, use, and express emotions skillfully. Skillful in this context means not being overly concerned with any particular emotion that might arise. How we express that emotion is far more important, for it is the expression in action that determines whether it is harmful or beneficial to ourselves and others. Through this we gradually become more skilled at utilizing the various experiences to advance on the spiritual path.

Of all of the meditation techniques, however, insight meditation is the most important because it allows us to see into the nature of things. Without insight we cannot really cultivate our wisdom consciousness. We may be able to train our minds to become a little more calm and learn how to express our emotions in a healthy, constructive fashion, but without insight we will never overcome the habituations and conflicting emotions of our deluded consciousness. We might be nice people who do no harm to anyone and even want to help others, but without insight we will never be able to transcend our ordinary state of being.

Insight meditation reveals all of our experiences to be based on a distorted type of thinking that misperceives and misinterprets everything. This becomes more discernible if we scrutinize our consciousness; we see that it is not passive, simply receiving information through the senses. Consciousness is an active agent that determines how and what we perceive and how we employ our interpretative schemas. Our misperceptions and misinterpretations then lead to the development of fixation (*dzinpa* in Tibetan).

We have to gain insight into how the mind imputes all kinds of fictitious characteristics and attributes to things. If we lessen that mental tendency to reify everything, all the other practices will fall into place. Without this insight into the nature of things, it is not possible to make the transition from ordinary deluded consciousness to our wisdom consciousness.

It bears reiterating that when you become a buddha you are totally transfigured. Shakyamuni Buddha was an ordinary human being originally, but that does not suggest he was still just another human being after attaining enlightenment. He was not just another human being; he was a human being who had become completely transformed. When we follow the spiritual path, we also have to think of becoming an elevated being and of loosening our attachment to our normal human characteristics and human conditions. The state of enlightenment is not simply an altered psychological state. It is a state of being that is truly transformed and illuminated with the spiritual qualities and attributes of our innate wisdom consciousness that we as ordinary sentient creatures can hardly fathom. It is to become a truly rejuvenated and transfigured human being, which is the goal that Buddhist practitioners have been aspiring to for the past 2,500 years.

5

THE
FOUR PRELIMINARIES

___

THE FOUR PRELIMINARIES SERVE AS A BRIDGE BETWEEN THE
exoteric and mystical approaches to enlightenment. Even though these
preliminary practices are an integral part of the exoteric and esoteric
systems of the Mahayana, the way I have introduced them here is somewhat different from their usual presentation. I have followed the Kagyu
and Nyingma understanding of these important practices, and the language that describes them is therefore commensurate with the vocabulary of the rest of this book. Terms such as *the nature of the mind* and *the
ground of being*, which are indicators of the mystical approach, will also
be found in this chapter.

The four preliminaries belong to the common preliminary practices (*tummong ngondro*) of Tibetan Buddhism. The fundamental objective of these preliminaries is to remind ourselves constantly why we are
practicing. These practices are traditionally done at the beginning of
every session of meditation as a supplement to the main practice, because they help to reinforce our motivation and prevent us from lapsing
into laziness and complacency.

Without thinking about the preciousness of our body, the fragility
of our lives, the essentially dissatisfactory nature of cyclic existence, and
how our lives are determined by our habitual karmic patterns, it would

be very easy to yield to our habitual tendencies and allow our motivation to lapse. Sometimes Westerners mistake the preliminaries for something basic and inessential to their spiritual practice and think of tranquillity and insight meditation as a superior form of practice. On the contrary, it is essential to found all of our meditative practices on these preliminary contemplations, because without them our practice will be unstable and without foundation. If we ignore the preliminaries, we will practice only when we feel like it and thereby fail to maintain a sense of urgency about our spiritual goals.

It is fairly common for people to be enthusiastic about their practice at the beginning of the spiritual path, especially if some life situation has triggered their search. Some people are driven to spiritual practice out of despair or unhappiness or some kind of health scare or because they just got divorced. After meditating for a while, they begin to feel better and go back to their old ways as if nothing were the matter—until the next time disaster strikes. We have to remind ourselves that even when everything is going well there is no insurance that our lives will continue in a positive direction. People often think that if they eat well, exercise properly, and have a loving partner, a loving family, and rewarding work, this will guarantee them a long and happy life. The truth is that people die suddenly from unexpected causes all the time, regardless of their healthy lifestyle, careful intentions, or fortunate circumstances.

These contemplations are not presented to make us morbid or morose but to help build a real appreciation for our opportunities while we have them. If we do not think about the precious human body, impermanence, the sufferings of samsara, and karmic cause and effect as we do spiritual practices, we may not commit ourselves to their transformative potential. If we think that each new day is just another day, we will never generate the motivation to do anything much. Each day is *not* just another day; it is a day that is going to determine what direction we take in the future. If we think that each day and each moment is precious, we will appreciate our lives more and feel motivated to pursue our spiritual goals. These four preliminaries are designed to strengthen our resolve to approach spiritual practice in this way.

What follows is a detailed discussion of each preliminary and the meditative exercises to be incorporated into our daily practice. While it is also of enormous benefit to devote entire meditation sessions or retreats solely to these preliminary practices, it is recommended that you spend five minutes or so on them at the beginning of every session of meditation, regardless of what your main practice might be. You can spend a minute or so on each preliminary or you can meditate on them together.

It is traditional in Mahayana Buddhism to begin every meditation session by taking refuge in the Three Jewels (Buddha, Dharma, and Sangha) and generating an enlightened heart (*bodhichitta*) for a few minutes. We take refuge in the Three Jewels to remind ourselves of our commitment to take the spiritual journey and attain enlightenment for the sake of all beings. It is said in the traditional literature that we take refuge in Buddha, Dharma, and Sangha because they are the only true friends we have—all other sources of refuge are impermanent, subject to change, and will inevitably let us down. The compassionate and caring attitude of the enlightened heart must be present in our practice to remind us of our commitment to others. This is the fertile ground of goodness from which all spiritual qualities grow. It is also important to remember to dedicate any merit we may have accumulated through our practice to other beings. This is a form of rejoicing in our love and compassion for all beings and helps to create wholesome dispositional qualities within our own mind-stream.

THE PRECIOUS HUMAN BODY

In this first meditation, we contemplate the preciousness of our human body. This contemplation on the precious human body is considered extraordinarily important, because most of us do not realize that something is precious until we have lost it. It is part of our human affliction that we take what we have for granted. This encourages us to look at the rarity and preciousness of our opportunities by treasuring our human body as the basis for enlightenment. We are blessed with a sound mind and body, and we should learn to rejoice at our good fortune and the invaluable opportunities for spiritual practice that this provides, rather than dismissing our body as an inferior material thing. The traditional teachings advise that if we really meditate on the preciousness of our human body and learn to appreciate how difficult it is to obtain, this will have a profound effect on our spiritual progress and guarantee an unwavering motivation to leave the samsaric state behind.

According to the Kagyu and Nyingma schools of the Tibetan tradition, a so-called precious human birth involves more than just having a sound mind and body; it describes a human embodiment that has access to Buddhist teachings and the leisure to pursue them with diligence. Traditional Buddhist teachings say that while any human rebirth is difficult enough to obtain, a precious human body is rarer and more valuable still, because it represents the perfect vehicle for following the spiritual path. It would be extremely foolish, then, to let our opportunities slip away after being given this chance to do something significant with our lives. It would be akin to discovering a valuable treasure on a remote island, then returning home without it despite the hardships of the journey.

The Eight Leisures and Ten Endowments

Our lives have to include specific leisures and endowments to qualify as a precious human rebirth. The potential of this kind of rebirth is compared to a destitute person accidentally finding a rare and valuable gem, because in both cases a life that initially promised very little is suddenly transformed into one of opportunity and joy. The truly precious human body is characterized by eight kinds of leisure and ten kinds of endowment.

Buddhist cosmology divides existence into six possible realms and says that we transmigrate through each of these as a result of our karmic traces and dispositions. These realms consist of the hell realm, the hungry ghost realm, the animal realm, the human realm, the jealous god realm, and the realm of long-lived gods. These realms can be viewed as either psychological states or physical realities. It is not hard to imagine the mental or existential realities of some people—even ourselves—as corresponding to the symbolism of these realms. The first four leisures, then, are defined as having a mind that has not taken us into the hell realm, the hungry ghost realm, the animal realm, or the god realms and thus inured us to the hardships and lack of leisure that these realms entail. The next four leisures include not being born among uncivilized people, among people who hold erroneous views, in a place where there are no Buddhist teachings, or mentally or physically impaired.

The ten conditions defined as endowments include five that relate

to ourselves and five that relate to our environment. The five endowments that relate to ourselves are that we have been born in a center of
advanced culture, we have been endowed with acute mental and physical faculties, we have a sense of moral values, we have maintained our
spiritual understanding, and we have reverence for spiritual things. The
five endowments that relate to our environment consist of being born
in a place where the Buddha has appeared, where he has made the gift
of the teachings, where his teachings are still alive, where they are followed by religious communities, and where these communities have a
sense of sensitivity and compassion for the suffering of others.

If we have no moral or spiritual sensitivity, dedicate our time and
energy to worldly goals and distractions, and have no interest in
searching for solutions to our human quandaries, then our human
body cannot be defined as precious. We may have a sporadic enthusiasm for spiritual pursuits and engage in some wholesome activities, but
if our minds are not consistently turned toward beneficial activities, we
are fickle and unreliable and of no benefit to ourselves or others in the
long run.

We are considered to have a precious human body only when we
sincerely listen to Buddhist teachings and contemplate the meaning of
what we have heard. Even that is not sufficient in itself. The meaning
has to make an impact on us so that we become transformed by our
spiritual practices and can make a difference to the lives of others. If our
spiritual commitment is as unwavering as a mountain, our human body
can become a vessel that holds everything precious and worthwhile in
life. While some people may be able to hold only some of these qualities, others may become fit vessels for realizing the full potential of their
leisures and endowments. Therefore, we should aspire to commit to
spiritual practices without delay and concentrate on lessening the temporary distractions of mundane life.

MEDITATION

Settle yourself on a comfortable cushion, take refuge in the Three
Jewels and arouse enlightened heart, then imagine that your body
possesses all the attributes necessary for the attainment of enlight-

enment. Regard your precious human body as something that you have newly discovered and finally come to appreciate. Contemplate your exceptional good fortune in having found a teacher who can give you spiritual instruction. Then think that even if you have met such a teacher, it is not easy to actually apply those teachings in your everyday life. Nor is it easy to have the sustained resolve to advance on the spiritual path. If you want to realize the profundity of these leisures and endowments for yourself, you have to look at your own precious human body and think: "I am going to utilize this body by turning my mind to the Dharma. I will do this by listening to the Buddhist teachings and then applying the teachings to my life circumstances." Conclude the meditation by dedicating any merit you have accumulated to the welfare of all sentient beings.

The Difficulty of Obtaining a Precious Human Body

The possibility of obtaining elevated and noble states of being exists only because we possess a precious human body that is furnished with the eight leisures and ten endowments. We should not squander this opportunity by allowing time to slip away but practice diligently and generate a feeling of joy. It is important to give rise to joy when we do this contemplation. We must learn to appreciate how blessed we are with the opportunities that we have, instead of thinking that other people are better off than we are or projecting our opportunities into the future so that we squander the present moment.

The years slip by very quickly if we are not attentive, and these opportunities may be easily lost along with them. Instead of finding fault with ourselves, we should generate joy and excitement about our current good fortune and turn our tendency for mental projection about ourselves and our lives in a positive direction. For example, instead of thinking, "Someone else is always better off than I am" or "I am too fat" or "I am old and undesirable," we should think, "I am a good person and have the capacity to attain enlightenment in this lifetime." What we think has an enormous power to influence how we perceive, interpret, and react to things. It also determines the kinds of things we are motivated to pursue and incorporate in our lives.

If we appreciate our opportunities in this positive fashion, our inspiration to hear and follow the teachings and to engage in meditation can only increase. In fact, everything that we do in our lives will become more meaningful. We must engage in this joyful meditation on our great good fortune over and over. Everybody who has practiced the spiritual path and attained spiritual realizations and enlightenment has done so by capitalizing on the preciousness of their human body and by generating a sense of conviction and joy about their opportunities.

MEDITATION

Settle in the meditation posture, take refuge and generate bodhichitta, then feel a sense of joy in your precious birth and fortunate circumstances. Contemplate all the positive attributes you have in terms of the eight leisures and ten endowments and give yourself positive feedback about these good qualities. Think: "I am so fortunate to be blessed with these leisures and endowments. I have so many opportunities to cultivate and transform myself and can make a positive contribution to others through applying myself to spiritual practice. I am indeed blessed with wonderful good fortune and shall devote this body to the cultivation of the Dharma!" While thinking in this way, it is crucial to arouse joy in your mind at your rare opportunities and to think deeply about the truth of your situation. Conclude this meditation by making this aspiration: "From drinking the nectar of all that is noble and good, may all beings be free of meaningless distractions and purify their conflicting emotions." Then dedicate the merit to the welfare of all beings.

The nature of samsara is such that we can never stay in one place for any length of time. We are constantly on the move, both in this life and in the successive incarnations that define cyclic existence. No matter where we are temporarily stationed, we will never transcend the samsaric condition or be free of misfortune, loss, deprivation, and the ever-present fear of death unless we make a determined effort to transform ourselves on the spiritual path. The time that we have in this life is very brief. If life held nothing more than our mundane pursuits, it would be of no significance whatsoever. Whether or not we believe in rebirth, the most important thing is to make the most of this life. We have to really think deeply about this if we want a fruitful life. If we simply grow old and die, we will have achieved nothing. If, on the other hand, we can transform ourselves and do something to help others, we will have made a positive contribution to our world. If rebirth is a reality, as the Buddha said it is, we will move toward liberation from samsara—whether that is in this life or the next.

IMPERMANENCE

It is absolutely essential to do this meditation on impermanence as a preliminary to our daily practice, because even if we are fortunate enough to have a precious human body, that body is still mortal and easily lost. If we really examine our body, we will discover that it lacks any kind of immutable core and is actually more fragile than most other physical things. It is more akin to a bubble than to a rock.

Impermanence is not something that we should have any doubts about, for there is no question of its verity. We all have to die, and it is impossible to predict the time of our death. If we fail to make proper use of our body while we are still alive, we will have absolutely no control over what happens to it at the time of our death. It is only our spiritual practice that will help us at the time of death, for Dharma will both give us courage and peace of mind to face our death when the time comes and determine our experiences and direction in the post-mortem state. Furthermore, if we have misused our body and incurred negative karma, then suffering and pain will be our lot in future lives. Recognizing these facts will generate enormous motivation to practice the Dharma. Whatever pampering or nurturing we give ourselves should therefore be done with the view that our body is an aid for our spiritual growth rather something that we possess.

Death Is Ever-Present

No one in the known world has ever been able to escape death. External and internal threats to our lives are ever-present. Externally there are deadly weapons, fires, natural disasters, and accidents, and internally there are bodily sicknesses and mental ailments. We can also be put to death by the state, by an enemy, or by a felon. If we do not reflect upon our mortality in this way, our life will simply slip by. Even though we have been fortunate not to have fallen victim yet to any of the innumerable life-threatening causes and conditions, death can still arrive at any time of the day or night. In fact, whether we are alive or dead is often determined by a split second.

Although all living creatures must die, their physical dissolution does not signal the real end. Death simply means that one's consciousness becomes dislodged from one's body. That consciousness continues on a course that is predetermined by one's karmic inheritance. In light of this fact, we should compare our lives to the flow of a river. None of the rivers of the world remain in the same place; some rivers are long and some are short, and while they take different courses, they all ultimately end up in the ocean. In a similar way, our lives all end in death. Even though there may be no imminent threat to our life at the moment, this does not guarantee our longevity. Unforeseen circumstances may be just around the corner. Even if no sudden disruptions befall us, the time separating yesterday from today is only an instant. In the same way that day changes to night and night to day, our lives are unstable and quickly flash by.

MEDITATION 1

Take the meditation posture, take refuge in the Three Jewels, and generate enlightened heart. Think: "If even all of the galaxies eventually perish into entropy, why should I think that a mere individual like myself is not going to die? Even human beings far superior to myself have had to die, not to mention the countless numbers of sentient creatures who have died up to this point. No one can escape death. It is said that even gods are not immortal. None of the creatures that live on the earth, below the earth, or in the sea and sky can escape death. Even the sun and moon and all the continents of this earth will perish one day. In fact, this precious body is so fragile that my demise became inevitable as soon as I was born. My body does not remain the same even for an instant and could disintegrate as quickly as a bubble."

MEDITATION 2

Next, meditate on the fact that your body is a product of causes and conditions. Because everything that is caused is subject to impermanence, and everything that is impermanent will cease, you experience all kinds of mental torments, conflicting emotions (*klesha*), and discursive thoughts (*vikalpa*) when you do not relate to your body properly. Instead of thinking of your body as a possession that you need to protect, and thereby developing distorted views that only increase your mental agitation, regard your body as an instrument on the spiritual path. Think: "I will make constructive use of this body and train my mind to gain respite from this relentless turmoil."

MEDITATION 3

Even though time does not stand still, you have leisure and therefore the opportunity to do something that will be of benefit both to yourself and others. This can be achieved only by following the spiritual path. If you fail to do this, you will always be bound to cyclic existence and never have any freedom of movement. The resolve to make your life meaningful and significant has to come from the depths of your being so that you refrain from entrusting your life to worldly things. Reflect: "The time of my death is uncertain, and so is its cause. I am not going to waste my time getting caught up in superficial pursuits that only bring temporary relief."

MEDITATION 4

If you evaluate your situation properly, you will recognize that your circumstances are unique because you have a precious human body and contact with living spiritual traditions from which to draw inspiration and guidance. In this meditation, compare your body to a boat, the teachings to navigational skills, and yourself to the captain of that boat. When all three essential ingredients are present in this way, it would be highly delusional not to take advantage of this unique situation. If you do not put effort into achieving liberation from samsara, you will only have deceived yourself, and there will be no one but yourself to blame. Therefore, contemplate: "My precious human body will decay, grow old, and then be lost. I am going to use it as a boat to cross the ocean of samsara. The teachings and spiritual instructions that I receive are the navigational skills to safely cross these turbulent waters of inexpressible pain and suffering." Conclude your meditations by dedicating any merit that may have resulted to the welfare of all sentient beings.

The Defects of Ignoring Impermanence

The fundamental defect of the human condition is the general laziness, complacency, and passivity that prevent us from engaging in self-reflection. As a result, we are carried along by the external happenings of this world, constantly thinking about winning, maintaining our projected self-image, and indulging in unbridled hatred, envy, pride, and so forth. We become greedy and hoard everything that we can lay our hands on, while growing ever more unmotivated, restless, and argumentative. If we pass our time in this way, there will be no escape from the relentless torment of samsaric forces. Ironically, even though we become completely caught up in pursuing such limited goals, most of them remain unrealized because of the agitation and confusion that ensue from our states of mind. We have to ask ourselves how much more of a failure it is to neglect to pursue the real goals in our lives. Our ultimate goal should be to put an end to this relentless samsaric torment, and we must motivate ourselves toward that goal.

MEDITATION

Take the meditation posture, then take refuge in the Three Jewels, generate enlightened heart, and motivate yourself by contemplating impermanence in this way: "The previous buddhas attained their spiritual goals as a result of their own motivation. Before they became buddhas, they were also ordinary human beings. It is solely as a result of my own laziness that I have remained an ordinary sentient being. There are numerous buddhas who were in no better position than I am, and they were able to attain the ultimate fruit of the spiritual path. Therefore, it is due to my own karma that I am still wandering around in samsara. I will now devote myself with fervor to becoming free from this condition. Until I attain my goal, I am living on borrowed time because life is so brief and uncertain." Once again, conclude the meditation by dedicating the merit to the welfare of all beings.

———

It is only by contemplating impermanence that we become reflective enough to recognize which things are worth pursuing and which are not. We also learn to see exactly what our confusions arise from, because our experiences of dissatisfaction and frustration initially come from a failure to reflect upon anything. When we start to think in this way, there will be less likelihood of squandering our time in an unreflective fashion. Nor will we be as likely to become entangled in disputes and conflicts; constantly feel embittered, angry, and vengeful toward others; or indulge in negative thoughts and emotions. If understood properly, the teachings on impermanence have a sobering effect, just as if one had been awoken from a dream. Our approach toward everything that we normally deal with—material property, friends, acquaintances, and family—will also be changed. As a result, we will no longer be afflicted by a fear of losing what we have or not getting what we want. Our extreme reactions toward things will lessen because we will come to realize that it is only our attitude that hardens and stultifies as time goes by; the things themselves never stay the same. In other words, we change very little in our world through unreflective attitudes. We simply put our mind into a straitjacket, which restricts our involvement in life and ensures that we continue in a negative, alienated direction indefinitely.

Through persevering with this meditation on impermanence, we will begin to realize that our samsaric minds are out of sync with the world. As a result, our entrenched mental habits begin to loosen and our mind becomes more workable, pliable and amenable to training. It is only at this point that our mind becomes truly open to spiritual transformation. As a result of this softening and transformation, we start to go through life with a sense of ease—we will sleep with ease, rise with ease, move about with ease, and sit with ease. We will even be reborn with ease after we die. Most important of all, we will be able to practice with ease and enter various spiritual states of mind in an easy and untroubled manner. In brief, everything will cease to be a source of difficulty.

THE UNSATISFACTORINESS OF SAMSARA

Having realized that human life is precious and impermanent, we have to truly comprehend that the samsaric condition is the source of our suffering and pain. Samsara does not afford us any real sense of comfort or security. Conditioned existence is ephemeral, and unless we do something about it, we will continue to experience all kinds of suffering. The Buddhist teachings identify three types of suffering: the suffering of suffering, the suffering of change, and the suffering of conditioned existence. These three encompass all the dissatisfaction and pain in samsara. In this meditation, we should remind ourselves of the sufferings of samsara and seriously ponder the benefits of doing something to overcome the samsaric condition. If we do not, the causes and conditions that give rise to these painful experiences will never cease, and as long as they persist, we will suffer the consequences.

Most of us never really pay attention to the things that bring about comfort, peace, and happiness, nor to what causes the opposite of our well-being. As a result, we are at a loss to know what to do to promote our happiness and avoid further painful experiences. Everyone desires happiness, yet we know that everybody is unhappy on one level or another. Despite our desire for happiness, we manage to do the opposite of what is beneficial for ourselves through not being attentive to our mental and physical behaviors. If we do not reflect on these things and make an effort to deal with our conflicting emotions, we will continue to be slaves to our unruly minds. Allowing our minds to rob us of any genuine satisfaction and happiness in this way is sacrificing a great deal for very little. Allowing ourselves to be constantly cheated in this way is the result of ignorance. It is our distorted views of subject and object that give rise to our conflicting emotions, which create the unwholesome and destructive behaviors that contribute to our unhappiness.

MEDITATION 1

Assume the meditation posture, take refuge in the Three Jewels, and generate enlightened heart. As long as you are trapped in cyclic existence, you will never be free of the mental torment caused by your conflicting emotions. A whole gamut of things, from an elementary physical level to a very personal mental level, can be the cause of unpleasantness. If even a brief experience of pain is unbearable, how much more so is the sum total of relentless samsaric suffering, all with no end in sight? Generate a deep sense of sadness at not having found a way out of your condition, and think: "The suffering that I experience is like being trapped in a burning house, being stalked by wild animals, or being put in prison by the state. I am trapped in a very painful and unpleasant situation. I have not found a way to escape from it. These sufferings and pains are too great to enumerate, because anything and everything can be the cause of pain. This samsaric state is like being consumed by conflicting emotions that are like raging fires with nothing to put them out."

MEDITATION 2

Contemplate this next series of thoughts, which are based on the desire for happiness. Being habituated beings who act on impulse, we never experience any prolonged periods of peace. We are in this predicament because of our lack of reflection on what is beneficial and what is harmful. Therefore, think: "All sentient beings in the samsaric state are no different from me. They also are suffering, and they too want happiness. Like me, they do not understand the real causes of happiness. They end up creating more pain for themselves in their pursuit of happiness, all the while being deluded that they are doing something to improve their situation. Our behavior is like that of a moth burned through its attraction to a flame. Or like a wild deer that gets killed by hunters through its attraction to the sound of a flute. Or like a bee trapped inside a flower through its attraction to pollen. Or like a fish pierced by a hook through its attraction to a fisherman's bait. Or like an elephant, which has no natural enemies in the wild but gets mired in a swamp through its attraction to mud baths. In the same way, sentient beings are constantly duped and deceived by the very things that increase their suffering."

This situation is the result of failing to understand what things are beneficial or not beneficial to our well-being. Reflect: "All sentient creatures behave in this fashion because they are motivated by the conflicting emotions of deluded mind, excessive desire, anger, jealousy, and pride. In spite of my imprisonment, I have never learned from my experiences and have become a repeat offender. Each time I suffer the consequences of my actions, the punishment increases, yet I continue to offend until I am executed."

MEDITATION 3

Suffering exists wherever there are living beings, so as long as there is existence there will be suffering. Reflect: "Suffering is concomitant with having a mind. I have lived many times before and will live many times again. It is impossible to count the number of lives I have already had, and it is impossible to count the number of lives I will have in the future. Unless I do something about it now, I will have to experience the unpleasantness of samsara over and over without respite. Even if I am reborn in more privileged circumstances, I will still experience the suffering of separation, the suffering of not getting what I want, the suffering of coming in contact with what I do not want, and so forth. Whatever pleasures I experience will only be temporary and ultimately of no consequence. Therefore, unless I do something about this now, there will be no escape."

Mind and Mental Events

In order to appreciate just how we have become inured to this unsatisfactory situation and how we perpetuate our imprisonment, it is crucial to gain some understanding of the functions of our ordinary consciousness. After all, it is our mind that perceives certain things as pleasant, unpleasant, or neutral, and as a result pleasurable, painful, or indifferent experiences are generated. Everything we experience is dependent upon the activities of our consciousness in this way.

In Buddhist psychology, consciousness has three different aspects: The first is the sensory aspect, which is strictly related to our eye, ear, nose, tongue, and touch sense consciousnesses. The second is the intentional aspect, which is how our mind becomes conscious of the objects with which we make contact through our senses. The third is the cognitive aspect, which thinks, remembers, and reflects.

The sensory consciousness is neutral and simply apprehends something in the phenomenal world. The intentional consciousness immediately seizes on an object and cognizes it as either this or that. This aspect of consciousness simply intends toward objects in a general way, without discriminating between the specifics of individual objects, but a mental fixation automatically arises from that perception. It is the cognitive aspect of consciousness that is either attracted or repelled by what is cognized through our sense impressions, because everything we experience is individually sorted and interpreted by this aspect of the mind.

The dissatisfactions of samsara are caused by the interactions and reactions of these three aspects of the mind, because through them we seize upon individual objects, and this then gives rise to our different emotional responses. These emotional responses can be divided into the three general types: excessive desire, excessive aversion, and ignorance. Although they are described as different functions, these three aspects of the mind operate almost simultaneously and in unison; they are ever-present in each moment of cognition.

These aspects of consciousness give rise to mental events. It is these mental events that seize on the specific features of our experience. The primary aspects of the mind seize on the objects of consciousness, and the mental events seize on the specific features of that experience. Although the mind and mental events can be distinguished in this way, they really occur at the same time. The fundamental point is that at first there is cognition, and then there is a mental act in response to that cognition.

In terms of our experience, anything we perceive as a source of pleasure will give rise to craving; anything we perceive as a source of displeasure will give rise to aversion; and anything we perceive as neither will give rise to ignorance. Over time our tendency to interpret things in this way conditions the mind to perceive certain things auto-matically as painful and other things as pleasurable. These specific in-terpretations gradually become entrenched in our mind-streams, so that whenever a certain object is perceived we immediately associate it with either pain or pleasure. This applies to everything, from fairly simple processes of perception to more complex interactions with the external world. For example, if you perceive somebody to be an attractive per-son, you will experience sexual desire for him or her, while somebody perceived as threatening will give rise to aversion.

When our reactions to things become habituated like this, they de-velop into dispositional properties that become part of our character traits and personality. Karmic seeds are laid in our stream of conscious-ness through the interaction of the mind, the object, and the meaning that we attach to that object. This fundamental duality of mind and ob-ject gives rise to the perception of self and other, and our physical, men-tal, and verbal actions reflect this habituated interpretation as a result. It is also crucial to understand that our discriminations are invariably mo-tivated by the conflicting emotions of excessive desire, hatred, and ig-norance. It is the combination of our mind and mental events—or the discriminations and conflicting emotions—that causes the dissatisfac-tions of samsara.

This description of the workings of the mind does not apply to en-lightened beings, because enlightened beings apprehend things imme-diately, not in the dualistic fashion just described. We only manifest these three aspects of the mind because we perceive everything in a du-alistic fashion. Enlightened beings operate from the mode of true com-passion, where they no longer distinguish between self and others but simply respond to the needs of others from the genuine intention to ameliorate their suffering. It is this compassionate attitude that we most need to cultivate in our actions and thoughts.

MEDITATION

Settle yourself in meditation, take refuge, and generate enlightened heart. You need to ponder the manner in which the mind and mental events give rise to the fixations and conflicting emotions of your consciousness and appreciate how this conditions and habituates the dualistic way you relate to your experience. Initially, with an untrained mind, it is very difficult to discriminate instinctively between what is beneficial and what is harmful. As suffering is caused by engaging in negative forms of action and happiness is generated by engaging in positive forms of action, you must train yourself to recognize wholesome modes of behavior. As long as you engage in unwholesome forms of action, you will descend farther and farther into samsaric misery and dread. Engaging in positive activities is the way to put an end to suffering. However, unless these wholesome actions are imbued with compassion, they will not be genuinely wholesome in nature. Everything you do should be done with bodhisattva intent, so think: "I will only engage in wholesome actions with compassion in order to bring an end to samsaric dissatisfaction." Then dedicate whatever merit you may have accumulated to the benefit of all beings.

Overcoming Samsaric Fixations

To Buddhists, the six realms of existence are what constitute the samsaric realm for migrating sentient beings. Our karma compels us to take rebirth continuously in one or another of these realms without respite. As mentioned earlier, these are the hell realm, the hungry ghost realm, the animal realm, the human realm, the demigod realm, and the realm of the long-lived gods; we cannot find any relief from relentless samsaric toil in any of these realms. In the hell realm, we suffer because of mental paranoia and delusions about being persecuted, beaten, and maimed. The suffering of hell consists of perceiving potential or actual harm to oneself in everything that transpires in life. The sufferings of the other realms are commensurate with the kind of rebirth we have earned. The hungry ghosts suffer from irremediable hunger and thirst, animals suffer from ignorance and domination, the demigods suffer from fighting and jealousy, and the long-lived gods have to relinquish their privileged lifestyle in one unexpected and irredeemable loss. Every suffering we endure in these realms is in direct proportion to our own misdeeds; the kind of suffering, the length of suffering, and the intensity of our suffering all result from the physical, verbal, and mental acts of our lives.

MEDITATION 1

Take the meditation posture, go for refuge, and generate enlightened heart. You have to find a way out of this difficult and unpleasant situation, because there will never be any relief from samsaric turmoil in any of the six realms. If you do not seek liberation from this state now, you will transmigrate through samsara indefinitely. It is not possible to attain liberation from samsara unless you actively seek it. You have to think that the samsaric condition is comparable to a prison and that you must find the means to achieve your release from it. The essence of this means is yourself, and you should proceed on the journey of liberation from that premise. Reflect: "I have two choices. I can continue with my old habits or I can try to reverse my inclinations. I am truly fortunate to have been born a human being. If I had been born in another realm or other situation, I would not have this opportunity to find relief from my samsaric condition."

MEDITATION 2

Changing our habits is not as simple as being woken from a deep sleep, in which our dream turned into a nightmare. This is not how we wake from our samsaric stupor. If that were possible, we would not need many buddhas. One buddha would be sufficient, because he or she could simply awaken sentient creatures, one by one, caught up in the samsaric dream. Unfortunately, even buddhas do not have that kind of power. The choice to wake up is an individual one; it cannot be made by somebody else on our behalf. So reflect: "Liberation is something that I must achieve. I am going to put all of my effort into achieving this freedom."

MEDITATION 3

Whenever we are required to endure a little bit of hardship in order to do things that are of benefit to us, we have little or no patience. However, we tend to show enormous patience toward negative, destructive activities that we should not tolerate. The buddhas have said that we should be ashamed of this kind of erroneous view. It is compared to being in a hole in the ground where sunlight cannot enter. Even the radiance of an enlightened being is unable to penetrate the depths of our ignorance, and we stumble and grope around in darkness. Although the buddhas are capable of providing assistance and guidance on the path of liberation, if we make no effort to escape the darkness of our lives, their presence is of no use to us. Meditate thus: "It is up to me to do something about this. I can seek assistance from the buddhas, bodhisattvas, and other teachers while I endeavor to find liberation."

MEDITATION 4

You should not feel discouraged by the extent of your suffering, but understand that it is all a result of your conflicting emotions. There are many different kinds of conflicting emotions; some are forceful and virulent, others more subtle and insidious. Reflect: "I experience this kind of suffering as a result of my own mistaken views, which are dependent on my delusory states of mind. If my delusory states of mind diminish in power, they will have less influence over my body, speech, and mind, and the suffering that I experience will decrease accordingly."

MEDITATION 5

To overcome suffering, you have to deal with your conflicting emotions because suffering only increases whenever these emotions are stirred up. Reflect: "Paying attention to my mental states will help me find release from the harmful states that fan my conflicting emotions. From this day forward, I will deal with my experiences differently. I will pay attention to my behavior, to how I use words, and to the thoughts and emotions that arise in my mind. I vow to cross the turbulent waters of samsaric suffering and reach the shore of nirvanic peace, and I will achieve this goal by engaging in the appropriate spiritual practices. I will make use of my spiritual practices day and night for the benefit of myself and others. May I accumulate the necessary merit and wisdom to attain buddhahood." Conclude this meditation by dedicating the merit to the welfare of all sentient beings.

———

To genuinely engage in enlightened forms of activity rather than merely wholesome moral actions, we have to do more than simply good works. The real cause of samsara lies not in our failure to engage in wholesome actions but in the failure to generate wisdom. In addition to compassion, we need to cultivate wisdom, for wisdom is what cuts through to the heart of our existential condition. In fact, true compassion can only arise from wisdom, because without an understanding of emptiness (shunyata), we will always be bound to a dualistic perception of our world and ourselves.

Wisdom will arise only if we realize that the things we take to be real and substantial are not real and substantial at all. All of our negative habits and distorted views come from failing to understand how things really are and fixating instead on how they appear. This is how we misinterpret everything. This fixation gives rise to the belief in our psychophysical constituents as a self and to the misapprehension of objects perceived through our sense consciousnesses as real and substantial. This in turn disturbs the mind and gives rise to discursive thoughts and conflicting emotions. Negative forms of behavior ensue so that eventually we are led back to our experiences of suffering and dissatisfaction and to the further production of discursive thoughts and conflicting emotions.

It is only by realizing the nature of the mind and the nature of things that we reverse this downward trend into samsaric existence. From that realization will come a direct perception (*pratyaksa*) of the luminous, spontaneously arisen wisdom that is perspicacious in nature. This wisdom manifests in an unceasing manner, quite unembellished by the dualistic notions of subject and object. It is only the failure to recognize this self-luminous state that has led us to our entanglements in the dualistic fixations that create our samsaric suffering. If we want to put an end to the dissatisfactions of samsara, we have to put an end to our delusions. We must make no mistake about this: As long as our delusions persist, our samsaric suffering will continue incessantly. It is therefore imperative that we grasp the nature of things to be devoid of inherent existence and realize that there is no self-existing subject or object that is ultimately real.

KARMIC CAUSE AND EFFECT

Although suffering is an all-pervasive aspect of the samsaric condition, individual beings experience it in their own unique and personal ways. In order to understand the variety of both suffering and temporary happiness, we have to investigate the notion of karmic cause and effect. Every individual carries his or her personal history of karmic predispositions, tendencies, and imprints. It is these imprints and tendencies that are responsible for our varied individual experiences. In other words, our own particular sufferings have to be understood in relation to karmic cause and effect, because we do not have specific experiences by accident or chance. The whole gamut of our experiences is contingent upon the karmic causes and conditions in our mind-streams.

Whether we are in the conditioned state of samsara or the unconditioned state of nirvana is completely dependent upon our actions. Action, in turn, is dependent upon the mind. While the nature of the mind is primordially pure and untainted by our actions and their results, a multitude of things still impinge on the relative existence of our ordinary deluded consciousness. Our karma should be viewed as a sculptor who molds the details of our existence or like a shadow that always follows us. We cannot share our karma with anyone else, just as our painful and pleasurable physical experiences are ours alone. Reversing our karmic flow is also extremely difficult. It has the force of a waterfall and can either lift us up or plunge us into the depths of despair. In that sense, karma is like the ultimate tyrant.

The Eight Levels of Consciousness

In order to understand karmic cause and effect from the perspective of our personal experience of suffering, a deeper look at the workings of consciousness is required. According to Yogachara theory, there are eight levels of consciousness that operate in the samsaric mind. The first five levels relate to the faculties of sense consciousness (sight, sound, smell, taste, and touch), the sixth level to the empirical consciousness (*vijnana*), the seventh to the afflicted consciousness (*manavijnana*), and the eighth to the basic consciousness (*alayavijnana*).

We perceive the phenomenal world through our sense consciousness; discriminate and classify what we perceive through our empirical consciousness; react with excessive desire, aversion, or indifference with our afflicted consciousness; and leave karmic imprints from these actions and reactions upon our basic consciousness. In other words, all of our wholesome or unwholesome actions leave imprints on the basic consciousness. They are stored there and reactivated to generate further potential experience of samsaric suffering (if they are unwholesome imprints) or experiences that are more in tune with liberation (if they are wholesome imprints).

It is important to understand where these karmic imprints and habit patterns reside in our being. This basic consciousness is unconscious rather than self-conscious, because even though it is the source of all of our mental experiences it does not recognize itself. It is said to be like a mirror, because while a mirror has the capacity to reflect various objects it does so without being self-illuminating or transparent. However, while this level of consciousness remains oblivious of itself, it does have the capacity to differentiate between self and others.

This basic consciousness is also said to be neutral, because it does not tend toward either wholesome or unwholesome states of mind. It simply provides the impartial ground for all types of karmic imprints to take root. Nor does this basic consciousness have any kind of essence or ultimate reality. It simply perpetuates our deluded perceptions on the relative level by being the repository of our karmic traces and dispositions. Another way of saying this is that when the karmic traces and dispositions are eliminated completely, the basic consciousness dissipates along with them. The world that we perceive through this filter of deluded consciousness is known as the samsaric world.

When we embark on the spiritual path and start to direct our consciousness toward the attainment of liberation, our consciousness as a whole becomes attuned to spiritual emancipation. It is through purifying the basic consciousness of its negative karmic traces and dispositions that we attain the state of liberation. With this revolution in consciousness, all the necessary qualities and attributes required to advance on the spiritual path will become manifest from the nature of the mind in due course. This will lead to the realization of the ultimate ground of being, which in itself is emptiness.

The five sense consciousnesses arise from the basic consciousness but are themselves nonconceptual. They are conscious of things purely in terms of sensory impressions. The basic consciousness is comparable to a mirror, and the five sense consciousnesses to the images reflected in that mirror. The empirical consciousness is what cognizes the objects that are apprehended by the sense consciousnesses. This gives rise to the seventh level—the afflicted consciousness—which reflects upon the perceptions of the previous six levels of consciousness and generates various responses to them.

This level of afflicted consciousness immediately follows any form of mental event. For example, if we only vaguely perceive a physical object without any comprehension, that perception occurs on the level of basic consciousness. If that physical object is perceived and apprehended as something—a table, for instance—that particular act of apprehension is followed by the afflicted consciousness, which gives rise to all kinds of conceptualizations, categorizations, likes, dislikes, and so forth. All of this occurs within a split second.

From this explanation of how the levels of consciousness work we can understand how karma is created. As the afflicted consciousness discriminates between things as desirable and undesirable (on the basis of the previous impressions and judgments that have been stored in the basic consciousness), the conflicting emotions that this generates give rise to various physical, verbal, and mental actions. These actions then leave further karmic imprints in the basic consciousness, which lie dormant until they are again activated by further reactions from the afflicted consciousness. It is also important to note that the karmic imprints that are left in the basic consciousness do not remain there unchanged; they too can decrease or increase depending upon existing conditions.

Although the basic consciousness is neutral, this does not imply that this level of consciousness is a state of purity. It is still tainted by ignorance. It is only the ground of being that is pure and untainted. The ground of being—or the nature of the mind—has been pure from the beginning, and this element gives rise to the actual possibility of enlightenment. This ground of being is more fundamental to our nature than the basic consciousness. It is the innately pure ground of luminous bliss, from which the very possibility of enlightenment arises (more will be said about this in chapter 7).

In order to realize this ground of being, we need to utilize two forms of purification. One is innate because the nature of the mind is intrinsically pure in itself, and the other is acquired because we still have to purify our basic consciousness by engaging in various forms of spiritual discipline. In that sense, the basic consciousness itself cannot really be used as the basis for the liberation of the mind at all. In fact, there has to be a fundamental revolution of that basic consciousness—it has to be transformed from the unconscious container of our delusory states to a spacious, boundless awareness that is fully conscious and depleted of all its hidden elements. The basic consciousness is subject to change and is transformed through the exhaustion of the traces and dispositions that reside there. Only then will the basic consciousness dissipate into the spacious luminosity of the nature of the mind and manifest as undeluded wisdom consciousness, or yeshe in Tibetan.

Karmic Bondage
and the Two Accumulations

We can see that our mind has a great deal of potential. It can transport us to elevated states of existence or plunge us into the lowest, most demeaning states, all as a result of our karma. Our unwholesome karma is created by ten different types of actions, three of which are physical, four verbal, and three mental. Our wholesome karma is also created by ten actions, which are diametrically opposed to the unwholesome actions. The three unwholesome physical actions are willful killing, stealing, and improper sexual acts. The four unwholesome verbal actions are lying with the intention to deceive, slander in order to cause friction, idle gossip, and harsh words. The three unwholesome mental acts are covetousness, harboring harmful thoughts toward others, and wrong views. Unwholesome karma is generated through these avenues, and wholesome karma is generated through their opposites. For example, instead of taking lives, we save them; instead of stealing, we try to practice generosity; and so forth.

Our experiences of pleasure and our rebirth into elevated states of existence are the result of engaging in wholesome actions, while the degraded states that we experience are the result of unwholesome actions. If we experience a long life free from illness, with good looks and charisma, this is not due to good luck but a consequence of the accumulation of wholesome karma in our past. If we are afflicted by all manner of suffering and are unattractive in appearance, this is likewise the result of unwholesome actions in our past. It is also our karmic patterns that determine our different opinions, qualities, and character traits.

We must rely on positive actions to gradually distance ourselves from the samsaric condition and come closer to liberation. Positive actions alone are not sufficient, however, because they lead only to the accumulation of merit. Merit may take us to elevated states of existence, but those states will decline again once the accumulated merit has expired. It is essential to engage in the two accumulations—the accumulations of merit and wisdom—if we hope to secure the ultimate freedom of enlightenment. The accumulation of merit relates to the development of compassion and arises from wholesome actions; the accumulation of wisdom relates to realizing the nature of the mind and arises from engaging in the practices of tranquillity and insight meditation. Engaging in these two accumulations will purify the twofold obscurations of the mind, known as the two veils: the veil of conflicting emotions (*klesha-varana*) and the veil of cognitive distortions (*jneya-varana*).

MEDITATION

Settle yourself in meditation, take refuge, and generate the enlightened heart. While we are in samsara, we continually engage in either planting karmic seeds or reaping the fruits of those seeds. We should try to abandon unwholesome actions and the causes and conditions that allow unwholesome seeds to flourish. We should try to engage exclusively in activities that will lead us to liberation, for if we do not create the necessary causes and conditions, we can never hope to attain the fruit of liberation. Some karmic seeds bear fruit in the short term, some in the long term, and some may even be deferred to another lifetime. It is certain, however, that they will all ripen eventually. Contemplate the benefits of performing wholesome actions in terms of your temporal and ultimate goals and think: "From this day forth, I will endeavor to save lives, practice generosity toward others, and conduct myself in sexually moral ways. I will always tell the truth and refrain from negative talk or gossip about others. I will cultivate benevolence, compassionate thoughts, and correct view."

KARMA AND DEPENDENT ORIGINATION

We should not regard the karmic causal link as having some kind of intrinsic reality, for then we will become fixated on the notion of cause and effect. Karmic cause and effect has to be understood in the context of the principle of dependent origination (*pratityasamutpada*). That is, although karma appears real enough, it has no intrinsic reality, and we should not think of it as something real, inevitable, and mechanical. Some people do hold to this kind of karmic theory—which is very similar to the Protestant notion of predestination—and thereby interpret karma to mean that we are effectively preprogrammed. While our karma is responsible for bringing us all kinds of pleasurable and painful experiences, these are just like insubstantial dream experiences. We cannot say that the karmic causal link exists or does not exist, because its true nature is nondual.

In terms of the accumulation of merit on the relative level, we have to think very seriously about the karmic causal link. But from the ultimate point of view—the view that arises from the accumulation of wisdom—we have to understand the insubstantiality of karma. Just as our dreams have no substantiality of their own but still affect us while we are dreaming, karmic cause and effect has no intrinsic reality. However, as long as we have not awoken from the samsaric state of ignorance, we will continue to suffer from karmic consequences based upon our merits or demerits.

Everything that occurs within our experience and our basic consciousness has a dependent relationship. As long as the karmic traces and dispositions remain, the basic consciousness will function as a kind of unconscious subterfuge to our being. When the traces and dispositions are completely removed, the basic consciousness will also dissipate into the transparent clarity of luminous bliss.

To illustrate this complex relationship, we can use the analogy of a candle wick and its flame: The flame is dependent upon the wick in order to burn, but in burning it consumes the wick and eliminates itself. Similarly, all our karmic traces and dispositions (including those that have been created from the accumulation of merit and wisdom) can be exhausted if we train our mind in various spiritual practices, including tranquillity and insight meditation. The basic consciousness will gradually be fundamentally transformed by these methods, and when all traces of defilements and obscurations vanish, the full mani-festation of enlightenment will emerge.

Karma is dependently originated because it is only after certain causes and conditions that karmic cause and effect comes into opera-tion. Nor does the theory of karma imply that particular results will in-evitably come about. There are measures that we can take to preempt the possibility of our karma ripening. To quote an example from Shan-tideva, the Indian Mahayana master, "If we cultivate patience, all the karma we have accumulated through anger and hostility will diminish."

We have to develop a proper understanding of the karmic causal link in relation to dependent origination and engage in the accumula-tions of both merit and wisdom. Only this will allow us to eliminate the effects of our karma on the relative level and enable us to gain in-sight into the nature of ultimate reality.

MEDITATION

Contemplate the benefits of creating merit and developing more amiable, helpful habits. Not all habits are bad, and it is important to develop habits that are beneficial for our spiritual growth. This is achieved through the accumulation of merit. Then ponder the need to eventually go beyond all habits and develop a spontaneous disposition whereby our behavior is automatically wholesome and beneficial, producing only positive karma. This is attained through the accumulation of wisdom. Reflect: "I will engage in the skill-ful methods of compassionate activity to accumulate merit, and I will practice tranquillity and insight meditation to accumulate wisdom. In this way I will aspire to become an elevated being who spontaneously acts for the benefit of all beings." Then dedi-cate whatever merit you may have accumulated to the benefit of all beings.

While we remain in the conditioned state of existence, we can ac-cumulate virtues and aim toward the liberation of nirvana, or enlight-enment. If our mind is predisposed toward virtue, it will automatically orient itself toward the accumulation of further virtue. The goodness of ourselves and our community will increase through being predisposed to wholesome actions in this way.

We can only see the effects of our actions in daily life and can never really know the causes. We try to understand what we see from all kinds of perspectives, using political, social, economic, genetic, environmental, and theological theories to help explain the huge variations in people's experiences of suffering. The karmic hypothesis is one such theory. Karmic theory does not contradict the explanations given by political scientists, social scientists, or cultural theorists. It can accommodate these explanations quite easily, for it says that these situations exist as a result of karmic cause and effect. The Buddhist explanation emphasizes, however, that we ourselves are responsible for what happens; there is no external agent to be held responsible for our experiences.

The point of karmic theory is to encourage us to behave in a way that is beneficial to others and ourselves. If we try to live in a wholesome fashion and leave the kind of impression on others that inclines them to act in a similarly wholesome way, we can still hope for a better world.

GENERATING COMPASSION

We should be aware of and compassionate toward the many human beings who fail to respond to spiritual concerns and who fail to see their predicament. When they attempt to follow the teachings, they fail, because the meaning has not penetrated their minds and they have developed no understanding of what they heard. There are other people who have experienced change and impermanence in their lives—a death in the family, sickness, or other personal hardship—and suffered the consequences but have not been moved by any of this. In fact, such people go about their lives as if they were going to live for an eon, devoting their time to trivial matters without giving any serious thought to themselves. Still others are deprived of the opportunity to fully utilize their fortunate circumstances because their emotions rage like an uncontrollable fire and they never experience any peace of mind. There are others who are so aggressive that they are either filled with rage or overwhelmed by competitiveness and envy.

People can be afflicted in a variety of ways. These afflictions determine all kinds of unwholesome and negative behaviors, such as finding weaknesses and flaws in others or disparaging others. In fact, many people pursue this kind of behavior with immense zeal. There are other people whose afflictions are of a painful nature, and they endure intense suffering as a result of different mental and physical torments. Despite all this hardship, however, they give no thought to addressing their suffering. They neither learn from their suffering nor become wearied by it and give no thought to questioning their mental attitudes. Still others are fairly educated in spiritual matters, but their understanding is only an intellectual one that has not penetrated to their inner being. As a result, they become conceited about their knowledge of various subtle philosophical distinctions and start to regard others as immature and ignorant. Instead of realizing that they are victims of their own conflicting emotions and are consumed by the fires of an agitated mind, they allow this fire to burn up all that is good and precious in themselves.

MEDITATION

Settle yourself in the meditation posture, go for refuge, and generate enlightened heart. Then contemplate the importance of not squandering your precious time. Think of all the beings that suffer in one way or another from their afflictions, and give rise to the aspiration to achieve enlightenment for your own and others' benefit. Generate great compassion for all beings by thinking, "I will endeavor to bring myself and others to the state of enlightenment." Then recite the following prayer:

> May the lives of ailing sentient beings be extended and made
>   meaningful.
> May those who are suffering from hunger or thirst obtain
>   sustenance,
> Those who are afflicted by external fears become fearless,
> And everything that beings desire be granted exactly as they wish.
> May all sentient beings do good and swiftly attain enlightenment.

May those in power rule with justice,
Governments be of service and ministers be endowed with
*   wholesome qualities,*
And the public remain in peace at all times.
May all sentient beings be free from all possible forms of suffering.
May they attain liberation,
Their minds be free of unwholesome states,
And their time devoted to realizing their true nature.
May there be bountiful harvests in all the lands.
May there be no sickness or any threat to life,
No conflict between self and others,
And peace and prosperity everywhere.
May limitless sentient beings in the ten directions be free
*   from suffering.*
May whatever they put their mind to bear fruit,
And may they attain bliss
As a result of the merit accumulated from this prayer.[1]

Then imagine that all sentient beings have benefited from your aspiration, all the terrible things in this world have decreased, and good things taken their place. Finally, dedicate the merit to the welfare of all beings.

———

While these teachings are extremely important, we should remembere that they are only preliminaries. Their purpose is to motivate our practice. We do not have to dwell interminably on these contemplations and make them an all-consuming obsession. The point is not to make us panic about our mortality and the fact that time is passing. It is just that we can so easily slip back into complacency and laziness. The preliminaries arrest that tendency and so are of enormous benefit to both our spiritual practice and the way we approach our lives. It is only by thinking about the preciousness of our body, how impermanent all our opportunities are, how dissatisfactory our temporal experiences ultimately become, and how trapped we are by our habitual responses to things that we will maintain our motivation to engage in spiritual practice and take stock of our lives.

These meditations are a form of skillful method. They are not necessarily a description of how things are; they are a prescription for what
we should do. These contemplations simply help us to see the relevance
and the urgency of spiritual practice. We are all suffering, even if it is
not always the obvious suffering of emotional loss or mental and physical pain. We experience the suffering of change and the suffering of
conditioned existence. It is through contemplating these things that our
sufferings are overcome, because unless we become spiritually conscious in this way, we remain in a state of denial about our lives. We will
just go about our business without being aware of what is really going
on. Despite this focus on suffering, however, Buddhism is not pes-
simistic; Buddhist philosophy simply states how things are. It constantly
says that all these sufferings can be overcome. The heart of Buddhism is
practice—and this consists of ways to lessen both our own suffering and
pain and the suffering and pain of others.

6

THE
FOUR IMMEASURABLES

THE FOUR IMMEASURABLES ARE A PRACTICE THAT ALLOWS US TO enter into a dialogue of compassion and wisdom with the world instead of seeing the world as a reality to be rejected, resisted, defied, and escaped from. These meditations are designed to bring about the type of feelings, emotions, and thoughts that will have a positive effect on our character. Many of our actions are unhelpful and self-destructive because they stem directly from our unexamined egocentric attitudes. Meditating on the four immeasurables provides the opportunity to reorient ourselves and transcend our limited, self-absorbed states of being. It also counteracts our unconscious tendency to rationalize our selfish acts, because often even our altruistic actions are shot through with selfishness.

These so-called immeasurables are called *Brahmaviharas* in Sanskrit, literally, "abodes of Brahma." The Buddha suggested that by meditating on immeasurable love, immeasurable compassion, immeasurable joy, and immeasurable equanimity, one would become divine, become more like a god.[1] Each of these immeasurables, then, can be defined as a "divine" quality. When we begin to understand that we have the capacity to develop these qualities, we can rise above our ordinariness and become a special kind of being. This is what we have to aspire to, not in a competitive sense but in the spiritual sense of transcending our familiar egotistic state in order to function from a higher level of being. In the sutras, the Buddha made many references to becoming like gods, by which he meant that one can become an elevated being.

THE IMPORTANCE OF THE FOUR IMMEASURABLES

Buddhist practice is about putting an end to suffering. While we may never be able to overcome suffering altogether until we attain buddhahood, we can still reduce our suffering by cultivating and dwelling on things that are good and valuable. We become what we put into ourselves. It follows that if we think about immeasurable love, immeasurable compassion, immeasurable joy, and immeasurable equanimity, we will become a loving, compassionate, joyful, and stable person.

The cultivation of love, compassion, joy, and equanimity is connected to the notion of skillful means (*upaya*), which is directly related to the six paramitas, or transcendental actions of the Mahayana bodhisattva path. A bodhisattva is not yet a fully enlightened being but someone who is progressing toward enlightenment using compassion and wisdom as the method. The practices of the four immeasurables relate more to the aspect of compassion (the wisdom element is addressed in detail in the following chapters). These meditations are another form of skillful action that complements and supports the practice of the six transcendental actions in everyday life. To be more precise, it is the first four transcendental actions of generosity, patience, moral precepts, and vigor that are involved in the development of compassion. The final two transcendental actions of meditation and wisdom correspond to tranquillity and insight meditation and involve the development of wisdom. Through practicing the four immeasurables, our application of generosity, patience, ethical conduct, and vigor in real-life situations will draw from the expansiveness created by the immeasurables. To illustrate this point the Mahayana teachings refer to these practices as an inexhaustible world of goodness.

As we engage in this type of practice, our mental stability will become strengthened. Normally our minds have rigidity and fixity but not stability. We have to understand that we are stuck in a particular mode of being and thinking, with no flexibility of mind. If we can develop stability without fixity, it will help us develop the kind of character traits we require to sustain our spiritual journey.

It is only from the stirring of emotions based on love, compassion, joy, and equanimity that we can gradually become a person who is loving, compassionate, joyous, well-grounded, and not given to extreme mood swings and instability. Many people are extremely generous and caring one moment and then, without warning and seemingly for no apparent reason, are spiteful and vengeful the next—usually toward the same person and on the same day! To fully appreciate the importance of this type of meditation, we should not think, "What good is it just to think about this sort of thing without actually doing anything?" Acts of love and compassion come from *being* a loving and compassionate person. While we must recognize that there is a difference between practicing these healthy emotions in meditation and applying them in daily life, there is nonetheless a strong connection between the two experiences, because the meditation and the action inform and influence one another.

These qualities are called immeasurable because we can apply them in an unrestricted fashion during meditation. When we engage in the practice of the transcendental actions in everyday life, we do so in a specific environment, and there are a limited number of players involved in any given situation. In the context of meditation, though, there should be no limit to what we can do. Through the use of imagination, we can expand our love and compassion in an almost boundless fashion. Practicing positive emotions such as love and compassion in this fashion is eminently more beneficial than giving attention to negative, unconstructive, and unhealthy emotions, which tend to produce a sense of gloom and hatred about life. Worse still, they encourage us to develop a sordid sense of spiritual conceit. Spiritual practices that focus on all that is negative about the human condition will never allow us to flower into more spiritual, happy, and loving beings. Instead, we will turn into shameful, self-hating moralists.

EMOTIONAL ENRICHMENT

People behave destructively as a result of their lack of skill in managing their emotional lives. We often see, hear, or experience this in our daily life. When we think about our emotional tendencies in this way, we begin to appreciate the need for practices like the four immeasurables and the benefits they might have for our well-being. This approach trains us in a very practical, efficient way of expressing ourselves. It is important to acknowledge that we can develop these skills in relation to our negative, unhealthy emotions—it is not the case that our emotions are so intrinsic to our natural instinctual urges that they are beyond educating.

Some Buddhist practitioners have the impression that they should aspire toward some kind of stoic indifference through meditation, like the Stoics of ancient Greece who advocated a state of complete dispassion. People who adhere to this view say that meditation should be a way of achieving a stoicism that prevents the rise of strong emotions, which lead automatically to our downfall. That is a completely mistaken interpretation of Buddhist practice. Buddhism simply encourages us to *manage* our emotions so that their full potency and destructiveness is acknowledged.

Practices such as the four immeasurables aim to modify, manage, and creatively utilize our emotional intelligence, to borrow a phrase from Daniel Goleman.[2] This is possible for "ordinary" people as well as those who lead a monastic life. As Shantideva, Nagarjuna, and many other Indian Buddhist teachers pointed out, it is actually how we normally experience and express our emotional repertoire in the so-called real world that diminishes our capacity to function fully, rationally, and responsibly.

Meditating on the four immeasurables involves both mental purification and healing, which lead to self-enrichment. This enrichment can come about without our having need to obsess over our internal processes. Normally, when we explore our inner mental world, we dwell on all the negatives, such as how hurt, rejected, denied of love, or grief-stricken we feel, or on all our hopelessness and inadequacy, or on our insecurity and anxiety about the future. We see danger in what is to come tomorrow, forgetting that yesterday was just as dangerous!

When we spend any time looking at ourselves, this is what we always end up focusing on. We only become more and more entangled through this approach, and while desperately seeking clarity, we are swept up in ever deeper states of confusion. In fact, every time we obsessively focus on our inner mental states and personal issues, we lose clarity. The time we spend dwelling in and harboring these negative mental states and processes never leads to answers about life's problems; it only makes us more bewildered. Genuine cultivation of self-reflection, such as contemplation of the four immeasurables, will gradually allow us to recognize the unconscious influences that come from our deep-seated psychological programming. This programming is based on cultural and religious biases, gender differences, our individual psychological makeup, and everything else that serves to limit our ability to embrace sentient beings and feel connected and intimate with them.

The four immeasurables have the capacity to heal as well as purify the mind. It is through engaging in this practice that our conflicting emotions and delusions are lessened. We gain respite from our normal, disturbed states of mind while engaged in this meditation, and in so doing are able to see ourselves in a positive light. We all need these positive experiences in great quantities. As a result, our capacity to care, share, give, and feel for others becomes enriched. When we feel love for someone, for example, we are also enriched. Consequently, having love, compassion, joy, and equanimity can have a stabilizing and strengthening influence on our character and temperament. We admire saintly or enlightened beings precisely because of the personal qualities they exhibit, and these qualities have their source in the generous attitudes and perspectives we have discussed. In fact, the greatest quality that anyone can have is the capacity to connect with others and have a positive effect on them. This produces mutual benefit for oneself and others.

BRIDGING THE GAP BETWEEN SELF AND OTHERS

Cultivating the four immeasurables is concerned with alleviating not just the suffering of others but also our own suffering, thereby narrowing the seemingly unbridgeable chasm that separates us from others. When we regard others as completely separate from ourselves, we view everyone in one of just two ways: on the one hand there are the so-called worldly people, who do everything only for themselves, and on the other hand the so-called spiritual people, who do everything for others. One type of person is supposed to be self-serving and egotistical, the other type self-sacrificing and altruistic. This dichotomy presents its own problem, because even if we do not realize it, self and other cannot be separated so easily. In fact, conceiving this separation between self and other to be possible at all is the source of all our conflicts. The Buddhist teachings emphatically state that the notion of an autonomously existing self is completely imaginary. This imaginary notion is regarded as one of the gravest illusions from which we can suffer and the most difficult to relinquish. It is the primary cause of untold misery.

Describing the self as illusory does not suggest that there is no such thing as a "self" at all—we need to be clear about this. It is only that our empirical, conventional self is completely determined by our characteristics, dispositions, and mental life in general, including socially produced ideation. This conventional self is not some kind of independent, unchanging, undefinable, mysterious psychic substance. While it may be inherently difficult for us to gain a direct insight into the Buddhist notion of selflessness (*anatman*), it is not difficult to develop an intellectual understanding of it. We should approach this understanding as more akin to the notion of soullessness than to the complete absence of a self. We are soulless to the extent that we define *soul* in the metaphysical or theological sense as a kind of immutable psychic substance.

A lot of the confusion on this topic arises from incorrect translation. The Sanskrit term *atman* denotes "soul." However, many Western translators have rendered the term *atman* as "self" and consequently interpreted the Buddha's rejection of atman as an advocation of selflessness. Peter Harvey is one recent author to have written a helpful book on this topic of anatman from the perspective of early Buddhism.[3] If you read the Buddha's words carefully, you will see that he denies only that which we assume to be unchanging and permanent. He never refuted the fact that we have an individual self-identity of some kind. There is also a very interesting discussion of the Buddhist notion of self, the Brahmanical notion of *atman* and the concept of buddhanature by David Seyfort Ruegg that is worth looking into to gain a more thorough knowledge of the historical and philosophical background to this debate. This discussion is based upon later Mahayana Indian and Tibetan sources.

Since Buddhists do not believe in a soul or subscribe to a notion of God as an entity that can influence our spiritual practices, one might then assume that the cultivation of love, compassion, joy, and equanimity is just an exercise to produce certain psychological states. As I have mentioned, this is not true. The notion of saintliness (*aryan*) is extremely important in Buddhist practice. We can either attain elevated states of existence or conversely—or, as a cynic might say, more likely—descend into very low forms of existence. Buddhist literature repeatedly states that, even without subscribing to the notion of rebirth, if we lose our senses and neglect ourselves, the force of our habits can propel us into very depraved and subhuman states of existence. These will be lives where undesirable states of mind such as anger, brutality, and cruelty are dominant.

SELF-TRANSFORMATION

Even though we are speaking about self-transformation in these practices, it is not some kind of detached concept of the self that we are trying to transform. It is the various character traits or dispositional properties that determine and define who we are, what we become, and how we see ourselves. Our efforts should definitely go toward developing the character traits and dispositional properties that will allow us to develop in a positive direction, both as ordinary human beings and as spiritual seekers. By focusing on others through the four immeasurables, the self will become transformed without our ever having to focus exclusively or obsessively on our own well-being. Practicing the Buddhist approach to compassion in everyday life is not about doing what is right but about doing what we consider to be good and valuable. This contrast between what is right on the one hand and what is good and valuable on the other is based on the difference between morality and ethics in Western thinking, whereby morality is said to relate to moral guidelines and ethics to what is good and valuable. In the context of Buddhist spiritual self-transformation, what is good and valuable is what contributes toward building our character. If too much emphasis is placed on so-called self-discovery, we might well find nothing much worth discovering. A person empty of any character or truly impoverished within, who is shallow and superficial, will find that there is no such thing as a self to discover. Alternatively, those who engage in the practice of self-cultivation and have become enriched through dealing with themselves in relation to others will find that something truly worthwhile has developed in their character. As a result, they become people of depth and integrity.

Certain contemporary Buddhist secularists emphasize the benefit these practices have for our own sense of self-worth. They highlight the need to focus on our own individual experience as a yardstick for our psychological and spiritual requirements, repeating their mantra, "You have to rely on your own experience." I have great reservations about this emphasis on individual experience. We cannot be too careful about how we can deceive ourselves here. Our experiences change from minute to minute, hour to hour, day to day, so how can we put our trust in anything as fleeting and untrustworthy as experiences? This cult of experientialism, which is so prevalent in all quarters of the modern world, from psychotherapy to politics to New Age spirituality, has to be regarded with a degree of caution. If I think something is important and worthwhile, it also has to be something others can relate to and engage in with the same degree of certainty if it is going to be of any benefit to them. Too much emphasis on our own experience can cause our practice to collapse into total subjectivism and solipsism.

If these practices are formalized in a way that encourages us to seek our own gratification as an end in itself, without a deep respect for the needs of others or any real consideration for the practice of love and compassion toward others, the practice becomes lopsided and unbalanced. Consideration of our own needs and the needs of others has to be kept in equal balance at all times. As a matter of fact, our own experiences will become transformed by our paying attention to the experiences of others. How much our notions about ourselves, our way of seeing things, and our experiences of emotions and feelings become transformed is proportionate to how much attention we give to others.

As Shantideva and other Mahayana masters have pointed out, the more we concentrate on our own experiences to the exclusion of others' experiences, the more our mental agitation, frustration, and despair will increase. The more attention we pay to the experiences of others, the more we will automatically view our own experiences differently. As a result, it will become easier to be more loving than hateful, more compassionate than resentful, and more joyous than given to bouts of depression.

THE WISDOM OF EQUANIMITY AND DISCRIMINATION

The mind is capable of two levels of functioning: One level is an all-encompassing, undifferentiated state, and at the other level discrimination is employed. We will never overcome our mental afflictions unless we can access the undifferentiated state of consciousness. We nonetheless require both levels of consciousness in order to function in the world. The first level of consciousness is described in Buddhist discourse as the wisdom of equanimity and the second level as the wisdom of discrimination. The wisdom of equanimity refers to the ultimate perception of the sameness or evenness of all things and the recognition that nothing is more valuable than any other thing in terms of its intrinsic nature. On the relative level, things *are* different, and it would be impossible to function in the world if we did not perceive these differences. The individual attributes and characteristics of things are apprehended by the wisdom of discrimination.

We are trying to generate this all-encompassing, undifferentiated state through the practice of the four immeasurables while in everyday situations maintaining our sense of discrimination. For example, if we want to help those who are most in need of help, we do not aim to treat them the same as people who need no help at all. We have to be able to discriminate in order to recognize and attend to the person actually requiring our assistance. People often think Buddhism requires us to love all sentient beings equally in all life situations. While we should love all sentient beings equally in our imagination, how we go about caring for others in everyday life will be determined by our circumstances, our abilities, and the inner and outer resources that are at our disposal. This has more bearing on what we are able to achieve than the actual requirements of the recipient of our help.

There are many Buddhist stories that at first glance appear to belie this logic, such as those found in the Jataka Tales of the Buddha's previous lives. There is a story, for example, of the Buddha deciding to sacrifice his own life in order to be food for a hungry tigress who had recently given birth to cubs, so that the tigress and her cubs could live. These kinds of parables should not be taken literally but rather seen as praises to the qualities of love and compassion and the importance of generating them in our contemplative state. We are not expected to emulate such actions in real life. Proof of this takes only a moment's reflection on the Buddhist notion of karma, for allowing somebody to take our life is a morally impermissible act according to karmic theory. We can see, then, that it is very important to differentiate between generating love, compassion, and so forth in a contemplative state, and performing acts of love and compassion in daily life in the context of the transcendental actions of generosity, moral precepts, patience, and vigor.

Some Westerners mistakenly believe wisdom to be related entirely to nondiscrimination. This common misconception arises from the erroneous idea that discursive thoughts are anathema to meditation and must be eliminated. It is made very clear in the Buddhist teachings that even an enlightened being functions on the levels of both nondiscrimination and discrimination, as they are equally necessary conditions for functioning in the world. That is why these two levels of mind are classified as separate aspects of wisdom.

THE PRACTICES OF THE FOUR IMMEASURABLES

We must learn to empathize with and have sympathy for others, and this requires the ability to imagine ourselves in their position. We have to imagine what it would be like if we ourselves were to have their worries, their sadness, and so forth. We train ourselves to develop this kind of empathy through a combination of imagination and visualization, practiced repeatedly; they can be done both in retreat situations and as a daily meditation. They are recommended as a complement to Mahamudra meditation techniques, as part of daily practice, irrespective of what our main practice might be.

Begin by settling on a cushion and adopting the meditation posture (described in chapter 8), before closing your eyes and slowly practicing a series of visualizations. First, settle your mind in tranquillity meditation by not encouraging or following your thoughts. This does not imply that you suppress or eradicate the thoughts that have arisen; simply let your thoughts be. A helpful technique for this type of meditation is to concentrate on the exhalation and inhalation of your breath. Imagine that all the disturbing thoughts and emotions are leaving your body with the exhalation of the breath, and that peace, serenity, and a sense of spaciousness are entering your body with the inhalation of the breath.

Each of the meditation exercises has a similar format, as follows, When your mind has become sufficiently calm, first think of a person whom you love or are extremely fond of, such as a relative, spouse, or friend. Then do the same visualization in relation to someone whom you dislike, then toward someone who is merely an acquaintance. These three different kinds of beings are regarded as the three objects of meditation. They must each be meditated upon from the different perspectives of past, present, and future. After imagining these different individuals, slowly expand the visualization to include all sentient beings. (This refers to all living creatures, not just human beings.) The Mahayana teachings also counsel us to expand our visualization to include beings on other planets and even in other galaxies, as a way of completely challenging our limited concentration on the small circle of significant others whom we fixate upon as friends, enemies or nonentities.

In the meditations on love, compassion, and joy, we also divide the visualization into two aspects: with and without an object. The former involves generating the requisite emotion toward a particular person or persons, and the latter involves simply resting in an all-pervasive, radiating emotion without focusing on anything.

The notion of rebirth can also be included in the practice if you wish. To do so, expand the visualization of the three different types of people to encompass their previous lives. You might think, "This person whom I dislike with such passion may well have been my best friend in my previous life, and this person whom I love so intensely might have been my worst enemy in a previous life." While this is actually true, you do not have to include this aspect of the practice, as it is not a precondition for its success. When we are learning to relate to our emotions in a less biased and more empathetic and generous way, it is helpful to bear in mind that in the Buddhist teachings there are three components to integrating our emotional experience. There is the feeling component of an emotion, the experience of the emotion itself, and the thoughts that are attached to that emotion. We have to look at our emotions in terms of all three components if we are to see the fixations that lie behind our emotional responses and learn to connect with others in a more compassionate way.

Another indispensable factor in these practices is that meditation on the four immeasurables *is* the result. We do not practice the meditation on love in order to give rise to love; the "practice of love" *is* the giving rise to love. The meditation on compassion *is* the giving rise to compassion. This may seem extraordinary, and you may doubt the efficacy of simply imagining love and compassion in your meditation and wonder, "How can I give rise to love and compassion by thinking about it?" This doubt arises only because you are thinking of love and compassion in terms of your actions rather than your state of mind. It is important to realize that if the thought of compassion has arisen in your meditation, then compassion itself has arisen. Do not regard this meditative exercise as some kind of prelude to something that will be more real in postmeditation. Of course, the actual experience of love and compassion may be more profound when it occurs in daily life, but meditating on love and compassion *is* the experience of love and compassion nonetheless.

Immeasurable Equanimity

Immeasurable equanimity (*upeksha*) begins with the development of a state of mind that is without aversion, attraction, or indifference. Equanimity is actually the most important disposition because the love, compassion, and joy that we are ultimately trying to generate have to come from a mental space that is uncluttered by mental activity. This is the contemplative state, which is the natural state of being—we could call this the ground Mahamudra. This spaciousness of the mind is said to be the most important of the four immeasurables, because without it love, compassion, and joy can all become corrupted by the investment of all manner of notions about self and other.

We generate this spacious state of mind through realizing how relationships are constantly unstable and moving as a result of shifting circumstances. We must be clear that equanimity does not imply indifference, for indifference is a state of mind that is closed off. Equanimity, on the other hand, is a spacious state that notices the fact that relationships are always in movement, that nothing about them is fixed. This open state of mind is intimately engaged with our experiences, but it is not fixated on them. While developing this open, unfixated state of mind, we should be aware of the dual function of this contemplation: While the aim is to develop a genuine state of equanimity, simply doing this meditation will result in freeing up the mind.

VISUALIZATION

Settle yourself in tranquillity meditation and then give rise to the mental images that follow from that state of tranquillity. You will find that if you begin these practices from a genuinely calm state of mind, the appropriate emotions will arise without your having to generate them. This practice begins by meditating on a loved one. Evoke the image of someone you are particularly fond of or have deep attachment to, and when that person is vividly present in your mind's eye, ponder your past and future relationship. Perhaps that individual was a nonentity to you in the beginning, then became an acquaintance, and is now somebody you are extremely fond of. Then imagine that this individual will not remain a friend in the future. Contemplate the changing circumstances that might adversely affect your relationship with that person, and notice how your feelings can move from deep affection and fondness to indifference and aversion.

Meditating in this way allows us to develop a shift in how we view others, including those whom we hold dear. We develop a greater appreciation for the fact that the individual in question is not some kind of self-existent being. Instead, who we think the person is and what he or she means to us is greatly affected by our and their changing circumstances as well as the changing circumstances of the relationship.

Next, perform the same meditation in relation to someone for whom you feel intense dislike. Visualize someone who is a constant thorn in your side, and deliberately make all the person's unpleasant attributes vividly clear. Think about the person you dislike in relation to the past. He or she may have initially been insignificant to you or may have actually been a close friend. Then think about the person in relation to the present, and then move into the future and imagine further changing circumstances. For example, that person might move to another city or country and become insignificant once more. Or the person could become an ally, perhaps because you are brought together by a common enemy.

The third step is to imagine someone with whom you are unfamiliar or about whom you have no definite opinion. Think of that person in relation to his or her past and future. Perhaps in the past that person was a friend but due to the shifting pattern of your circumstances has drifted away and now hardly features in your life at all. Think of examples of changing circumstances, and imagine that this person has become your friend again or has become an adversary through a different set of conditions.

This exercise is meant to help us understand that what makes someone a friend, an adversary, or insignificant to us is contingent on multitudinous external factors. There is nothing preset in terms of our relationships, and this uncertainty means that all kinds of possibilities can and probably will arise. When we really understand this to be so, we can view all these possibilities with whatever degree of equanimity we can muster.

Equanimity does not connote that everything will remain on an even keel at all times. It simply means that the ups and downs of life will no longer be interpreted as major upheavals. We will always be subject to fluctuating experiences, because life's circumstances are always changing. New and unexpected things may be just around the corner. Sometimes things work out and sometimes they do not. I am sure even enlightened beings have bad days due to the situations in which they are placed. His Holiness the Dalai Lama, for example, had to escape from Tibet because it was very uncomfortable for him to stay in Lhasa. Being reduced to the status of a refugee could have made him lose touch with reality if he were just an ordinary person. For many years the Dalai Lama was not as well known and popular as he is today. When he first escaped from Tibet, nobody knew of him other than the Tibetans. He underwent an amazing series of difficulties and faced formidable obstacles as the leader of a refugee community. It was his practice and his level of attainment that enabled him to work with such difficulties. Not only does he not bear any ill will toward the Chinese, but he consistently instructs us to generate love and compassion toward them. This is not something an ordinary person could have achieved under similar circumstances.

Immeasurable Love

The practice of immeasurable love involves learning to experience the fundamentals of a loving feeling, often described in Buddhist literature as loving-kindness (*maitri* in Sanskrit; *champa* in Tibetan). Loving-kindness is an emotion that is not compromised or diluted by other conflicting emotions or feelings. It is a love that is pure, for want of a better word. It can be applied to both romantic love and love for family and friends. It is also a love that we can learn to generate for all beings, in sympathetic and empathetic response to the existential condition. Love in this context is defined as wanting someone to be happy. The most important aspect of this practice is the feelings and emotions that we generate. What is happening externally is actually of no consequence; it is the subjective experience of love that is the key factor in this meditative exercise.

VISUALIZATION

Generate a state of equanimity and then begin the visualizations. As before, generate love in relation to the three types of people. It is much easier to generate love for someone you are already very fond of, so begin by visualizing such a person. Start with wanting your loved one to be happy, and gradually extend that aspiration to include all sentient beings. When visualizing a particular person, think: "What would make this person happy? What does he or she desire and need on a physical, mental and spiritual level?" It might be immediate kinds of material or financial recompense, the restoration of health, finding a lost love or a new love, or perhaps a loftier ideal such as discovering meaning in life. Whatever his or her wishes, imagine vividly that the person to whom you are sending love has received the fulfillment of his or her desires and is visibly affected by your love and generosity. Picture the person as happy, joyous, and completely content. When you finish this meditation, return to resting in a state of equanimity for a short time.

It is important to return to the practice of equanimity. You can arouse strong feelings engaging in these practices, and equanimity is a way to keep from getting swept away by unrestrained emotions. Otherwise you may begin to feel somewhat overwhelmed by the whole experience and find it hard to continue the meditation.

Next, give rise to the image of a person who is an acquaintance or a stranger. A neutral person is visualized next in the sequence because it is easier to generate love toward an acquaintance than someone for whom you feel antipathy. Visualize that person, whoever it may be, and think about what would make this person happy on a physical, mental, and spiritual level. Imagine that whatever he or she desires, needs, and dreams about is fulfilled as a result of the love that you are sending out. Picture the person being enveloped by this love and receiving the full benefit of it. When you have concluded, return to the state of equanimity.

Next, think of someone you dislike. Imagine wanting this person to be happy and to have everything he or she needs. If your dislike has arisen from perceiving the person to be aggressive, obnoxious, or arrogant, imagine that this aggressive nature has been mellowed and softened and that he or she is becoming happier, more joyous, and less aggressive toward you and others as a result. If your dislike is the result of some other characteristic, visualize the same process of amelioration of that factor.

As you become proficient in this meditation, you should incorporate an ever-increasing number of sentient creatures into your visualizations. Expand it to include all living creatures that you know of and all living creatures that you do not know of, such as those that live in your city, your country, or the world, and even farther out to other planets or galaxies if you wish. When you have completed this visualization, return again to the state of equanimity and remain in that state for a time.

That concludes the meditation stage that is known as loving-kindness with object. After this, return to a state of equanimity and then generate a loving state without thinking of any specific individual or any kind of object of your love. This is called objectless loving-kindness meditation. This has to follow from the loving-kindness meditation that employed an object as the focus of love. In this latter exercise, you generate an all-pervasive, radiating love and then just rest in that state of being, which is the ground Mahamudra.

———

It is crucial to understand how love can become diluted by excessive attachment or possessiveness. It can swiftly convert into hatred and become intermingled with other negative emotions, leading usually to destructive forms of behavior. People often object to the notion of detachment when it comes to love, saying that we cannot really love someone if we do not have strong attachment. They therefore regard the Buddhist notion of detached love as practically impossible. According to Buddhism, though, attachment interferes in myriad ways with our capacity to truly care for others; it is a complex emotion that is often intermingled with various other negative emotional states and ideas, which become all jumbled together and cloud the mind. True affection and true caring can be separated from attachment. Attachment implies that we have a need to be affixed to the object of our care—whether it is a thing, a person, or an idea—for our own security. The fundamental basis of this is fear. If our attachment is too strong, however, we no longer own the thing—it owns us!

A moment of reflection will help to dispel these fears and objections. The evils of strong attachment are revealed in the all too familiar occurrence of domestic violence and people engaging in criminal acts. In any case, Buddhist teachings have never said that nonattachment means that we should not have affection, nor is it said that gradually we will have fewer and fewer emotions until we transcend any kind of emotional experience whatsoever. The teachings say that as our understanding of emotions and feelings for others increases, we will recognize that they are always moving and changing.

The love that we are trying to generate in this practice is incapable of such selfish and corrupted responses. It has to be pure, all-encompassing, and plentiful. Detached love does not equate with mediocrity or lack of heart; it indicates a withdrawal of selfish motivations and possessiveness. It is possible to love without needing to control or manipulate the object of our affection. As this love is only being practiced in our imagination in this context, it has none of the limiting factors of place and time that otherwise might inhibit our emotions.

Immeasurable Compassion

The next meditation is immeasurable compassion (*karuna* in Sanskrit; *nyingje* in Tibetan). As with the meditation on love, this has to be a pure compassion untainted by selfish concerns. We practice this meditation in order to develop an all-pervasive compassion toward all beings. We should be especially careful to avoid allowing our compassion to degenerate into sentimentality or gushing emotionalism. The basic definition of compassion in Mahayana Buddhism is the desire to alleviate the suffering of others. Almost all of us have had moments of feeling compassion for others, but these moments are episodic and often tainted with less savory emotions. As such, our compassion is not part of our character, which is exactly what this practice is meant to bring about—it will help us become more compassionate and more loving people; and as a consequence, all of the other virtuous qualities will begin to flourish in us as well.

VISUALIZATION

After settling your mind in equanimity meditation, practice the meditation on compassion by thinking about the three types of persons. First, think of someone you have great affection for—a friend, associate, partner, or family member—and then contemplate that person's unhappiness. Ask yourself: "Why is this person unhappy and suffering?" Think of that person's predicament and his or her specific instances of suffering, and generate a strong feeling of compassion and sympathy. You have to imagine that your compassion is having an effect. Imagine that whatever has been causing the person's suffering—ill health, mental instability, family problems, financial problems—is addressed and attended to as a result of your compassion. Picture the person finding relief and respite from his or her anguish and gaining real and lasting comfort and ease. Then go back to the state of equanimity.

Turn your meditation practice to an acquaintance now. Think about his or her specific problems—they could be drug related, or domestic, or simply agonizing loneliness—generate compassion toward the person. Remind yourself that this person's feelings *do* matter, even though you are not particularly intimate with him or her. Generate a real feeling of concern, a feeling that you really want to alleviate this person's difficulties and hardships, whatever they might be. Imagine the person beginning to respond to your sympathetic feelings of kindness and care. Imagine doing things for the peson, such as giving material aid, saying soothing words, or providing psychological and spiritual counsel. Last, imagine that the person's suffering and its source have been overcome, and he or she is beginning to feel joyous and uplifted in spirit.

When you have completed this visualization, remain for a

while in the state of compassion without thinking of anything or anyone. Allow compassion to well up inside you, radiate outward, and spread in all directions. Remain in that state for a while before returning to the calm and restful state of equanimity, without thinking about anything at all.

Next, visualize someone you despise, and again think of that person in terms of his or her suffering. Whatever you find to be a source of difficulty or tribulation in relation to this person, acknowledge that this factor is a problem for him or her as well. If, for instance, the person is selfishly egotistic or overbearing, generate compassion by regarding that characteristic as the cause of his or her own suffering. As Shantideva explains:

> As ordinary sentient beings
> We are not the master or mistress of our house.
> We are at the mercy of our uncontrolled emotions,
> Entrenched habitual patterns and unconscious tendencies.

Contemplate the reality that the person you dislike is also a victim of his or her emotions and tendencies and is suffering from that. Occasionally the person may admit to having emotional or other problems but is unable to handle them except through aggression and bad behavior. Imagine these tendencies diminishing and the person becoming less self-centered, less inconsiderate, and so on, depending on the quality you find irksome. Thinking along these lines in different situations, imagine the object of your meditation becoming happier and more amiable as the result of the compassion you have directed toward him or her.

Following this exercise, again remain in a state of unrestricted or objectless compassion, without thinking of anything or anyone as the recipient of your compassion. Just rest in a state of radiating compassion before returning to the state of equanimity again.

As with the meditation on immeasurable love, the practice of immeasurable compassion has to shift gradually from a focus on a few people to increasingly numerous sentient beings. You begin with peo-

ple in your immediate vicinity, then expand that to your city and re-
gion, then to the whole country, the continent, and beyond until you
have included the whole world and the galaxies. This is why this practice refers to immeasurable or infinite qualities—it involves boundless
love and compassion toward all beings. It is also said that these feelings
of love and compassion should be generated toward beings that have
existed in the past, exist in the present, and will exist in the future. In
other words, you should include absolutely everyone. It is important
to remember that these meditation practices should be undertaken
from within the spacious state of mind that comes with the meditation
on equanimity. Otherwise, we can easily get caught up in all kinds of
self-deception. We may think we are generating love and compassion
toward others, but really we are just satisfying our own emotional
needs. Sometimes our effort to express positive emotions toward others is just a disguised yearning for love and compassion for ourselves.
Buddhists would call that an impure motivation. If we have the spacious state of mind that comes from equanimity, there is room for a
genuine self-love and self-caring that is not narcissistic and that does
not fill our own egotistic needs for attention and self-nurturing. This
is extremely important. Even in the early sutras, the Buddha said that
love and compassion for others and love and compassion for oneself
have to be related. People who hate themselves can never love someone else. Self-hatred is a destructive fixation and one of the root causes
of our emotional problems. Friendliness toward ourselves is therefore
especially beneficial and transformative.

Immeasurable Joy

The next meditation relates to immeasurable joy (*mudita* in Sanskrit; *de*
in Tibetan). This too should be uncontaminated by the ever-present
and insidiously polluting influence of negative emotions. Joy is a feeling of upliftedness that we should generate slowly in meditation. It has
to become a part of our disposition, so that we are predisposed to feeling like a relatively cheerful person and are not given to bouts of depression or self-loathing. To be that kind of person, we have to first
create and generate the feeling of joy and then habituate ourselves to it
through repeated practice.

VISUALIZATION

Do this practice with the three types of individuals as the objects of your meditation and by beginning and ending each segment with the meditation of equanimity. When you visualize someone for whom you feel affection, you take joy in the person's achievements and good qualities and rejoice in the person's health and well-being. When you take acquaintances and people you dislike as the object of meditation, imagine that they are extremely happy and satisfied, without feeling any sense of jealousy. Rather, partake in the joyous celebration of their newfound happiness. Also think that joy is all-pervasive within yourself and that you are completely at ease.

You should feel joyous that all sentient beings have secured happiness. Here, you should mainly visualize people who are happy. Think that they have attained this happiness all by themselves, and rejoice in their well-being. Think: "May sentient beings who are experiencing happiness not cease from experiencing this happiness. Until they attain their final goal of enlightenment, may they always be accompanied by happiness and well-being."

Begin this practice by thinking that the suffering of one individual has ceased and that he or she has attained a long-awaited happiness. Then gradually expand this to include all sentient beings in the world and the galaxies. Continue with this practice until you have imagined every conceivable living being to have attained that state. Imagine each person bathed in happiness, and celebrate this fact by thinking that everyone is deservedly happy. Then generate a feeling of joy because everyone is happy. After that simply remain in a state of great joy without thinking of any object. You should simply be filled with happiness and remain in that high spirit for a short while before returning to the state of equanimity.

Having a joyous disposition does not mean we will not experience pain or discomfort from time to time. We may experience those things, but nothing will be so bad as to make us feel helpless and without hope.

It is also important to note that feeling unmotivated has a great deal to do with having a poor opinion of ourselves. From a Buddhist point of view, that is just another extreme form of egotism. Self-loathing, feeling bad about ourselves, and being harsh on ourselves are all expressions of egocentricity. Meditation on the immeasurables is an excellent means of dissolving this self-deprecation. During meditation on immeasurable joy, we may in fact feel a sense of elation that can lead to distraction. If this happens and your mind becomes too tumultuous and active, meditate on equanimity without attachment and view everything in the same fashion. Elation is a more temporary experience of upliftedness than joy and does not last. You simply experience a rush of exhilaration and then feel flat again. This does not mean that you should not be elated from time to time, but you have to overcome that elation and not mistake it for real joy.

MAKING PROGRESS WITH THE FOUR IMMEASURABLES

These meditations must be done over and over again. They address our negative states of mind while circumventing the need to dwell on any one of them. If we meditate on love, our anger, aggression, and hostility will decrease proportionately. If we meditate on compassion, our attachment, greed, and neediness will start to diminish. If we meditate on joy, our experience of envy will be reduced. The meditation on equanimity acts as a corrective for conceit, egocentricity, and selfishness. Instead of trying to get rid of overwhelming desire, engulfing anger, or resentment, we find that these negative emotions will dissipate from our fundamental makeup through meditation on the four immeasurables. The feelings of guilt, shame, fear, and confusion that we generally harbor will come to rest without our having to deal with them directly. Their power diminishes as we become more accustomed to these emotions, and their ability to make an impression on our minds grows correspondingly fainter.

The exercise in equanimity is really an exercise in learning how to let go of our fixations. As I stated in chapter 3, all of life's problems and travails come in large part from our habit of fixating on things. We becoming fixated as a result of things we think about, our emotional investments in them, and the strong feelings with which we relate to them. The ability to let go comes from developing a spacious mental attitude. This may not free us completely, but it will at least unfetter us. I would like to share the following story by way of illustration.

A Jewish disciple went to her rabbi to seek his advice. She said, "I'm in desperate need of help or I'll go crazy. My husband, my children, and my in-laws are all living in a single room, and our nerves are on edge. We yell and scream at one another. The room is a hell." The rabbi thought for a while and then said gravely, "Do you promise to do whatever I tell you?" The disciple replied earnestly, "I swear I shall do anything." "Very well," responded the rabbi, "how many animals do you have?" "I have a cow, a goat, and six chickens," was the reply. "Bring them all into the room with you," the rabbi instructed, "then come back and see me in a week." The disciple was appalled, but she had promised to obey, so she brought the animals into the room with the rest of her family. A week later she came back to her rabbi looking pitiably distraught and declared, "I'm now a complete wreck. The dirt, the stench, the noise—we are all on the verge of madness." "I see," said the rabbi. "Now I want you to go back home and take all of the animals outside." The woman ran all the way home to do as her rabbi requested. She came back to visit him the following day, her eyes sparkling with joy, and said, "How sweet life is. The animals are out and the home is a paradise. It's so quiet and clean and spacious!"

If that spaciousness exists, emotional intelligence will arise automatically, because this intelligence comes from a lessening of fixation. Our vision has become so narrowly focused that we miss almost everything that is going on, and our emotional intelligence becomes dimmed and distorted. According to Buddhist thinking, we do not have to resolve our issues—we simply have to learn to let them dissipate so that they effectively become nonissues.

Many of the great figures in modern history—at least those who merit our admiration, such as Mahatma Gandhi, Nelson Mandela, and the Dalai Lama—rose above their experience of oppression, torture, imprisonment, and great loss to emerge as strong, wise, visionary leaders. If they had not let go of their past and had instead made an issue out of every little incident or trauma, they would not have become the great beings that they did. Nor would that approach have made them happier or more content.

It is fundamental to our spiritual progress to realize that our thoughts and emotions are not solid entities. They are transitory and constantly in motion. Within that transitoriness there is also a profound stability. Some people make the mistake of thinking that because Buddhism emphasizes transience so much, it does not really cherish the notion of stability. That is not true. Stability does not come from things remaining the same, because that would only be stultifying, a form of imprisonment. We may take refuge in that inertia, but that comfort is illusory, because it is just a fabrication of our own mind.

In reality, nothing stays the same, so we are better off being realistic and accepting that fact. Stability has to come from embracing the fact that everything is in motion. It is the same with our emotions and the people and things we care about. We are constantly interacting with things, people, and other living creatures and never have a static position from which to interact with the world, for the simple reason that there is no such fixed position. Acknowledging and accepting this dynamic state of affairs is how we learn to transcend our ordinariness. This is where all growth comes from. If we cannot embrace this dynamic state of flux, we will always be trapped in our ordinariness and can never aspire to become a bodhisattva, let alone a fully enlightened being.

Even though there is no one right way to practice the four immeasurables, they are generally practiced in the order presented here, with one exception. In the traditional exoteric teachings of Mahayana Buddhism, we start with contemplation on love and follow that with the contemplations on compassion, joy, and equanimity. In this instance I have followed the lesser-known practice of putting equanimity first. The reason for doing so is twofold. First, equanimity functions as a stabilizing force for the emotions of love, compassion, and joy and helps to ensure that they do not overwhelm us or become tainted by our tendency to privilege our own selfish concerns. The second reason is that equanimity is something of a doorway to the unbiased nondiscrimination of the nature of the mind, which characterizes the Mahamudra tradition of spiritual practice and which can ultimately give rise to the spontaneous expression of love, compassion, and joy.

There is also a reason the contemplations are combined as a whole. Attachment may arise when we generate love, so we meditate on compassion to counteract that. Mere sentimental feelings may arise as a result of meditating on compassion, so we meditate on equanimity to counteract that. Equanimity may deteriorate into indifference or apathy, so we generate love again from that open state. In this way, the immeasurables counteract each other and create a natural equilibrium in their meditative expression.

We tend to think that if we have some kind of problem, we need to do something drastic to counteract it. These meditations on the four immeasurables are a far subtler way to deal with ourselves, as we can do them without ever concentrating on ourselves. We do not have to think, "I must change; I should not do this anymore; I can't stand it anymore." If we think in this way, our problems will just become an overwhelming burden. Even though we are constantly referring to love, compassion, joy, and equanimity here, we are not talking about them in relation to what we do but as a meditative exercise of self-enrichment. While many people make the reasonable assumption that love and compassion are forms of *doing*, and that that is where the proof of them lies, if we are not loving and compassionate by nature we will find it almost impossible to be loving and compassionate in our actions. These meditations are important because they help us to narrow that gap between being and action.

The Mahayana teachings say that practicing the four immeasurables is akin to tending a garden. If a garden is well watered and well tended, everything in it will flourish. When we cultivate immeasurable love, immeasurable compassion, immeasurable joy, and immeasurable equanimity, this may not include all of the virtuous qualities we need in order to become bodhisattvas, but it will create the favorable mental conditions for us to develop in that direction. Love, compassion, joy, and equanimity are the precondition for becoming a bodhisattva; they ensure that all the other virtuous qualities of a saintly being will flourish. If love, compassion, joy, and equanimity are absent, the other virtuous qualities will have no way to flower.

Therefore, when we practice the six transcendental actions in everyday life, we must combine them with these immeasurables. If we practice generosity, we do so with an element of love, compassion, joy, and equanimity. It is the same with the practice of patience, moral precepts, and vigor. The four immeasurables are not meant to dictate the specific practices that we do on a daily basis; they simply assist us in doing our regular practices with those positive states of mind, and we will then do them better. Everything we do should be imbued with these mental attitudes, and the efficacy of the practice of the four immeasurables will naturally flow from this.

We should always aim high and have high expectations of ourselves. However, having high expectations in terms of what we do does not imply that only doing something remarkable is worthwhile. The little things also count. Even if we are doing something we consider insignificant, its success should be measured in terms of the quality of our actions, the excellence with which we execute our aims. We should always feel good about the things we have done, however small, and treat our apparent failures in a positive way. If we think we have failed at something, we should not dwell on that failure except to try to understand how to prevent a similar mistake in the future. It is essential to cultivate this kind of attitude as part of our spiritual practice.

It should be remembered that the four immeasurables are only mental exercises, intended to transform us by training in thinking about others. Although we tend to think we can transform ourselves only through deliberate thinking about ourselves, the Mahayana Buddhist perspective teaches that we do the greatest service to ourselves when we concentrate on others. All of our Buddhist practices need to be combined because each practice is designed to complement another practice. If we can combine them successfully, we will have a tremendously comprehensive method to deal with all aspects of ourselves as human beings, enabling us to benefit others accordingly. In the Mahamudra tradition, we develop a calm mind through tranquillity meditation, gain more insight into reality and the nature of the mind through insight meditation, and complement these by developing more wholesome attitudes and tendencies through practicing the four immeasurables.

PART TWO

GROUND
MAHAMUDRA

7

BUDDHA-NATURE

We come now to a discussion of ground mahamudra and some of the more philosophical elements of Mahamudra meditation. The notion of the ground—also called the basis—is a key concept for Mahayana and later forms of Buddhism. *Ground of being* refers to the Mahamudra itself, or to our true nature, our authentic state of being. In Mahayana Buddhism, this ground is also known as buddha-nature. I will begin with this more widely known concept from the perspective of the exoteric approach and then proceed to link the idea of buddha-nature to the mystical notion of the ground of being, or ground Mahamudra.

THE EXOTERIC PERSPECTIVE

In Buddhism the stated aim of spiritual practice is to attain enlightenment, or buddhahood, which requires that we bring about a fundamental change in our state of being. It may seem obvious that in order to do this, we need to utilize and gain a deeper understanding of our awareness of the mind, yet the question arises: How can our normal consciousness—our conceptual mind, which is far from perfect—attain a state of perfection? Our normal consciousness does not have the freedom to shift suddenly to a highly elevated state, for our ordinary consciousness is thoroughly habituated to delusory perception. But we do need to attain enlightenment. Where would the ability to do so come from? The answer, according to the Mahayana literature, is that it comes from our own authentic natural state of being, known as buddha–nature, which is fundamentally and innately free of conflicting emotions.

As we have already discussed, buddha–nature is not confined to the normal functionings of our mind, so it could be said to be a transcendental state, in that it is not contained by the thoughts, emotions, feelings, and egotism that define our conventional empirical reality. It is the undeluded aspect of our mind. Nevertheless, it is not itself a state of transcendence, because it is fully immanent in our experience in the sense that it does not exist outside our mind. The most important point is that buddha–nature is not something hidden or beyond our reach.

Buddha–nature is called *tathagatagarbha* in Sanskrit: *tathagata* literally means "thus gone," and *garbha* means "essence." In Tibetan, *tathagata* is translated as *de sheg*, which signifies "arriving at peace," and *garbha* is translated as *nying po*, which also means "essence." *Tathagata* therefore refers to someone who has gone beyond suffering and arrived at the seat of peace, a synonym for our own innate wisdom. It is this wisdom that enables us to leave the turmoil of the samsaric condition (our ordinary normal condition) and arrive at the state of liberation (the state of peace). In other words, tathagatagarbha, or buddha–nature, refers to our innate spiritual nature. This spiritual nature must be understood as a given, something we already *are* in essence.

THE MIDDLE WAY

In the course of the development of Mahayana Buddhism, during its travel from India to Tibet, China, and Japan, there have been many new and noble interpretations of buddha–nature.

Despite the numerous ways in which the concept of buddha–nature has been assimilated into various Buddhist schools, one thing remains unchanged: buddha–nature has to be understood within the context of the middle view, whereby we do not fall into either the extreme of complete indulgence in the worldly aspect of life or the extreme of single-mindedly focusing on otherworldly, metaphysical concerns. This middle view is an alternative way to understand the human condition.

Roughly speaking, throughout history there have been two principal ways of understanding the human condition. The first is empirical, whereby human beings are seen as the sum total of their physical and psychological constituents. That perspective leads to a particular kind of self-understanding without reference to the transcendental dimension, confining itself to the empirical domain. The other way is to view the self or an aspect of the self as in some way disconnected from the world. The self is thought to be an immutable, permanent, self-existing soul or metaphysical self. That perspective will obviously lead to a completely different type of self-understanding from the materialistic one, and the focus here is firmly placed on the transcendental at the expense of the empirical.

From the Mahayana point of view, the notion of buddha-nature, the indwelling of our spiritual nature, transcends both of these self-understandings. The empirical self cannot be a vehicle to transport us to the state of enlightenment because it is contingent on ever-changing psychophysical conditions. Alternatively, a psychic substance such as a soul or metaphysical self is equally unable to serve this purpose, because it is defined as a fixed entity existing beyond dynamic processes. Hence the concept of buddha-nature has to be understood as the middle way that avoids these two extreme views. It is not reliant on something that is constantly changing, nor is it reliant on something that is unchanging and metaphysical. The Tibetan version of the *Mahaparinirvana-sutra*, which was translated from Chinese sources, makes this point:

> This buddha-nature is not in reality atman [metaphysical self]. It is for the sake of sentient beings that the self is spoken of. Whereas by virtue of the existence of causes and conditions the Tathagata [Buddha] has spoken of not-self as "self," in reality there is no self. Though he has spoken thus, this was no untruth. It is because of the existence of causes and conditions that it is said that the self is not-self. Whereas saying that self exists, in reality it is with a view to the world of beings that it has been said that there is a self. But that was no untruth either. The buddha-nature is not-self, and if the Tathagata has spoken of self this is because a designation has been employed.

To gain a proper understanding of ourselves, we need certain concepts to steer us in the right direction. In the Mahayana scriptures, buddha-nature is presented as a way of understanding ourselves that does not fall into either of the two extremes. If we do not understand this properly, buddha-nature could become just another version of the atman theory. We would then become fixated on a fictitious concept that simply does not correspond to any real-life experience. Buddha-nature is not a metaphysical self, nor is it reducible to the sum total of our physical and psychological states. It has a spiritual reality that goes beyond our everyday psychological states while still being something that *is* experienceable. We often talk about "having" buddha-nature and see quotations from the scriptures such as "All sentient beings are in possession of buddha-nature." Taking this literally could be quite misleading. We do not *have* buddha-nature as we have other kinds of characteristics as part of our psychological makeup or personality. Buddha-nature is what we *are* in essence; it is our own primordial nature, which is in reality a spiritual one.

Many popular books on Buddhism written for Western audiences speak about buddha-nature as if it were some psychic state that we can access during meditation. This explanation has to be viewed with suspicion, because it implies that we are nothing but mere permutations of physical and mental states. Again, that would be a foundation too precarious on which to build a spiritual practice. If we were a metaphysical self, on the other hand, that would be too abstract and remote (and, from a Mahayana point of view, too fictitious) to be immediately accessible in meditation. Both these options, for different reasons, are too unreliable to serve as the basis for building spiritual insights. A humorous story illustrates the need to have an innate capacity in order to succeed at what we wish to achieve. A young composer once visited Mozart to consult him on how to develop his talent. "I would advise you to start with simple things," Mozart advised him. "But you were composing symphonies when you were a child!" protested the young composer. "That is true," replied Mozart, "but I didn't have to ask anyone for advice on how to develop my talent."

THE WORKING BASIS

In traditional Buddhist literature, buddha-nature is often referred to as the working basis. For example, one of the early chapters of Gampopa's *Jewel Ornament of Liberation* devoted to buddha-nature is called "The Working Basis." Here Gampopa explains that we can become enlightened because we can rely on this basis. We cannot rely on the notion of a soul or some kind of metaphysical self because of its abstract nature. He argues that even if the soul existed, according to Mahayana reasoning, since it is immutable and unchanging, we must have been born with it, and it must remain indissolubly with us. It is difficult to determine how such an unchanging entity would aid us in our self-transformation. To be functional, it would have to become involved with change. Furthermore, because everything we experience is subject to change, something that is unchanging and immutable cannot become evidently manifest in our stream of consciousness and thus can have no impact on it. Asked whether the metaphysical self and buddha-nature are the same, the Dalai Lama replied:

> No. The term *atman* has a different connotation; it refers to a self or person completely independent of the psychophysical aggregates. *Atman* is a self that can be identified apart from body and mind. This kind of self is refuted in Buddhism. The clear light or the buddha-nature itself is not the person or a sentient being but the basis of such a being. It is part of the consciousness and is therefore the basis of a designation of a sentient being of the self or a person, but it is not the self itself.[1]

People often say that the difference between buddha-nature and the soul or atman is all semantics and that in reality they are the same. A Buddhist would insist that it is not just a question of semantics or verbal and conceptual distinctions, because buddha-nature is not and has never been thought of as some kind of unchanging psychic substance. Buddha-nature is that element in the consciousness that remains resistant to the delusory workings of the mind. The notion of an essentially undeluded consciousness is not an invention of Mahayana Buddhism. The Buddha himself made references to this idea in his early discourses. For example, in the Pali sutta *Nguttara-nikaya*, the Buddha had this to say about the essence of consciousness being luminous and pure and immune to defiling tendencies:

> This mind, monks, is luminous, but it is defiled by stains that come from without, but this the uninstructed folk do not understand as it really is. Thus for the uninstructed folk there is no cultivation of the mind. I declare that mind, monks, is luminous and is cleansed of taints that come from without. This the instructed noble disciple understands as it really is. Thus for the instructed noble disciple there is cultivation of the mind, I declare.

In this Pali sutta, Buddha refers to the nature of the mind as luminous and sees the defilements as adventitious, which means they are not intrinsic to the mind itself. The word for luminosity is *pabhasar* in Pali and *prabhasvara* in Sanskrit. It would be one extreme to say there is no self at all apart from the self-identity constructed on and around our psychophysical constituents. That would be a nihilistic view. To say that there is a metaphysical self is the other extreme and represents an eternalistic view. The concept of buddha-nature therefore offers the middle way between these extremes. It refers to that element of consciousness that is pure and has remained resistant to the delusory states of mind. This is the working basis that Gampopa takes as so essential for the spiritual path and the reason it is possible for us to attain enlightenment.

ENLIGHTENMENT IS POSSIBLE

As our buddha-nature is not subject to rapid fluctuations (as our psychological states are), and as it is not elusive, mysterious, and completely impervious to change (as the metaphysical self is), it can serve as a stable foundation for spiritual insight. Buddha-nature, then, has to be understood as our indwelling spiritual nature. It is important to point out that just because the word "buddha" is included in the concept of buddha-nature, we should not infer that it applies exclusively to Buddhists. Of course, it originated as a Buddhist concept, but buddha-nature exists in every being.

It is because our true nature is buddha-nature that enlightenment is possible. Without it, the aspiration to attain enlightenment would merely be wishful thinking. There is nothing in our ordinary physical and mental states to suggest that they have the capacity to lead us out of the murky world of samsara, for the vicious turning of cyclic existence is characterized by periods of temporary happiness and periods of extreme pain, suffering, and despair. In fact, it is our very psychological workings that perpetuate this cycle.

The second reason we are able to aim toward enlightenment, according to the Mahayana teachings, is that it is the conflicting emotions, and nothing else, that prevent us from recognizing our innate spiritual nature. If there were no conflicting emotions, we would understand our own true nature already and would not have got lost in the fictitious pursuit of self-knowledge. All of our distorted and deluded thoughts and our emotional conflicts of anger, jealousy, greed, hatred, pride and ignorance serve to perpetuate the deluded consciousness.

The Mahayana sutras compare buddha-nature to the sun and the conflicting emotions to clouds. The negative emotions are said to be black ominous clouds and the positive emotions to be white clouds. In both cases, they are only temporary obscurations that are unable to dim the brilliance of the sun. Likewise, our conflicting emotions do obscure our minds temporarily, yet they are unable to cause any harm to the original purity of our mind, our buddha-nature or the ground Mahamudra.

The third reason we can realize this nature is our innate capacity to develop saintly qualities and attributes that in turn empower our efforts to overcome defilements. They do not have to be newly transplanted and cultivated, as would something foreign introduced from outside of ourselves—they are native to ourselves. We already have all the redeeming, elevated qualities and attributes that we admire in highly evolved beings, although those qualities remain in a state of potential at this point. Naturally, with encouragement, we can learn to cultivate and develop that potential. Knowing this will boost our confidence and lessen doubts and uncertainties.

If the qualities that we require for liberation needed to be imported from outside ourselves, we would always have a nagging suspicion that they might not take root. On the other hand, if they already exist in dormant form within ourselves, we can be assured that they will grow if we nurture them. The metaphor used in the Mahayana sutras is the planting of a field. If one takes an exotic plant and attempts to grow it in the desert, there will be little likelihood of success. And yet one can grow any plant in a fertile area that is conducive to growth. It is the same with virtuous qualities.

One could that say consciousness by nature tends toward enlightenment. Our spiritual practices are designed to encourage that tendency rather than introduce something new to consciousness. We should therefore think of spiritual practice as encouraging what it is already natural for us to do. It is not natural for us to exist in a deluded state—that is the aberration that leads us away from the luminous bliss of buddhahood.

This is why we speak of samsaric existence as going astray and why buddha-nature is referred to as our original dwelling place, our original home. Our buddha-nature is where we belong, where we should be; it is not anything new or foreign. It is unnatural for us to have been thrown into a deep state of confusion. To use a Christian expression, spiritual practice is a way of responding to the "original calling" of buddha-nature. We are simply responding to that call of our spiritual nature and returning to it. We do not *have* buddha-nature; we *are* buddha-nature. Our essence is spiritual, and we need not manufacture it in any way; it is the given condition of our fundamental state of being. This is why it is said that the defilements that obscure buddha-nature are only adventitious.

BEYOND THE NOTION OF SELF

From the general Mahayana point of view, it is necessary to develop a sense of confidence in ourselves as we progress along the spiritual path. How we go about cultivating this is therefore very important and yet often misunderstood. In a pragmatic sense, the idea of buddha-nature is useful in counteracting our reliance on the empirical ego as the object or reference point of our self-perception. There is a danger in this as well, however: We can fall into the trap of thinking of buddha-nature as the "big self," or the "real self," and the empirical ego as the "little self." From a Buddhist point of view, the notion of any kind of self is always problematic, and that word needs to be accurately defined.

We think in terms of self-cultivation, but this is not about forming another self-image of who we think we are. We do need to develop self-confidence and a healthy sense of our own self-worth, but that confidence must stem from our own true spiritual home, our original dwelling place, for only that is reliable. Other attempts at boosting our self-confidence will always be undependable, because whatever self-image we form will always be vulnerable to the challenges posed by re-ality. This is because any self image is constructed; every little piece is required to stay in its place—and this is not possible. No doubt we tem-porarily feel better and stronger personally for having done some work on ourselves, but if we fail to examine our entrenched delusions and habitual tendencies, all such superficial efforts will reveal their cosmetic nature, and any positive effects will fade, or something will go wrong again and our confidence will be shattered. If we feel comfortable in ourselves in relation to our own true nature, whatever we think we are on a relative level is less likely to be affected by what happens to us. In this way, our buddha-nature has to be understood as something we can rely upon, something we can experience. It is not an abstract principle, hidden and inaccessible.

In the West today, there is a tendency to psychologize everything, which I believe is a form of reductionism. This can be particularly destructive when applied to spiritual endeavors. When Buddhists refer to deluded and undeluded states of mind, for instance, this is meant in the context of the spiritual path. It is not simply a case of seeing how one's mind operates; we need to be led to a deeper understanding of self and ultimate reality. We generally assume that consciousness is a "thing," or at least a mental entity of some kind, and therefore a single entity. On the contrary, according to Buddhism, consciousness is something that has many elements and many dimensions. We are capable of having far greater experiences of it than we currently do. The idea of an "expansion of consciousness" is a reasonably good analogy here, especially if we remember that this thing called consciousness is not a unitary thing. In Buddhist thinking, all our psychological experiences are regarded as defiled by layers of delusions. The things that we think about and perceive, the emotions that we experience—even if they are altruistic—are never entirely free from delusions. Delusory states are much more than just neuroses or other forms of mental disturbance. They are spiritual maladies akin to the theistic notion of sin, although they would not be defined in quite the same way. Nevertheless, as such, they require spiritual ministration rather than mental health treatment.

According to the Buddhist view, psychological neuroses and emotional disorders arise from our delusions, but the delusory states themselves are more than mere psychological disturbances. Consequently, a well-adjusted, happy person would not be regarded as undeluded and beyond the need for spiritual ministration. Buddhist spiritual practices and meditation methods are not just designed for unhappy people; they are for all of us who search for a deeper meaning in life. This is why spiritual insight is liberating. Everything else we experience on the delusory level is imprisoning because it narrows our vision and our capacity to perceive ourselves and the world. Mahayana texts often use the analogy of a person who has developed cataracts and perceives everything through a cloudy, obscuring film.

The metaphor sometimes used in Western psychology compares

the self-image we create to a mask or persona that we project toward others, and this is understood to be the core of the problem with ego and attachment. But Buddhism has never suggested that we should dissociate from self-images completely or that this is even possible. Without any persona whatsoever, we would not be able to function. We all have to play multiple roles in our lives—as a parent, a wage earner, a friend and so on. The real problem arises when we think of our persona— the multiple roles we necessarily play as a member of our society— and then feverishly cling to it as being indistinguishable from ourselves. This close identification with our self-image is what we should be wary of. Yet to think that we should not be projecting any kind of image whatsoever in our interactions with others is idealistic and impractical.

OVERCOMING CONFLICTING EMOTIONS

The only way to realize our buddha-nature is by overcoming our conflicting emotions. We therefore need to have a clear understanding of what conflicting emotions actually are. Our conflicting emotions are akin to, but should not be equated with, the idea of being in some way tainted by sin. Conflicting emotions are not related to any theological concepts in Buddhism, however, in either their nature or their origin. Nor are they neurotic states as understood in Western psychology.

Conflicting emotions have to be seen as aberrations, a word that suggests something uncharacteristic and unnatural. An illness or disease is an aberration to health, for instance, and has to be overcome or removed. Our conflicting emotions are like this, a disturbance to our well-being, and are therefore aberrations that need to be corrected.

The conflicting emotions are said to have two sources, known generally as the two veils, so called because they obscure or veil our ability to recognize things as they are—our true nature, the true state of affairs in relation to ourselves and others, and our ability to directly perceive ultimate reality. The first veil stems from unhesitating distorted ways of thinking and is primarily responsible for the development of our erroneous views and perspectives on things. Consequently, it is referred to as the veil of cognitive distortions. The other veil bears on the emotional aspects of our being and is labeled the veil of conflicting emotions.

Everything we experience is obscured and overlaid by these defiling veils, which is why it is said we live in the illusion of samsara. If these conflicting emotions are unattended to, as is normally the case, they gradually become more virulent and insidious and subtly cause the progressive corrosion of our sense of awareness, leaving our mind listless and torpid. The conflicting emotions have a dimming effect and originate from ignorance. As the conflicting emotions begin to affect our consciousness, there is a growing loss of sensibility, awareness, and sharpness of the mind. Correspondingly, the power of consciousness is greatly reduced, becoming rigid and resistant to change.

The varied ways in which we suffer from our deep-seated and constantly reinforced habitual patterns is an unmistakable indication of our loss of consciousness, and hence self-control, in our emotional life. The diminution of the power of consciousness through conflicting emotions and delusions leads to well-established habits—usually negative and self-destructive ones—that become entrenched in our sense of who we believe ourselves to be. Our habitual responses to others through our words, deeds, and demeanor will also have a beneficial, detrimental, or neutral impact upon both them and ourselves, depositing further traces and dispositions in our basic consciousness that then become converted into latent tendencies and dispositional properties.

How We Acquire Conflicting Emotions

Before discussing the ways in which our conflicting emotions are acquired, I would like to relate a famous Zen story that illustrates how mental projections function in the mind. The dying wife of a Japanese man told him she would come back to haunt him if he ever married or took a mistress after her death. Some months after her death, when he fell in love again, he was not surprised to see her ghost walk into the house and accuse him bitterly of infidelity. This went on night after night until he was at his wits' end, and he went to consult a Zen master about what to do. The Zen master asked him, "What makes you so sure that it is a ghost?" The man answered, "She knows every single thing that I have ever done or said or felt." The master gave the man a bag of soybeans and told him not to open it. Then he instructed the man, "When she appears tonight, ask her how many beans there are in the bag." That night, when the man asked the ghost how many beans there were in the bag, it could not answer and fled, never to return. The man returned to the Zen master and asked him how this could be. The master replied, "Don't you think it is strange that your ghost knew only the things that you knew?"

Our delusions are perpetuated by a lack of awareness that results from the fact that we are never fully conscious. Only a buddha is fully conscious. By removing the conflicting emotions, we will access the acuity and awareness of buddha-mind, becoming more like a buddha and less like an ordinary sentient being. According to the *Mahayanuttaratantra*, the classic fifth-century Mahayana text on buddha-nature, there are four different avenues through which conflicting emotions become active as the traces and dispositions of our mind-stream.

The first is the avenue of the senses and sense impressions. When certain delusory states of mind are entrenched in our stream of consciousness, everything we see, hear, smell, taste, touch, and cognize is already tainted by our traces and dispositions. Nothing enters our consciousness without being interpreted in some discriminatory manner. For example, when we see something, we do not simply see it for what it is. Rather, we immediately react to that object with attachment, aversion, or some other form of discrimination. We may be looking at a car, but we are thinking, "Oh, that is a beautiful car. I have to have it." If we see an attractive person, we immediately respond to him or her as an object of desire. It is a very personalized perception of things because it is all dictated by our well-defined likes and dislikes. It is the same with the other senses, such as hearing. What we are accustomed to finding appealing we hear as a pleasant sound; what we do not like to hear is rejected as a disturbing cacophony that we want to tune out.

Second is the avenue of self-perception. This describes the fact that everything we experience is generally processed with reference to ourselves: It is seen as "belonging to me." We are always thinking, "I experienced this, I saw that, I thought this." Gradually and insidiously, this reinforces our thinking of ourselves as a particular kind of person, a unique discrete entity.

Third is the avenue of the causes and conditions that prevail at a given time. This refers to one's natural and social environment, which one can influence and also is affected by. Nobody functions in a vacuum, so to speak. Environmental conditions and the internal conditions of our being are interrelated in a myriad of ways.

The fourth avenue is the avenue of homogeneity. The idea of homogeneity basically means that our preceding physical and mental states will determine our subsequent physical and mental states. In other words, we will be able to find a clear causal relationship between what precedes and what follows in terms of our experience. For example, if we have been in an agitated, negative mental state, with harmful thoughts and the stirrings of violent emotions, then our ensuing mental state is likely to be similar.

In order to achieve liberation from these unconscious stresses and dispositions that are responsible for our deep-seated habit patterns, we need to work with the conflicting emotions. This we can do through the practice of meditation. The word *liberation* (*moksha* in Sanskrit; *tharpa* in Tibetan) suggests we are imprisoned in a world that is created by our own deluded consciousness. The possibility of finding an escape from that world into a more expansive space implies other ways of being; there is more to what we call *mind* than we normally realize. This idea of attaining enlightenment by overcoming our adventitious conflicting emotions is a radical understanding of the spiritual process, and it has largely escaped or been ignored by many modern interpreters. For instance, a frequent criticism of Buddhist meditation is that it does not deal with emotional issues sufficiently to eradicate our psychological problems. We cannot regard meditative insights as the same as psychological insights; meditation would then have to address the meditator's specific psychological problems. But meditation has a different goal. Spiritual insights have to be viewed as illuminations of our own true nature, insights into the nature of our delusions.

CONNECTING WITH OUR SPIRITUAL NATURE

Meditation takes pride of place in Buddhism, valued more than any other spiritual or religious activity (or nonactivity) because it is in and through meditation that we learn to become more conscious of how our minds function. There are many different meditative methods in Buddhism, but all are designed to increase our awareness and to decrease our conflicting emotions, enabling our spiritual senses to reawaken. Again, the idea of reawakening the spiritual senses is not equated with flashes of psychological insight. They are of a different order. To experience our buddha-nature is to experience a breakthrough from the confinements of our ordinary consciousness.

Some books on Buddhist meditation suggest that awareness is the key to awakening and that by simply being aware we can overcome delusory states of mind. Being aware is, of course, the first step, but it is certainly not the complete method of becoming fully conscious. When we practice being aware during meditation, we are engaging in a mental act. That mental act of awareness is just a convenient device; it is not in itself liberating. Unfortunately, some longtime practitioners of Buddhist meditation have labored under the misapprehension that psychological awareness is itself the complete path. They complain that while their minds are more calm, all their emotional rubbish remains unprocessed and unresolved. They then feel disillusioned with meditation and become nihilistic and cynical. This is why I keep emphasizing the importance of insight meditation in Buddhism. Without this practice, we will not gain insight into our mind, and without insight our delusions will not lift. If our delusions do not lift, then emotional problems will always recur in one form or another. We may undergo therapy to address a particular psychological problem, but if later on we develop another problem, it also will need to be addressed by psychotherapy. Failure to appreciate this has led some practitioners to rush to therapists to discuss the trauma they have suffered because of meditation! Here again, one is reminded of the importance of learning and developing the correct view.

Being aware and learning to connect spiritually in the context of meditation is not about being aware in the ordinary sense. We are talking about an awareness that relates to a dimension of being of which we are normally oblivious. It is important to note this distinction, or we could end up practicing a psychological state of awareness rather than a meditative type of awareness. Disillusionment can occur when the meditator fails to connect with a deeper level of being. Meditation is not about being aware of our psychological states, nor about simply learning to be attentive and present.

We have spoken at length about what the experience of our true nature is *not*: It is not an egotistic experience or a psychological experience, and it requires the removal of defilements. Hence we have defined it through a largely negative vocabulary. This is difficult to avoid, as our true buddha-nature is not a thing to be characterized and evaluated. According to the Mahayana teachings, being in touch with our own true nature is a transcendental experience, untainted by dualistic notions of perceiver and perceived, subject and object. It is an all-encompassing state within which one no longer distinguishes between self and other. This is liberating because there is no boundary; we have broken out of the egotistic shell. We arrive at that state of buddha-nature, ground Mahamudra, now, in the present. If we can allow ourselves to do that, without continuously being compromised by various delusory states of mind, even if only for a short time, then we are already there. We can then see that it is not something inaccessible, hidden, or far beyond our reach.

That liberating experience is something we *can* attain. How deep and how stable that experience is will depend upon our own capacity. Fortunately, there is a kind of momentum involved, whereby the recognition of this more expansive reality in everyday life will become more emphatic and our thinking, experience, and actions will be steadily freed from egotistic needs and desires. They will come from a deeper level of being, which is more reliable and more consistent and therefore possesses the potential to uplift us.

This is what is indicated by the term *tathagatagarbha*. As I said earlier, *tathagata* means "thus gone." Actually, it can imply both coming and going at the same time, so "thus come and thus gone" is a more accurate rendering. *Garbha*, as I said, means "essence." So *tathagatagarbha* is the intrinsically pure and incorruptible nature of all beings, which is both transcendent and immanent in our consciousness. Only when awareness leads us to become fully conscious of our own spiritual buddha-nature does awareness cease to be a mental act. According to the Mahayana teachings, it will then become a radiant expression of buddha-nature, which in the Mahamudra teachings is the realization of ground Mahamudra.

TRADITIONAL PERSPECTIVES ON BUDDHA-NATURE

Having given a general overview of the Mahayana concept of buddha-nature, I would now like to link this concept specifically to the understanding of ground Mahamudra. There are many different ways to understand buddha-nature within Buddhism, and many different methods are employed to achieve the reality that is described and formulated. The various perspectives all state that buddha-nature is a kind of reality, but they differ as to what that reality actually is and how we should best go about realizing it. We do not have to decide which of these diverse (or perhaps seemingly conflicting) perspectives is true. Different perspectives on buddha-nature bring about different experiences, all of which lead to the same goal.

In Buddhism, it is openly conceded that having different terminologies and different concepts gives us a different understanding of something. Multiple perspectives are valued because particular perspectives will necessarily yield corresponding understandings. Sometimes people become annoyed by these multiple perspectives and begin to question which one is real and which ones are false. The Buddhist position is that they are all true within their given context. They are also necessary because in Mahayana Buddhism the teachings have to accommodate the needs of a diverse range of people, all potential beneficiaries of the Dharma. Any single perspective that is dogmatically thrust upon a multitude of diverse individuals will fail to inspire many and is unlikely to benefit more than a few.

Ideally, Buddhist teachings address our individual predicaments and spiritual needs and tally with our individual temperaments and outlooks on life. It is only natural to assume, given this imperative, that we will find some perspectives more suited to our overall worldview than others.

A cautionary pause is in order at this point, lest we veer into a libertarian authorization of any and all interpretations and viewpoints. This cannot be the case. Different perspectives have to form a coherent whole with an underlying thematic link between the variations, otherwise they would cease to be perspectives on the same thing. For instance, a botanist deals with different classes of floras, and different experts may hold contradictory views about these classifications, but their opinions still have to remain within the discipline of botany. There is no point in drawing from geology to support a particular position (apart from the fact that geological conditions may affect the health of plants). In the same way, our different perspectives on buddha-nature have to have the commonality of the Buddhist notion of tathagatagarbha. If buddha-nature is to be interpreted as no different from the notion of a soul, it ceases to be a perspective on buddha-nature at all. One has to maintain a healthy balance between dogmatism and nihilism in this way.

Broadly speaking, the teachings on the interpretation of buddha-nature are divided into the exoteric, esoteric, and mystical. The exoteric perspective is the same as sutric Mahayana, the esoteric perspective is the same as tantric Mahayana, and the mystical perspective is that held by the Mahamudra tradition. Other mystical traditions include the Dzogchen teachings and some schools of Zen Buddhism. Different terminologies can result from these differences in perspectives.

Up to this point, we have been discussing buddha-nature from the exoteric perspective. We now turn to the esoteric and mystical interpretations of buddha-nature as a way of leading into the Mahamudra understanding of the ground of being and the nature of the mind.

The Esoteric Perspective

The esoteric Mahayana perspective on buddha-nature offers yet another fascinating and rich interpretation of what is already one of the most valued and widely interpreted concepts in Mahayana Buddhism. Here, buddha-nature refers to our essential nature as the clear light of bliss, wherein clear light is seen as the same thing as buddha-nature. The perspective differs also in that buddha-nature is not seen as a mere potential for attaining enlightenment but is viewed as the mind itself, because the mind is described as the clear light of bliss. This clear light is also regarded as the luminous and blissful nature of awakening.

Through the use of radical tantric methods, we can realize the clear light of the mind very directly. Instead of gradually trying to reduce the conflicting emotions through meditation and the six transcendental actions, as we would in the exoteric approaches, Tantrism uses the visualization of deities and psychophysical yogas or exercises to bring about insight into the luminous bliss of the mind. There is no mention of gradually eliminating the conflicting emotions.

It is important to understand that the tantric iconographies of gods and goddesses are actually representations of our own conceptual mind. Instead of trying to reduce discursive thoughts and overcome negative emotions, we employ them in the practices directly. When we visualize deities and other iconographic images, we have to use our thoughts; it is impossible to do visualization practices without them. Instead of attempting to calm our minds by reducing thoughts, we use our conceptual activity to construct these divinities.

Tantric practice has two phases, generally known as the creative-imagination stage and the dissolution stage. In the creative-imagination phase, one deals with the gross level of conceptual activity, and in the dissolution phase, one deals with the subtle level of conceptual activity. When the functions of the gross level of consciousness begin to slow down and finally stop, the clear light of bliss becomes manifest.

The aim of tantric practice is to reach down to this level, which is actually a prethought level. One then arises from that state of absorption. Going back and forth between these two states of the mind will facilitate the realization of the luminous bliss of consciousness. In the creative phase of the practice, we are dealing with our normal consciousness. With the dissolution phase, we go deeper and deeper into levels of absorption until we are able to remain in the pure essence of consciousness. The tantric method is not simply about remaining in that state, however, nor is it considered that we have gone beyond the normal functioning of consciousness by having this experience. Actually, what has taken place is the transformation of the normal functioning of consciousness, which is one of the central goals of esoteric practice. The other goal is to have a deep and abiding experience of luminous bliss, and by so doing realize our innate buddha-nature as the enlightened state.

The Mystical Perspective

The understanding of buddha-nature in the Mahamudra tradition is identical to the understanding of ground Mahamudra explained in chapter 1. We do not resort to the methods of renunciation and purification advocated in the exoteric Mahayana approach, nor do we employ any of the methods of transformation found in esoteric Mahayana, or Tantra. The mystical approach of Mahamudra is the method of self-liberation. This very special method of practice is at the heart of the Buddhist mystical tradition, originating with the mahasiddhas of ancient India. Mahamudra method, along with the *mahasandhi* practice of Dzogchen, is the most exalted of the esoteric teachings in the Kagyu and Nyingma traditions of Tibetan Buddhism. As such, they are not themselves part of the esoteric teachings but the very apex of the Buddhist path itself.

As was described in chapter 1, the Mahamudra approach of self-liberation arose within the tantric tradition of India, yet it came to be regarded within the Kagyu and Nyingma schools as a complete path in itself. It is not surprising, then, that Mahamudra retains much of the tantric terminology and philosophical understanding of spiritual practice. One of these central tenets is that luminous bliss is the goal of spiritual awakening. The difference between them at this point is that the Mahamudra tradition advocates a direct meditative experience into the nature of the mind as the means of attaining this experience of luminous bliss.

In the Mahamudra context, buddha-nature is regarded as the nature of the mind, or sometimes as the nature of the Mind-in-itself. The nature of the mind is not seen as a potential for enlightenment but as the actual state of enlightenment. Hence our spiritual nature is understood in terms of a complete enlightenment that we already embody. In the exoteric path in particular, there is not this idea of enlightenment being a connection with our already present spiritual nature.

Both exoteric and esoteric approaches regard human beings as fundamentally flawed in some way and therefore impress upon us the need to change. The mystical perspective, on the other hand, does not view deluded and undeluded states of mind as radically different. It does not even recognize the real existence of impurities that require removal, for any distinction between purity and impurity implies a dualism that is antithetical to the Mahamudra understanding of ultimate reality. This ultimate reality is the ground Mahamudra. As Jamgön Kongtrül Lodrö Thaye declares:

> *Not produced by causes, not changed by conditions,*
> *It is not spoiled by confusion*
> *Nor exalted by realization.*
> *It does not know either confusion or liberation.*²

From this perspective, the only difference between an enlightened being and an ordinary sentient being lies in whether we know or do not know our own nature. If we understand our state of being from this perspective, buddha-nature is not the *cause* of enlightenment—it is enlightenment itself. The spiritual path is simply a matter of realizing the nature of the mind, which is utterly complete and perfect in itself and needs nothing added to it or taken away from it in order to be realized. As Rangjung Dorje, the third Karmapa, sang in *The Aspiration of the Mahamudra of True Meaning*:

Without realizing this, we circle in the ocean of samsara.
When realizing it, buddhahood is not somewhere else.
It is completely devoid of "it is this" or "it is not this."
May we see the vital point of the all-ground, the nature of things.[3]

It should be noted that the Mahamudra approach still utilizes the practices of tranquillity and insight meditation. In this instance, though, these two types of meditation are undertaken so that we remain in our own nature, not to gradually reduce conflicting emotions and increase virtues and wisdom over a period of time, as in the exoteric approaches. We are not trying to attain any particular meditative state per se; we are simply trying to remain in our own natural state, which is not separate from the nature of the mind, or buddha-nature. It is through this mystical illumination that we come to the realization of our own true nature.

The Significance of These Variations

The three main perspectives of buddha-nature—exoteric, esoteric, and mystical—may yield realization in different ways, but it is still the same state that is realized. Whether we call it buddha-nature, the clear light of bliss, the nature of the mind, or the ground Mahamudra, it is still the same spiritual nature. In other words, each of these approaches leads to the same realization but through a different method. Perhaps the experiences accompanying each realization will also be different, but what one comes to realize in the end is the same.

Some people find the exoteric perspective on buddha-nature to be best suited to their way of thinking; others find the esoteric perspective more appealing. Still others find the mystical perspective more in keeping with their predilections. Collectively these different perspectives and methods are known as skillful means because they are skillful applications of various teachings that promote a particular perspective on a certain topic. This is actually the function of the teachings. Please keep in mind that it is this last perspective of buddha-nature that has been appropriated in the Mahamudra teachings and that buddha-nature and the nature of the mind are the same thing in this mystical literature.

—

PART THREE

PATH
MAHAMUDRA

8

TRANQUILLITY MEDITATION

I_T CANNOT BE STRESSED ENOUGH THAT IN BUDDHISM, THE CALM_ing method of tranquillity is only a preliminary meditation practice. Despite the popular view, it is neither the most important nor the most valued method of Buddhist meditation. Some of the more recent popularizers of Buddhist meditation have been responsible for this misunderstanding, calling tranquillity meditation "insight" meditation, while omitting insight meditation, or vipashyana, from their books completely. These two types of meditation, tranquillity and insight, are in many ways quite distinct. Tranquillity meditation is important, as the considerable volume of literature on Buddhist meditation attests, but it does not by itself constitute Buddhist meditation. It is actually the foundation for insight practice, providing the requisite stability of mind to allow the awareness that is peculiar to insight meditation to arise.

BASIC PRACTICE

To begin the practice of tranquillity meditation, first find a comfortable cushion to sit on. A cushion that you can place under your buttocks is actually preferable to a larger type that goes under both legs and ankles. If the ground is too hard under the ankles, a large mat can be used in

addition to the cushion. One of the favorite cushions used by meditators is the Japanese *zafu*, which is also used with a square flat cushion
known as a *zabuton*. That is the perfect combination for sitting meditation.

The cushion for your buttocks is important because it provides
the requisite support for your back. The key to a good meditation
posture is to maintain a straight back or spine. Once that is established, you can place your hands on your knees with palms downward
or in your lap with the palms facing up, right hand resting on left,
thumbs slightly touching. The shoulders should be relaxed and the
mouth slightly open, with the tip of the tongue resting lightly on the
roof of the mouth. The breath should be even. The head should be
slightly tilted forward and the gaze cast downward, focused on a spot on
the floor or on a small object placed to anchor your visual attention.

The following exercises are often recommended for the beginner.
Inhale a breath of air, hold it for a second, and then forcefully release it
through the nostrils, imagining that you are exhaling all the tension,
anxiety, and tightness in your body. Do this three times, while trying to
maintain a general sense of being present and aware of both your body
and the external environment.

At this initial stage of tranquillity practice, do not worry about
watching thoughts or mental states. Simply be mindful of whatever object of meditation you are using as an anchor—this could be anything
from a piece of wood to a Buddha statue, or even objects of the other
senses such as soft music. As you gain proficiency with this practice, the
breath can be employed as an object of meditation. When there is
enough stability of concentration to use the breath as an object of meditation, focus on the incoming and outgoing breath exclusively, on
nothing but this.

Having progressed to this point, it is helpful to start counting your
breaths. The main technique here involves counting the inhalation and
exhalation of the breath as one cycle. The first cycle of inhalation and
exhalation is counted as one, the next inhalation and exhalation as two,
and the next cycle as three. After counting to three in this way, go back
to the count of one and start again. After pursuing this method of
counting for some time and developing some proficiency at it, increase
the number of breath cycles to seven.

Other considerations are to set aside a specific time for meditation
in either the morning or evening (the morning is always preferable)

and, if possible, to avoid meditating on an empty stomach or in a very stuffy or chilly room. If the room is stuffy, open a window so that the air can circulate; if the room is chilly, heat it.

In addition, try not to hold any tension in your chest while watching the breath in meditation. If your mind becomes too agitated, try to relax the posture by feeling the muscles in the shoulders relax. If you start to experience drowsiness, on the other hand, try to tighten the posture. There has to be a subtle balance of relaxation and slight exertion. This delicate exertion is necessary so that you do not lose the object of meditation through lack of attention or give in to distractions. If you become distracted by sensory stimuli, such as a startling sound or a vivid visual image, or if you find you have become lost in thought, simply remember to return to the object of meditation.

When distracted in this way, you definitely should not indulge in self-recrimination of any kind. It is common for meditators to think, "I should not have allowed my mind to wander. I didn't even see my mind being distracted," but we should not waste our time entertaining such thoughts. Simply return to watching the breath and try to feel at ease and fully present in the moment. It is important to generate a real sense of well-being during meditation. As the mind becomes more stable, you will gradually become more aware of your thoughts, even if you are not specifically paying attention to them. When thoughts arise, they should not be viewed as something bad. Simply let them go and return your attention to the breath. This is a method of relaxing that has nothing deliberate about it. Indeed, it is something of a paradox to "try" to relax, as effort and relaxation are contradictory terms.

The Meaning of Mindfulness and Nowness

The mainstay of tranquillity meditation is the practice of mindfulness: the ability to be in the present moment through not allowing the mind to become distracted. Being in the present should not, however, be understood as a dissociated, suspended state of being "in the now." It simply refers to a state of being aware or being present without becoming distracted by thoughts. Mindfulness can be defined as being fully conscious of the present moment through not dwelling on things from the past and not anticipating possibilities in the future. Mindfulness is practiced by not forgetting to stay with the object of meditation, such as the breath. If our attention wavers through our becoming distracted, or yields to an upsurge of emotion, we simply need to remember to return to the object of meditation.

When people ask, "What is mindfulness?" the popular answer is, "Mindfulness means to be in the present." But how is that to be achieved? A fundamental aspect of mindfulness meditation is remembrance—using memory as an aid to increase mindfulness. It may come as a surprise that the opposite of mindfulness is forgetfulness. Due to our well-entrenched mental habits, we are not psychologically equipped to be in the present and mindful without the aid of memory. Distraction can therefore be equated with forgetfulness, and mindfulness with remembrance. Forgetfulness leads to distraction, and distraction to a loss of attentiveness and mindfulness. This point is often lost on modern-day Buddhist teachers. Due to their obsession with "being in the now," they appear to have no concept of memory as a helpful tool for staying in the present moment. If we appreciate the role of remembrance in this context, we can better appreciate how to practice mindfulness by keeping forgetfulness at bay.

What is this state of now? All of our thoughts and emotions are based upon past impressions, and our present emotions and mental states are inevitably colored by them. If we become more observant and mindful of our mental states, we will realize that most of them are about the past or the future. However, this should not be viewed as a problem. When we become aware of certain thoughts, emotional states, and feeling tones (which may be about the past or the future), these thoughts do not themselves constitute a loss of mindfulness. Being in that current mental state—even if it is a state of remembrance—*is* being in the now, for we can only ever think about or react to the past or future right now in the present moment. When Buddhist literature mentions "not dwelling on the past or anticipating the future," it is saying we should not lose our awareness of the fact that these thoughts about the past and future are simply arising in our mind right now. If we lose our awareness of this process, we will yield to our unruly thoughts and emotions and become embroiled in their dynamism. When we become swept away by our thoughts in this fashion, mindfulness is completely absent.

If being in the now is not understood in this fashion, but instead as some kind of nonconceptual presence of mind, one is likely to give up meditation practice altogether in frustration eventually. When we become more accustomed to meditation practice, we naturally become more aware of our cognitive and affective mental states and will see that nearly all of them concern the past or the future. Subscribing to an interpretation of nowness that excludes thoughts about the past or the future can only frustrate our success at mindfulness practice. Even seasoned meditators find it impossible to exclude such thoughts. About this predicament the Kagyu meditation master Gampopa said: "When a meditator is learning to stabilize the mind, a state of meditative equipoise should not be regarded as something good, and an inability to experience meditative equipoise should not be regarded as some kind of failure."

How can we tell that we are in tranquillity meditation? Tranquillity meditation is nothing very mystical or esoteric. It is actually very mundane and ordinary in a way, because it is simply the ability to be cognizant or self-reflexively aware of certain mental states that we are experiencing. Awareness is an aspect of everyday life, but of course our level of awareness can vary from day to day and from person to person, as the following story depicts:

A heavy drinker met up with a friend at a bar. The friend saw that the man had bright red blisters on both his ears and asked what had caused them. The drunkard responded, "My wife left her iron on. When the phone rang, I picked up the iron by mistake." His friend thought this over, then asked what had happened to his other ear. "The damned fool called back!"

DISCURSIVE THOUGHTS

In the Buddhist teachings, the tendency to dwell on the past, anticipate the future, and discriminate between the types of thoughts and emotions we experience is known collectively as discursive thoughts. Discursive thoughts are based on a fixation on binary concepts at a fundamental level: things exist, things do not exist, things both exist and do not exist, or things neither exist nor do not exist. Binary concepts such as these are based upon the assumption that things have an enduring, independent existence, and we apply this assumption to metaphysical, spiritual, and moral concepts. This tendency, which in Buddhism is accepted as innate, is most virulent and strongest when it comes to seeing ourselves and others as separate. We tend to think of subject and object as independently existing entities. We also assume that our mind and body exist independently of one another. Spiritual concepts such as samsara and nirvana are also polarized, as are moral judgments about good and bad actions.

Discursive thoughts prevent us from realizing the true nature of things for the simple reason that in reality everything exists in relationship. Everything arises in dependence upon something else; some cause or condition enables a thing to come into being, supports its endurance for a certain time, and then eventually underlies its dissolution. For example, a tree may come into existence in dependence upon a seed situated in an environment conducive to its growth. It will grow in dependence upon nutritious soil, sun, and rain, and then wither and die during a drought, for instance. Natural calamities such as these are in turn brought about by a bewildering array of further causes and conditions. In this sense, nothing can be said to have an independent existence from its own side alone. Our thoroughly entrenched notion that things do have an independent, self-sufficient existence of their own is simply a mental imputation founded on ignorance.

As we become aware of discursive thoughts through mindfulness practice, we attach less and less value to them by interpreting them as good or bad. We should simply try to enter into, rather than create, a state of mental equilibrium. As long as we continue to put thoughts into the categories of good and bad, our mental agitation will never subside. No matter what discursive thought presents itself to your mind, simply notice it and let it be. You should neither encourage, dwell upon, nor try to get rid of these thoughts, but regard them as "just thoughts." This is a very important method of calming the mind. It is the same as the Buddhist notion of letting go, or not elaborating on the particular thoughts that come to mind. If you really investigate this meditation approach, you will realize that to judge discursive thoughts as either good or bad is merely to engage in further discursive thinking. This little story captures the essence of misperception well enough.

A monkey and a hyena were walking together through a forest when the hyena confided nervously to his friend that every time he walked past a certain bush, a lion leaped out and tried to maul him. The monkey responded, "Don't worry, I'll come with you. If the lion is there this time, I'll help you defend yourself." So they walked together past the bush, and sure enough, a fearsome lion pounced on the hyena and almost tore him to shreds. When the hyena had escaped and the lion disappeared, the monkey came down from the tree he had sheltered in and went over to his friend. "Why didn't you do anything to help me?" the hyena gasped. The monkey replied, "You were laughing so much I thought you were winning."

THE MAHAMUDRA VIEW
OF DISCURSIVE THOUGHTS

Many meditation systems regard discursive thoughts as anathema to meditation practice, but this is not true of the Mahamudra approach. In this tradition, we simply observe how the thoughts arise, how they persist, and how they dissipate. We do not try to eradicate negative thoughts or cultivate good thoughts. This is called the practice of nonacceptance and nonrejection, and it is a very special technique of the Mahamudra system because it regards tranquillity meditation as a way of *settling* the discursive thoughts rather than eliminating them altogether. The Mahamudra technique is preeminently concerned with allowing the mind to settle naturally; there is no attempt to forcefully remove discursive thoughts or experiences of negative emotions.

Even within the Buddhist context, this is quite a radical view considering Buddhism's central tenet of karma, which postulates a causal nexus operating within the workings of the mind. To briefly review the discussion on karmic cause and effect, negative thoughts and emotions give rise to negative actions, which bring about negative karmic effects and consequences. This in turn leads to painful experiences, both for the actor and for the recipient of those actions. These negative effects begin to affect our mind and leave negative karmic imprints in our mind-stream. Thus, the whole vicious process is repeated over and over in a seemingly endless cycle, binding human beings and other living creatures to the samsaric condition.

The general exoteric Buddhist teachings say that to free ourselves from this bondage, we have to foster a positive outlook by cultivating loving-kindness and other positive attitudes and virtuous thoughts. This will cause wholesome karma, which will give rise to wholesome karmic effects and leave wholesome karmic imprints on our mind-stream, thus reversing our samsaric imprisonment. The meditation methods employed reflect this philosophy and seek in the same way to actively purify the mind-stream toward the goal of wholesomeness. This approach would, without a doubt, be viewed as the most laudable spiritual pursuit in most Buddhist contexts.

So too with the Mahamudra teachings, we have to view the karmic process in exactly this way during our everyday activities, for it is imperative that we increase everything positive and reduce everything negative, destructive, and debilitating in our lives. In the context of Mahamudra practice itself, however, the matter stands rather differently, because here we are concerned purely with contemplation, not action. In meditation, we resist the imperative to privilege wholesome thoughts and actions. We learn to suspend judgment about our discursive thoughts and cognitive and emotional states. In order to reduce the proliferation of our mental activities and attain tranquillity, we do not regard some thoughts as good and in need of cultivation and other thoughts as bad and in need of elimination.

Of course, there are many complementary practices specifically designed to help us generate wholesome thoughts and mental states, such as the four preliminaries and four immeasurables. Here again, it is essential that we understand the context within which we are meditating, what it is we are meditating on, and what we are meditating for. In the four preliminaries, we meditate on aspects of conditioned existence in order to imbue ourselves with enthusiasm and joy and have the motivation to persevere with our practice. The four immeasurables are designed specifically to help us cultivate wholesome mental states. In the practice of Mahamudra tranquillity meditation, we do not preoccupy ourselves with thoughts of loving-kindness or wishes to alleviate the suffering of others. We treat all thoughts as the same in order to gain sufficient distance and detachment from our current mental state, which will allow us to ease naturally into a state of tranquillity without effort or contrivance. From this discussion, we can see how important it is not to confuse different meditative techniques.

MINDFULNESS OF MENTAL STATES

Having become accustomed to using the breath as an aid to establishing mindfulness, we can take a further step and turn our attention to our inner mental states as the focus of meditation, move on to the breath as our focus, and then apply mindfulness to the very cognitive and affective mental states that fixate on the past and future. The first thing we need to understand in relation to this practice of mindfulness of mental states is that human beings are thinking creatures. Not only do we think, but we attach values to the things we think about and to the thoughts themselves. We talk about having good and bad thoughts, virtuous and evil thoughts, illuminative and delusory thoughts, credible and incredible thoughts, fantasies, insights, and so forth. In order for the mind to settle, we need to suspend the value judgments that we impose on our mental activities. To maintain a state of equilibrium, we should avoid wishing for positive mental states to arise and resisting unwholesome mental states. Basically, this involves not getting bogged down by the twin afflictions of hope and fear. These two always go together, as this story illustrates.

A doctor decided that it was time to tell his patient the truth about his illness: that he was very ill and unlikely to survive for more than a few days. After delivering this news, the doctor asked his patient if he needed to settle his affairs and if there might be anyone he would like to see. "Yes," came the feeble voice of the dying man. "Who is that?" asked the doctor. "Another doctor," the man replied.

Our minds are normally governed by hope and fear, and this robs us of the opportunity to fully appreciate the true texture and flavor of our current mental state. It is essential that we not try to *create* a state of tranquillity but allow the mind to enter into tranquillity naturally. This is an important notion in Mahamudra meditation, that of nondoing. We do not *do* tranquillity meditation; we allow tranquillity to arise of its own accord, and it will do so only if we stop thinking of the meditative state as a thing that we need to do actively.

According to Buddhism, virtually all our experiences of pain, anguish, suffering, and torment have their origin in the dual tendencies of the human mind, namely wanting to have what one desires and not wanting what one does not desire. Due to this we swing back and forth between hope (*rewa*) and fear (*dogpa*). In those moments when we feel optimistic, we hope that everything will turn out well and whatever we do will bear fruit. We can just as quickly swing to the other extreme, fearing that we will not get what we want and things will turn out badly, allowing ourselves to be overcome by a deep sense of fear and dread. Even when we are pursuing our spiritual practices, that same dual tendency infiltrates our endeavours and disrupts our practices. This is why, in Mahamudra teachings, there is a constant emphasis on avoiding hope and fear in the context of our meditative efforts.

In order to resist becoming entangled in the above dual tendency, we should endeavor to rise above both hope and fear. Usually, either we hope that everything goes well and that only good things befall us (through making palpable progress in our meditation practice, for instance) or we allow ourselves to be plagued by self-doubt, fearing that nothing will go well. Due to their unfamiliarity, certain mental states can provoke fearful reactions; we may indeed feel as if we have entered uncharted areas. This should not surprise us unduly, for after all, meditation practice is a journey of exploration, and not knowing exactly what is ahead is part of it. The practice is to constantly return to the object of meditation whenever a distraction occurs. Just return to the current state of mind, where there is no hope and no fear—wishing for certain meditative experiences to arise and dreading the appearance of others. If hope or fear does arise, do not regard that as an obstacle or failing. Simply be aware of it without thinking that it is a good or a bad thing. In a manner of speaking, catching yourself in the act of distraction is the true test of tranquillity meditation, for what counts is not the ability to prevent thoughts or emotions from arising but the ability to catch ourselves in a particular mental or emotional state. This is the very essence of tranquillity meditation. As Gotsangpa said: "When a disturbing thought arises in the mind, simply focus the mind on that thought and rest in that state instead of reacting to it. The thought will then be liberated of its own natural accord."

The Obstacles to Meditation and Their Antidotes

The Mahamudra style of meditation does not encourage us toward the different levels of meditative concentration traditionally described in the exoteric meditation manuals. This meditation literature frequently lists nine levels of meditative concentration and four levels of meditative absorption. We will look at these nine levels later in this chapter, but for now it is important to understand their place in Mahamudra meditation. In the Mahamudra approach, they are not real indicators of progress on the spiritual path, and we need not be overly concerned with them. It is worth noting again that tranquillity meditation is not unique to Buddhism, and the levels of concentration associated with it are highly valued in certain Hindu traditions. The sole purpose of tranquillity meditation in Buddhism, however, is to create a favorable mental condition for the practice of insight meditation. The meditative absorptions of tranquillity meditation do not lead to an enlightened state of mind. It is only insight meditation that enables us to transcend our deluded states of mind and attain wisdom consciousness.

According to the Mahamudra teachings, the levels of meditative absorption that are conventionally promoted can be a real hindrance to our practice because they can lead to a lessening of conscious acuity. The value of meditative absorption is minimized for this reason, because it is considered imperative that we heighten our sensory awareness rather than diminish it if we are to practice insight meditation effectively.

In the traditional literature on meditation, we progress through different stages of meditative stabilization by detecting certain obstacles to our concentration and applying specific antidotes to them. Shantideva's instructions in the meditation chapter of his *Bodhicharyavatara* give a typical presentation of how to tame the mind, in which the meditator is compared to a wild elephant and mindfulness and awareness are compared to the implements used by the *mahout* to tame the elephant. The wild elephant in this instance refers to the mind that is given to unbridled, explosive emotions. The *Madhyamakahrdaya* for example, contains the following verse on this topic:

> *As the elephant of the mind wanders*
> *It should be bound with the rope of mindfulness*
> *Tied to the post of a mental image*
> *And tamed with the hook of awareness.*

In the Mahamudra context, all these obstacles can be subsumed under two main categories: mental agitation and stupor or drowsiness. These are the only obstacles with which we need concern ourselves. The two antidotes that we use to counterbalance them are mindfulness and awareness.

The use of mindfulness and awareness increases our ability to detect our permutational mental states, and they are the only tools we need to become skilled in the Mahamudra method. Initially, mental agitation often seems the greatest obstacle to mental stability. In fact, it is actually drowsiness and stupor that are the most difficult to overcome, because they elude detection far more easily than agitation. Drowsiness may even present itself to the unwary as a state of calmness and be mistaken for the stability of tranquillity meditation. It would not have the attributes of tranquillity meditation at all, though, which are the two qualities of mindfulness and mental perspicacity. The mind must be calm but free of stupor, drowsiness, torpor, and related mental states, including mild states of depression. In brief, tranquillity is the quintessential opposite of the excited state of mind, but it is not a state of dullness—which can be present in agitated states of mind as well.

Alternating periods of excitation and dullness will be a regular feature of one's daily meditative experience, but there is no need to be unduly concerned about this. The key to tranquillity meditation involves the ability to notice things, not to eliminate them from our consciousness. As our capacity to be attentive, conscious, and aware develops in the meditative situation, it will also begin to flow into our everyday lives as well. The story that follows may help to illustrate the importance of mindful engagement with the world.

The minister of a fashionable parish left the task of greeting his parishioners to the church's ushers. His wife eventually persuaded him to take on this task himself, arguing that he would end up not knowing his congregation if he did not make personal contact with them in this way. The following Sunday he took up his post at the church door and enthusiastically shook hands with the first woman to leave the service, welcoming her to the parish and saying, "I hope we will see you often at our service. We are always glad to see new faces." Somewhat taken aback, the woman replied, "Thank you, sir." Warming to his task, the minister added, "If you give me your address, my wife and I will come and pay you a visit one evening." The woman replied, "You would not have to go far, sir. I'm your cook."

TRANQUILLITY MEDITATION WITH AN OBJECT

The technical literature refers to two distinct methods of tranquillity meditation, which are called tranquillity with object and tranquillity without object, or, alternatively, tranquillity with attributes and tranquillity without attributes. Tranquillity with object involves using specific objects of meditation, such as a Buddha statue or the breath, to anchor our concentration, as we have already discussed. These sensory objects are simply used as a means to prolong our attention during our meditation practice. Tranquillity without object does not involve an object of concentration other than the mind itself.

We have a tendency to project expectations and interpretations onto our meditation experience, just as we do with many other things. These expectations and interpretations can even relate to experiences that we have not yet had. Following from this, we develop our own preconceived version of what meditative experience may entail, what it should be like, and what kind of results it ought to proffer. It is important to bear in mind that when one has no real personal experience of meditation as such, it is pointless to have expectations about it.

Cultivating tranquillity with object is meant to assist us in stabilizing our mind. At first we will develop only a rudimentary ability to stabilize the mind. This is often followed by an increased awareness of how agitated our minds are, and we may feel that our thoughts have grown even wilder than before. This is not true, however; it just appears that way because we have become more aware of what is actually going on in our mind. Instead of feeling that our meditation has been destabilized by this invasion of thoughts, we just take note of them. Nor do we regard disturbing thoughts and emotions as something that upsets our meditation. We simply allow them to arise, become aware of them, and then let them go—not commenting on or ruminating about our mental processes.

From the point of view of Mahamudra, the criterion by which we judge whether we are meditating or not is not whether we are exercising control over our minds but whether awareness is present. Awareness is far more important than controlling the mind. We must learn to relax the mind every time we employ a meditation object, for it is important not to analyze the object of meditation but simply use it to anchor the mind. Many people think that meditation is learning how to control the mind instead of relaxing it. If we try to control the mind, it will only become claustrophobic, and our agitation will increase. This is so because to stay in control requires energy, which then generates a state of mind that is anathema to relaxation. The traditional analogy for this is the life of a silkworm. Silkworms spend their lives producing fine threads of incredibly strong silk in which they entangle themselves, becoming prisoners of their own making. In a similar way, trying to control our thoughts and emotions only creates more and more discursive thoughts and emotions, which further mire us within our distorted perception of the world.

The principal technique of tranquillity with attributes is known as resting the mind. In the Mahamudra teachings, we are counseled to employ three techniques of resting the mind in tranquillity meditation.

Resting the Mind Naturally

In this technique, we must prevent the mind from straying from the object of meditation. It is very important to keep the mind free of any kind of contrivance, such as any artifice or creative act while observing the object, whether the object is a physical object, the incoming and outgoing breath, or mental states. The main point of the technique is an unforceful resting of the mind. An often-used image applied here is that of snow falling gently onto rocks and settling easily on the ground.

Resting the Mind in a Relaxed Fashion

In this technique, we allow the mind to enter effortlessly into a state of rest. The degree of effort people put into meditation can be indicated by how much they bemoan the hardship. People are always saying, "Meditation is so hard." This is because they have certain expectations about what the meditative state should be, and they try to fabricate a state that corresponds to those expectations. When this fails, they get infuriated and frustrated with their practice because it is so often full of struggle. The notion of effortlessness means not striving to attain any special kind of meditative state. We have to let go of the tension that binds the mind as a result of being too eager in our practice. The image used to illustrate this technique is cutting the cord that binds a bundle of wheat together. Once the cord is cut, the wheat will fall effortlessly to the ground.

Resting the Mind in Its Natural State

If we do not interfere with or contrive the flow of our discursive thoughts, they will dissipate by themselves into our natural state of being, or buddha-nature. We commonly see the meditative state as something completely different from our normal states of mind, which is why we frequently look for or try to create some altered state of consciousness through meditation. This becomes a hindrance rather than a help to our meditation practice, because we are constantly trying to acquire something that we do not have. It is this, more than anything else, that impedes our ability to be in the present. We must cultivate the understanding that meditation is about dealing with our current state of mind right from the beginning. Even if discursive thoughts surge up in our minds, we simply allow them to fall back into the natural state of the mind. The image evoked here is that of waves crashing back into the stillness of the ocean.

TRANQUILLITY MEDITATION
WITHOUT AN OBJECT

In the practice of tranquillity without object, it is not necessary to employ any external physical objects or the breath to anchor our concentration. The focus of meditation in this technique is simply the mind itself. From the Mahamudra point of view, we should not desire meditative equipoise nor have an aversion to discursive thoughts and conflicting emotions but view both of these states with equanimity. Again, the significant point is not whether meditative equipoise is present but whether we are able to maintain awareness of our mental states. If disturbing thoughts do arise, as they certainly will, we should simply recognize these thoughts and emotions as transient phenomena—they arise, they persist for a short while, and then they dissipate. The transience of thought is revealed by how difficult it can be to grasp a thought—when we try, it is already gone and another one has appeared in its place.

In tranquillity meditation without object, we sit in the same posture as before, but instead of gazing downward, we look straight ahead into space with the eyes wide open. We do not deliberately pay attention to whatever thoughts and emotions arise or do not arise in the mind, but with unadulterated simplicity we relax into a state of awareness without thinking about anything in particular.

In the practice of tranquillity with object, we were urged to observe our thoughts, but here we are not meant to be observing anything at all. We simply look straight ahead and allow discursive thoughts to come and go without paying any particular attention to them. It is a matter of allowing ourselves to slip into a relaxed state and then remaining that way with clarity and lucidity. Of course, we need to have established the stability of a mind that is at rest and free of dullness, for it is imperative that awareness be present at all times. Tranquillity without attributes has three stages, which will be discussed in turn. They are:

1. Stabilizing the agitated mind
2. Strengthening that stability
3. Achieving mental stability.

Stabilizing the Agitated Mind

This first step begins with an object of meditation, although it is important not to focus on that object too intently. The mind should be restrained from wandering from the meditative object, yet should remain relaxed. Simply make a phenomenological observation of the object without analyzing it at all. It is important not to mistake the object of meditation for the function of meditation, which is to enhance and develop your concentration. Just try to be aware of the object in question without grasping at it or trying to focus too intently. At times, your vision may become blurred, or you may feel that the object has moved, and so on. If that happens, stop focusing on the object for a while and gaze straight into space, trying to relax in that state without directing the mind to any particular object. Maintain a simple state of awareness without allowing the mind to fall under the influence of drowsiness or stupor.

Once you are able to maintain this awareness, your mind will slowly become lucid and you will experience mental ease. Beware of entertaining either hope or fear, and do not apply any kind of physical or mental exertion. If you become too concerned about maintaining meditative equipoise and eliminating disturbing thoughts, you will not be able to maintain a genuine meditative state. The object of meditation is now simply the mind itself. The thoughts and emotions are not so much used as an object of focus but simply kept in awareness and allowed to arise and dissipate of their own accord. Mahamudra experience is not created; it will arise spontaneously from the right frame of mind. If you know how to let your mind rest in this manner, you will no longer be disturbed by discursive thoughts but have a real a sense of spaciousness. It is also important not to evaluate your experiences for indications of progress and not to regard an inability to maintain this state for long as failure. If you can develop and maintain this sort of attitude, the disturbing thoughts themselves will reveal the innate nature of the mind.

At this stage, none of the experiences that arise in the mind are regarded positively or negatively. They are not judged as good, wholesome, and worthy of cultivation nor as hindrances and obstacles requiring abandonment. Cultivating this attitude will in time empty the mind of its unconscious content, and our karmic traces and dispositions will be purified. The purification of karmic traces and dispositions is not in itself a sufficient cause for enlightenment, however, for without insight into the nature of the mind and the nature of ultimate reality, we will continue to create karmic tendencies anew. Stabilization of tranquillity without attributes is, however, an important aspect of the spiritual path when used in conjunction with the development of insight.

Strengthening That Stability

The practice of meditation is fraught with obstacles, all of which, in the Mahamudra context, fall under the categories of drowsiness or stupor and mental agitation. There are other obstacles, such as laziness, that have to be dealt with through contemplating the four preliminaries, but in terms of tranquillity meditation these are the two real obstacles.

Even though drowsiness and stupor are closely related and categorized together here, they are quite distinct experiences. Stupor reflects a mental state deprived of clarity and lucidity. Drowsiness is connected to torpor. The experience of torpor is almost like falling asleep. Even if disturbing thoughts and emotions arise in the mind, we are unaware of them and unable to distinguish positive from negative meditative experiences. An old Zen story might be helpful in this regard. Master Soyen passed away at the age of sixty-one, leaving behind a most varied and sublime Zen teaching. Though he himself had never wasted a minute of his time, it was said that his students would sometimes sleep after the midday meal in the summertime. Soyen never said a word to his students about this. When Soyen was twelve years old, he studied philosophy with the Tendai school. One summer day, he had stretched out on the floor when his teacher was away and slept deeply for three hours. He was awoken with a start when his teacher returned to the room. His teacher simply stepped reverently over Soyen's prostrate body as if it were a distinguished guest and said, "Please excuse me, please excuse me." Soyen never again slept in the daytime.

If drowsiness or stupor occurs, try to expand your chest, straighten your spine, open your eyes, and gaze into the distance. It is also helpful to have some water in a container so that you can splash your face to refresh yourself. Cool the room down if it is too hot, or take off a layer of clothing. It also helps to shorten the meditation session by taking a number of breaks between sessions rather than sitting for extended periods. If drowsiness and stupor become a habitual problem, you may need to reduce the amount of food and liquid you consume, refrain from sitting in the sun or by a fire for too long, and make sure that you engage in regular physical exercise and breathing exercises. It is helpful occasionally to go for a walk and then cultivate mindfulness and awareness when you return to your sitting practice.

If mental agitation is an obstacle, try to relax the mind and body. Eat nutritious food, receive massages, and put on a few more layers of clothing. If your mind remains agitated, take a break instead of persisting with your practice. If the agitation is too intense and difficult to overcome, you may need to analyze the disturbing thoughts to see where they emanate from and what their content is. Ask yourself: "Are my thoughts about trivial day-to-day experiences, or are they about my meditation practice and spiritual concerns?" It is not the disturbing thoughts themselves but our conceptualization about these thoughts that disturbs us.

The real source of drowsiness and agitation is our own conflicting emotions. Therefore, any form of purificatory practice is extremely helpful. Another helpful method is to simply use agitation, drowsiness, or stupor itself as the object of meditation rather than attempting to apply antidotes. If drowsiness and stupor are recognized as a state of mind, and whatever state of mind you are in is seen as inseparable from the nature of the mind itself, insight will be gained without the need to abandon either of these mental states. As Rangjung Dorje, the third Gyalwa Karmapa, says in his *Prayer of Mahamudra*:

Let the waves of subtle and coarse thoughts calm down into their own place
And the waters of mind, without movement, come spontaneously to rest,
Free from the contaminations of discursiveness and sloth.
May I establish a still ocean of shamatha.

As this verse suggests, thoughts can be divided into coarse and subtle types. Some thoughts are immediately detectable because they are quite compelling in content; others are subtler, and it is only through developing greater awareness that we come to notice them at all. If there is no mindfulness and awareness in our meditation practice, both types of thinking will destabilize and despoil our meditative concentration. Torpor and dullness also act as obstacles to meditative concentration when they are not detected, for they can sneak up even when we are paying attention. Be that as it may, as Rangjung Dorje emphasizes, the way to overcome these obstacles is not by trying to forcefully prevent them from making their appearance, but by permitting them to subside by themselves and allowing mental clarity to arise by itself. You will gradually overcome these two obstacles in this way. When you have developed this ability, you can think, "Now I have achieved real meditation," and feel proud.

Actualizing Mental Stability

At this stage, we need to focus our minds on a particular visual object and then gradually expand that focus to include all objects in the immediate surrounding area. Next we choose a sound, smell, physical sensation, and mental image and try to focus on these sensory impressions one at a time. We then expand our focus to include the conflicting emotions that are generally considered something to be abandoned. After that we focus on virtuous thoughts, such as the practice of generosity, patience, morality, and so on, and then on neutral or trivial thoughts. As such, we turn our attention successively to positive, negative, and neutral emotions and to positive, negative, and neutral thoughts.

Traditional Mahamudra meditation manuals say that negative thoughts and emotions cannot be used as objects of meditation and must be abandoned. From the Mahamudra perspective, that approach will only cause further disturbing thoughts to arise. Again, we should not regard disturbing thoughts as harmful or as having a deleterious effect but instead accustom ourselves to simultaneously relaxing and focusing on our thoughts without reaction. Instead of trying to stabilize the mind by hanging on to a particular thought, we practice letting go of our thoughts by letting our attention rest naturally on their progress. Another fresh thought will always take the place of the last.

• • •

The function of tranquillity meditation is to maintain mindfulness and awareness, not to block out our thoughts and feelings, which is practically impossible to do in any case. Through this practice our thoughts will gradually stabilize. Even if things do not proceed like this and disturbing thoughts continue to arise, you should not feel disheartened. Simply be aware of them, because if you succeed in focusing your mind on thoughts, the thoughts themselves can become meditation.

Practice mindfulness and awareness intensively for a short time, then relax your meditation for a while, and then practice intensively again. Intensive mindfulness and awareness practice entails trying to detect everything that is going on in your mind, paying attention as carefully as you would if you were trying to spot an escaped prisoner in a crowd or walk with a pot full of boiling oil. These two images are used frequently to describe intense mindfulness practice in Buddhist literature. Shantideva gives a very graphic description of them in his *Bodhicharyavatara*. Relaxing your meditation means ceasing this intensive focus and maintaining instead a general sense of mindfulness and awareness, relaxing the mind into a sense of physical and mental well-being. As in the traditional analogy, we relax in the way a bundle of wheat falls to the ground when the cord that binds it has been severed.

You will gradually develop the necessary skill to deal with the two obstacles of mental stupor and agitation by practicing with intensity and relaxation. Do not become too fixated on any of these techniques or the order in which they are practiced. Experiment with your own needs and find out what works best for you. By way of encouragement, remember that without eliminating the obstacles of mental stupor and agitation and attaining a tranquil mind, we will never be able to gain insight into the nature of our mind and attain liberation from our mental conflicting emotions. As the first *Bhavanakrama* of Kamalashila emphasizes:

> Because the mind is shaky, like water, it does not settle without the foundation of tranquility. The mind that has failed to achieve settled equipoise can in no way understand perfect reality as it is."[1]

The middle *Bhavanakrama* also elaborates upon this point:

> Insight without tranquility renders a yogin's mind susceptible to the distraction of sensory objects. Because it is unstable, like a butter lamp exposed to the wind, it fails to attain the illumination of awareness.[2]

THE NINE LEVELS OF RESTING
THE MIND IN TRANQUILLITY

The three stages of tranquillity meditation without object are related to the following nine stages of resting the mind in tranquillity. They are all methods of practice and levels of attainment that provide a map for a meditator's progress from a distracted, unstable mind to the final level of mental equipoise.

Resting the Mind

As you begin to watch the breath, your mind will settle somewhat, and you will start to notice that your normal consciousness is in a constant state of agitation. This first stage of tranquillity meditation allows us an initial taste of some respite from that continuous agitation. You may find it extremely difficult to rest the mind initially, as the mind is a very fickle thing. For this reason, you have to make a determined effort at this point in order to reach the second level of mental rest.

Continuous Resting

You have to learn to stabilize these periods of calm and extend them by being mindful and learning to recognize your agitation and stupor while they are occurring. If you are able to rest your mind for even a couple of seconds, this can be gradually prolonged through the practice of mindfulness, and you will begin to experience definite periods when the mind is at rest alongside periods of distraction.

Patchlike Resting

At this level, your mind is sometimes calm and at other times agitated. Significantly, though, you begin to learn to practice mindfulness in both situations. This stage is about recognizing your distraction and using mindfulness to return to the practice of tranquillity meditation. In other words, if agitation occurs and you recognize it, your mindfulness has been maintained. The meditative state at this level is said to be patchlike because of the intermittent disruptions in the flow of meditative experience.

Close Placement

When you are able to bring the patchlike states of rest closer together, you have attained the next level. Here you can extend the state of mindfulness after agitation has occurred. At this point, you have become fairly proficient at tranquillity meditation. However, other problems may arise, usually more from boredom than from mental agitation. A distinct lack of interest in meditating may set in from time to time, and you may feel as if you are making little progress in the practice.

Pacification

To counteract your discouragement, there are methods of pacifying or taming the mind. Start by listing all the benefits gained from meditation: It allows you to feel more calm and collected and to experience less emotional turmoil, for instance. Think of these things during meditation to calm your mind and remind yourself that the mental exercise of meditation has made your mind more pliable and open to development. Think: "When I practice meditation, I'm less prone to conflicting emotions and do not get so overwhelmed by them." It is also important to remember that it is only through the practice of meditation that you can even imagine achieving liberation from the bondage of cyclic existence and thus aspire to achieve enlightenment. Therefore, you should also think: "Tranquillity meditation is not only helpful for my emotional conflicts; it is essential for achieving my spiritual goals. If I allow my mind to become dull, apathetic, and afflicted by emotions, I will not have the opportunity to travel the spiritual path."

Subjugation

To supplement this method of taming the unruly mind, which uses positive affirmation, contemplate the great drawbacks of failing to practice meditation. In this regard, think: "The harm that I suffer comes from having no control over my conflicting emotions and agitated mental states. I am constantly wasting my time in the confusion of disturbing thoughts or indulging in countless meaningless thoughts." If you examine the things that you think about and the emotions and feelings you have, you will realize very quickly that they are mostly of a negative nature in one way or another. Of the two types of thoughts and emotions that we can have, positive and negative, we indulge only in the latter. It is the emotions of anger, hostility, lust, unbridled desire, and so forth that tend to consume our consciousness, as well as the negative thoughts related to worry, fear, anxiety, suspicion, and paranoia. These disturbing thoughts and emotions prevent us from obtaining our ultimate spiritual goal and ensure that we remain in samsaric bondage indefinitely. Consequently, not only are we deprived of the opportunity to obtain the lasting happiness and the edifying peace of enlightenment, but we are also impaired in our ability to experience even temporary happiness and joy. It is essential to engage in this kind of contemplation at this stage in order to pacify the mind.

Thorough Subjugation

At this level, engage in reflection on the positive rewards of meditation practice and reaffirm your commitment to applying mindfulness and awareness. It is extremely beneficial to think along these lines: "It is only through the practice of tranquillity meditation that I have been able to attain relief from the relentless afflictions of my conflicting emotions and discursive thoughts. It is also due to this practice that I have any temporary experiences of pleasure and happiness. It is also only through this practice that I can realistically think of attaining liberation from the delusory, degrading state of samsara and aspire toward the exalted state of enlightenment and secure lasting happiness and joy."

One-Pointed Concentration

If you persist with the above practices and apply mindfulness and awareness without wavering in effort or resolve, you will attain one-pointed concentration. At this point you will have developed sufficient skills to deal with all of the obstacles to meditative concentration, including mental stupor and agitation in both their gross and subtle manifestations. Even if discursive thoughts arise, your mind will remain unwavering. This will be the result of the combination of mindfulness and awareness.

Meditative Equipoise

This final level is equivalent to the actual attainment of tranquillity and as such is the culmination of tranquillity meditation practice.

One could say it *is* tranquillity meditation. Even the notion of one-pointedness is no longer applicable here, because that still implies that some effort is being made to apply single-minded concentration. At this point, tranquillity meditation has become a natural state of being rather than something maintained through mindfulness and awareness. It is said that at this stage you have attained complete mastery over the pliancy of body and mind and will automatically enter into the state of tranquillity.

There are three essential stages to the process of meditative stabilization, which culminates in the complete state of tranquillity. The first stage is attained when awareness is present even while your mind is agitated, so disturbing thoughts disperse spontaneously. This kind of tranquillity is compared to snow falling on a boulder. The second stage is reached when a meditative state can be maintained even when disturbing thoughts arise. The mind is here compared to the gentle flow of a river. The third stage is accomplished when you gain the ability to maintain a sense of awareness in everyday life and your mind is consistently clear and lucid. This state is compared to the stillness of the ocean.

The meditative way of thinking that constitutes insight meditation requires a calm and stable basis in order to be effective, but no amount of mental calming will lead to meditative realization. If we do not have the mental training of tranquillity techniques, our minds will just be overwhelmed by conceptual proliferation during insight meditation. In his *Bodhicharyavatara*, Shantideva stresses that the meditation of tranquillity will not directly give rise to insight: "Only the person who is well endowed with insight as a result of establishing their shamatha meditation can eradicate their mental afflictions. Therefore, one should first seek tranquillity. Tranquillity arises as a result of detachment from the world and the generation of joy."

While insight meditation is referred to as analytical meditation, it is an analytical approach that requires a meditative way of thinking; and a meditative way of thinking requires a very serene and focused mind. Unless one happens to be one of those rare individuals whose minds are not given to mental agitation and tumultuous mood swings, tranquillity meditation is an essential prelude to, and support for insight meditation. Only the combination of tranquillity and insight meditation will give rise to the genuine state of the mind's luminous bliss, because the meditative state has to have both mental stability and clarity. Rangjung Dorje describes the result of tranquillity and insight meditation in these words in his *Prayer of Mahamudra*: "The great bliss, unceasing and without desire, unfixated luminosity, free from the veil of obscurations." Luminous bliss comes from two sources, tranquillity and insight. The bliss aspect arises from attaining a tranquil mind, and the luminosity aspect arises from cutting through mental fixations by gaining insight into the nature of our mind itself. It is this luminous bliss that is the ultimate goal of the Mahamudra meditative tradition.

9

INSIGHT
MEDITATION

———

Wʜᴇɴ ʟᴇᴀʀɴɪɴɢ ᴀʙᴏᴜᴛ ɪɴsɪɢʜᴛ ᴍᴇᴅɪᴛᴀᴛɪᴏɴ ᴀɴᴅ ᴛʜᴇ ᴘᴀʀᴀ-
mount role it plays in Buddhist practice, it is essential to realize that this
type of meditation *does* involve thinking. Unlike tranquillity meditation, in which we disengage from our thoughts, insight meditation actually employs thoughts as part of the practice. This might seem at
variance with the Buddhist characterization of the mind as inordinately
productive of thought to the point of being responsible for the delusory
experiences of our samasaric condition. Many Western Buddhists assume that all meditation is strictly concerned with the pacification of
thought. Even seasoned Western meditators show less enthusiasm for insight meditation than for tranquillity meditation. Many insight meditation courses that are offered in the West are not traditional vipashyana
but are rather traditional tranquillity meditation, and it is a misnomer to
call these practices vipashyana meditation. If the meditator's ultimate
aim is to quiet the mind and gain some semblance of mental composure,
tranquillity meditation is an adequate method. If, on the other hand, our
intention is to develop ourselves on the spiritual path, the matter is entirely different. Gaining real spiritual insight, overcoming delusory states
of mind, and attaining enlightenment are possible only through the analytical practices of insight meditation. In Buddhism, we believe that the

defilements, delusions, and obscurations of the mind are caused by what are known as two veils (*avarana*). They are called veils because they prevent us from seeing things for what they are; we are confined to perceiving things for what they seem. The first veil is known as the veil of conflicting emotions (*klesha-varana*). Generally, five conflicting emotions are desire, anger, jealousy, pride, and ignorance/indifference. Ignorance is mentioned because it is the precondition for the arising of the other four emotions, even though ignorance is not an emotion as such. It is also the basis for the other veil, the veil of conceptual distortion (*jneya-varana*). Therefore, ignorance serves as the basis for both veils.

Conflicting emotions bind us to the samsaric state, while conceptual distortions prevent us from attaining enlightenment. Conflicting emotions are contingent on conceptual distortions, which primarily manifest as our dualistic notions of subject and object and our primitive belief in the substantial reality of contingently arisen empirical phenomena. That is why insight meditation is so important in Buddhist practice, because it allows us to deal with conceptual distortions after tranquillity meditation has calmed the intensity of the conflicting emotions.

Whenever defilements and delusions are mentioned in this text, the reader should bear in mind that we are referring to both the veil of conflicting emotions and the veil of conceptual distortions. The combination of these two veils is responsible for producing various forms of mental disturbance. The primary mental disturbances that are mentioned in the traditional literature are: ignorance, shamelessness, recklessness, restlessness, greed, distorted views, conceit, hatred, envy, avarice or covetousness, worry, sloth, torpor, and skeptical doubt. Again, when mental disturbances are mentioned, the reader should keep in mind that this refers specifically to these elements, for these are the factors that Buddhism understands as the most harmful to our well-being.

As Buddhist practitioners, we should not be content with the mental equipoise of a calm state of mind. We need to recognize that the mind does not have any enduring essence and that, contrary to our deep-seated belief, there is no psychic substance to our being, such as an enduring self or soul. The thinking that characterizes insight meditation is not the usual discursive type of conceptual proliferation we have been discussing, but a type of thinking that is designed to cut through to the very heart of things—to pave the way for a direct insight into the very nature of ultimate reality itself.

The insight technique involves a kind of epistemological enquiry. It is not meant to deal with our specific thoughts and emotions or their significance to our individual history or psychic life. For example, if we have harmful thoughts, lustful thoughts, or confused thoughts, we do not try to work out where these thoughts have come from. We are not trying to construct an etiology of our psychic life, because the causes are endemic to our human condition and consequently are present in the very strategies we might employ to make sense of that condition. The insight technique is designed to dismantle our fixation on these thoughts and emotions, because it is our fixation that reinforces our biases and prejudices and dulls the lenses through which we "see through a glass, darkly."

The teachings of Buddhism do not suggest that greater psychological insight into our lives is unhelpful, nor that insight meditation will not yield some useful snippets of understanding about our personal problems. But this is not the aim of insight meditation, because this agenda is only temporal and partial in relation to our human condition. In fact, trying to see the whys and wherefores of our thoughts and emotions during insight meditation is the very thing we are trying to undermine, because it is these discursive thoughts that reinforce confusion about our true condition. The insight gained through this form of meditation is not concerned with understanding why we have certain thoughts; it is about recognizing that those thoughts have no enduring essence whatsoever. Thoughts are dynamic and expressive rather than inert, substantial, or material. The point of insight meditation practice is to recognize this, not to find out what mental causes gave rise to what mental states. We have to understand the *nature* of the discursive thoughts themselves.

It is important to make a distinction between our meditative goals and our everyday empirical goals. Buddhist teachings still encourage us to look for the causes and reasons for the things that happen in our lives, in the same way the Western traditions do. It is just that this is not identified as the purpose of meditation. Meditation practice has a much deeper and farther-reaching goal. We can have two different kinds of insight: One concerns the causes of things and the other the nature of things. It is the second kind of insight that is conveyed through meditation, and this takes priority over merely understanding how things have been caused—it is about understanding the nature of reality itself.

This is why analytical meditation is an indispensable practice in all schools of Buddhism.

The Mahamudra teachings counsel that we cannot understand the nature of reality without understanding the nature of the mind, and this understanding is the whole purpose of insight meditation. In light of this, it is both interesting and important to note that the Mahamudra teachings do not offer a comprehensive philosophical theory of mind as such. What they do offer is more akin to a phenomenological description of the mind within the context of meditative experiences.

It might be useful to define *phenomenology* at this point, as the following discussion of Mahamudra meditation is presented largely through this type of inquiry. Phenomenology refers to the inquiry into one's own consciousness and intellectual processes without regard for external causes and influences. It is a purely subjective investigation into the phenomena of the mind and focuses on the essential structure of experience itself. It necessarily involves suspending any preexisting theories we may have about the world and our own identity, seeking to base all observation on our lived experience as it happens prior to any kind of philosophical reflection.

The Nature of the Mind

The nature of the mind is a core concept in the Mahamudra tradition. It refers to the fact that the mind is empty of any essence and that this emptiness pervades all our mental events. A clear distinction is made between the empirical mind (*sem*) and the nature of mind (*semnyi*), defining them as the deluded mind and the wisdom mind (as discussed in chapter 4). However, Mahamudra is unique in that it declines to distinguish between these two types of mind—the empirical mind and the nature of the mind—in one singular circumstance: meditation practice. In meditation, we are not instructed to reject our thoughts and emotions as deluded and strive for some other transcendental state currently beyond the reach of our deluded mental states. Rather, we are encouraged to recognize the nature of the mind within the nature of thoughts and emotions themselves. In this way, the Mahamudra approach undermines all dualistic emphasis from the very beginning of the spiritual journey.

To understand the nature of the mind for ourselves, we need at first to use analytical tools to help us see how we create our own unhappiness through our distorted thoughts and conflicting emotions. Insight meditation should help us develop a certain level of conceptual understanding about our true condition through analysis. This conceptual understanding will at some point lead to a direct realization of the nature of the mind. During this process, however, we have to appreciate that our experiences will be affected and informed by our own predilections and personality. To a certain extent, then, we will come to the realization of the nature of the mind in a uniquely personal way, both in terms of when our realization dawns and the actual nature of our insights in meditative experience.

THE NATURE OF THOUGHTS AND EMOTIONS

The main thrust of insight meditation is how elusive, insubstantial, ephemeral, and intangible our thoughts are. Our thoughts are nothing in themselves. It is worth reflecting that this is a truth that we intuitively resist recognizing. Through insight meditation, we will come to realize that everything that occurs in the mind is empty of substance. That is the meaning of the traditional Mahamudra teaching that the nature of the mind is emptiness. This realization is not an especially mysterious or transcendent one. It simply means that everything we experience has no abiding or fixed nature and therefore has no real substance to it.

As discussed in the previous chapter, in the Mahamudra tradition, discursive thoughts are not regarded as a handicap or impediment to practice. They should not be discarded or even dismissed, but rather put to constructive use as a *necessary* tool for the generation of insight. Without disturbing thoughts and conflicting emotions, there would be no path and no insight. Disturbing thoughts and emotions are said to be no different than pieces of wood that we use to feed a fire; there is no fire if there is no wood. The mind that thinks, feels, anticipates, and experiences varied emotions is not separate from the nature of the mind. This does not mean the mind and its nature are the same; it means they have the same nature. The mind is the source of delusional thoughts while the nature of the mind does not know delusions of any kind. Therefore, we cannot understand the nature of the mind without them. If we can see this in meditation practice, we will realize that the very thoughts used to determine the nature of the mind are not distinct from the nature of the mind itself. As Gampopa explains:

"A meditator should not think of discarding thoughts, but instead should think of how wonderful it is to have these disturbing thoughts; how beneficial and indispensable these thoughts are to meditation. Without these disturbing thoughts, how would we recognize the nature of the mind?"

We should not think of discursive thoughts as a huge obstacle to meditation. In fact, as we become more acquainted with our thoughts—though it may seem absurd to think we can get closer to our thoughts than we already are—we will be able to perceive the thoughts themselves as expressions of our true nature. In Mahamudra literature, this is known as the dexterous play of the mind. The Kagyu lineage prayer says:

> The nature of thoughts is Dharmakaya, as is said.
> Nothing whatsoever, but everything arises from it.
> To the meditator who sees the dexterous play of the mind,
> Grant your blessing, so that the identity of nirvana
>   and samsara is realized.

The exercises in this chapter help us to get to know our discursive thoughts better. Through this familiarity we come to understand their nature and consequently gain insight into our own true nature. This simply means that the things that obscure have an inherent capacity to reveal as well. This fact is not appreciated by the dualistic mind, which is trained into thinking that everything is one thing or another.

It is simply not the case that the nature of the so-called obscurations of the mind that we are trying to overcome and the nature of the mind that we are counseled to recognize are separate or different. They are not separate in their essential nature. It is by recognizing that the nature of discursive thoughts and the nature of the mind are indistinguishable that we can prevail over the seemingly intractable obscurations of our minds. To take a traditional example, it is said that while milk and butter might be distinct substances, their nature is indistinguishably the same. This cannot be said about milk and sand. In the same way, the mind and thoughts have the same nature—the nature of emptiness. As Rangjung Dorje, the third Karmapa, emphatically states in his *Prayer of Mahamudra*:

> Since appearance is mind and emptiness is also mind,
> Since realization is mind and delusion is mind,
> Since arising is mind and cessation is also mind,
> Let me see through all mind's doubts.

This clearly indicates that the nature of the mind is not something that is transcendent, remote, or extremely difficult to access. To the contrary, the nature of the mind can be realized through understanding the mind in its ordinary manifestations. For this profound yet simple reason, the mind as a whole is often referred to in Mahamudra literature as ordinary mind. Gampopa describes this ordinary mind in these terms:

> If at this moment one wishes to achieve liberation from the cycle of existence, one must recognize ordinary mind, for it is the root of all things. That which is designated as "ordinary mind" is one's own awareness. Left in its natural state, this awareness remains unstained by any [nonordinary] perceptive forms, unmuddled by any levels of existential consciousness, and unclouded by dullness, depression, or thought.[1]

In essence, buddhas and sentient beings are the same. It is only owing to our delusion that we have failed to realize our nature, while buddhas have succeeded in realizing their nature. Not surprisingly, this also happens to be the reason we remain in delusions and buddhas are blissfully free of that same delusion. This point is reiterated in a different way by Rangjung Dorje in his *Prayer of Mahamudra*:

> *When it is not realized, one circles in the ocean of samsara.*
> *Realizing it, Buddha is not other.*

THREE ASPECTS OF THE MIND

The Mahamudra teachings identify three aspects of the mind: essence (*ngowo*), nature (*rangzhin*), and characteristic (*tsen nyed*). When the knowledge dawns upon us that the mind's essence is empty and its nature is innately awake and luminous, we will have gained a glimpse into the nature of the mind itself. Acquiring insight into the nature of the mind through the practice of insight meditation will give us the profound realization that of all our mental states and processes, none has sufficient power to corrupt and influence the fundamental purity of the mind or to compromise it in any way.

Essence

The essence of the mind is said to be emptiness, because the mind does not present itself as an entity or substance of any kind. In other words, the mind is not a thing. We inevitably use words to describe the mind in the same way we describe an everyday object such as a table, but mind is not like a thing at all. This is what meant by saying that the essence of the mind is emptiness. As Virupa, the twelfth-century Indian mahasiddha affirms:

> *But for its designation the mind is empty*
> *And nonconceptual, which is synonymous with mahāmudrā.*
> *It is empty from the beginning, like space.*
> *The essence of mind is unborn [emptiness]*
> *And is detached from any substantive reality.*
> *Like space, it is all-pervasive.*
> *Neither transferring nor transforming,*
> *It has always been empty and selfless*
> *From the very beginning.²*

Nature

The nature of the mind refers to the fact that we cannot experientially locate the mind anywhere or identify it as being anything because it is insubstantial, yet it cannot be said to be completely nonexistent, for the mind is innately endowed with amazingly rich and diverse cognitive capacities. This is one of the main reasons the Mahamudra teachings say that the nature of mind is luminosity. This luminosity of the mind has the dual function of illuminating and purifying the conflicting emotions. As the *Samputa* explains:

> *Mind defiled by passion and other uncontrolled impulses*
> *Is indeed the mind of cyclic existence.*
> *Discovering the mind's intrinsic lucidity is liberation indeed.*
> *Undefiled by lust and emotional impurities,*
> *Unclouded by any dualistic perceptions,*
> *This superior mind is indeed the supreme nirvana!*

The *Uttaratantra* explains the nature of the mind in these words:

> *Enlightenment is like the pollen in a lotus,*
> *Like the grains in wheat and gold in dirt,*
> *Like a treasure under the ground and seeds in a pod,*
> *Like an image of the Buddha in rags,*
> *Like a prince in the womb of a common woman,*

Like a heap of gold beneath the earth.
Thus the nature of enlightenment remains hidden in all sentient
*   beings*
Who are overcome by transitory defilement.

Characteristic

The characteristic of the mind refers to our general mental states and
processes, such as our thoughts, memories, feelings, and emotions. This
is often described as the unceasing play of the mind, because both deluded and undeluded states of mind are understood to be a manifestation, or display, of the same mind. Virupa makes this observation
regarding the characteristic of the mind:

> *If you realize the nature of the mind*
> *As revealed by the guru,*
> *Diverse forms of consciousness pacify themselves*
> *Into all-pervasive ultimate reality.*

Whereas the deluded states of mind throw up a confusing array of impure perceptions of the world, the undeluded states of mind give rise to
pure perception, such as that experienced by spiritually advanced beings. However, whether deluded or undeluded, both mental states are
referred to as the play of the mind. The word *play* is used to emphasize
that we ought not take these mental expressions too seriously, because
they are not real or solid in themselves.

As we have seen, the essence of the mind is emptiness, the nature of the
mind is luminosity, and the characteristic of the mind is the unceasing
flow of thoughts and emotions. Despite this distinction between how
these three aspects of the mind manifest, it is important to understand
that all three aspects have the same nature. That nature is the nature of
emptiness. In other words, the essence of the mind is emptiness, the nature of luminosity is emptiness, and the nature of what is called the unceasing play of the mind, with its various mental states and processes, is
also emptiness. As Maitripa elaborates:

> *As discursive thoughts arise from emptiness,*
> *This very thought has the nature of all-pervasive ultimate reality.*
> *The two have been inseparable from the very beginning.*
> *Therefore, these two have one flavor.*

If we fail to maintain this uniquely Mahamudra view, we will not profit fully from our meditation practice, because our minds will remain habituated to dualistic thinking. Normally, we employ endless binary concepts in relation to our experiences—permanence and impermanence, good and bad, self and other, and so forth. As a result, it is very easy for us to succumb to regarding certain states of mind as wholesome, virtuous, sacred, and rarefied and other states as deluded, vile, loathsome, and degraded. The Mahamudra practitioner must resist yielding to this type of conceptualization. Phagmo Drubpa, one of the great masters of the Kagyu tradition explained it this way: "Disturbing thoughts are the cause of awareness, so you should focus your mind with a sense of joy on these very thoughts themselves. If you try to eradicate your thoughts, they will become even more prolific. If, on the other hand, you realize that they do not have any enduring essence, there is no need to abandon them."

Mahamudra meditation provides us with a more permissive method of meditation that allows us to see our distorted thoughts and conflicting emotions with a more amiable and accepting attitude. We no longer need to regard discursive thoughts and conflicting emotions as the enemy; we no longer feel overwhelmed by our emotions, trepidations, sinful thoughts, and so on. The awareness we attain through this meditation has the capacity to expose the true nature of our discursive thoughts and immediately dispel our illusions. We see discursive thoughts for what they are: the passionate attachment to unreal and nonsubstantial things. This activation of luminosity enables us to come face-to-face with our own self-deception. Mahamudra meditation is designed to produce bliss, luminosity, and mental equilibrium or spaciousness toward discursive thoughts. Thus, the meditative state is characterized by these three attributes of bliss, luminosity, and mental spaciousness.

INTRODUCING THE NATURE OF THE MIND IN MEDITATION

A direct realization of the nature of the mind is hard to express in words. No one can convey its full meaning in either writing or speech. Even so, our understanding of it can be readily deepened through specific insight meditation practices. A number of helpful exercises based upon the Mahamudra approach follow here, along with a step-by-step approach to recognizing the nature of the mind. Please note that the key to success is maintaining awareness of meditative experiences during one's practice rather than foisting various interpretative schemas onto them.

The most helpful way to approach these exercises is to attempt only one per meditation session. As a prelude to the exercises, it is strongly recommended that you begin by contemplating the four preliminaries and the four immeasurables. Following this, do tranquillity meditation for a period of time, beginning one of the exercises after your mind has become sufficiently settled.

The following six practices represent the quintessential Mahamudra insight meditation instructions for recognizing the nature of the mind:

1. Recognizing the nature of the mind
2. Introducing the nature of the mind in a state of movement
3. Introducing the nature of the mind through sensory impressions
4. Realizing that the nature of the mind is emptiness
5. Establishing emptiness as spontaneously arisen
6. Realizing that spontaneously arisen emptiness is self-liberation

Recognizing the Nature of the Mind

The following exercises are designed to help us gain an initial recognition of the nature of our mind. If discursive thoughts arise during this period of resting in tranquillity, think of them as waves whipped up upon the surface of the ocean. No matter how fierce these waves are, they crash back into the ocean again without ever disturbing the stillness of its depths. Likewise, you should rest in a meditative state in spite of the arising of agitation, and regard discursive thoughts as waves on the ocean. If you are able to enter into the natural state of being and rest in that state, the discursive thoughts and conflicting emotions would not be able to subvert your mental stability. These exercises should be repeated over and over—they are extremely important. Although they may appear to be tedious and pointless at times, do not be discouraged. Just continue with the analysis regardless. If you persist, you will be rewarded handsomely with a deeper understanding of your mental functions. You will come to discover, perhaps gradually, that the mind is not an entity that is substantial and solid. It is hard to grasp this elusive ephemerality of mind, but it is exactly this difficulty that we are trying to engage in and experience. We need only refer again to the familiar statement, "the nature of the mind is emptiness."

MEDITATION 1
Recognizing That the Mind Has
No Inherent Existence Yet Is Fully Manifest

After you have settled the mind through contemplating the four preliminaries and the four immeasurables and then engaging in tranquillity meditation, begin the exercise by resting in that state of tranquillity for a while. When discursive thoughts have sufficiently subsided and no longer cause you any noticeable disturbance, remain with perspicuous clarity in that state. This state of rest should not be a state of mental blankness or vacuity. It should be alert and relaxed, but not so relaxed that you succumb to conceptual proliferations. In the traditional teachings, it is stated that the mind should rest like the sun free of clouds—vivid imagery indeed!

When various experiences arise, due to either sensory impressions or the inner workings of the mind, rest with them without fixation or clinging. The analogy used in the teachings is of an infant gazing at a visual display such as a fresco on the walls of a monastery. A child looks at such objects in a way an adult can rarely achieve because of the latter's accumulation of reifying concepts and ideas over the years. Without having to ask why, an infant effortlessly observes in a focused, relaxed, and above all natural way.

MEDITATION 2
Recognizing That Thoughts Are Elusive and Ephemeral

Even though thoughts rise and fall in tranquillity meditation, it is still somewhat a state of rest. Having rested the mind in this fashion for a period of time, we now come to the stage where we can begin the main practice of insight meditation with analysis. While resting in that state, ask yourself the following questions: "How does my mind rest when it appears to be at rest? In what manner does my mind rest? When my mind produces thoughts and emotions, how do these thoughts and emotions arise? What are these thoughts? Where do these thoughts occur? Where do thoughts come from and where do they dwell? When they cease, how do they disappear?" There are actually three distinct questions being asked here: The first is about the mind at rest, the second relates to how thoughts arise, and the third concerns the arising, persistence, and dissipation of our thoughts. Gampopa supports this view when he says: "The nature of thoughts is the authentic state. The only antidote that we need to employ in meditation is noninterference. Awareness is attained from the lucidity of the mind."

As humans we are thinking beings that think unceasingly, which makes it is possible to employ our discursive thoughts skillfully as part of meditation. It is vital therefore to grasp that the questioning in this practice must be about the thoughts themselves, not about the content of each particular thought. You are not asking yourself: "What am I thinking *about*?" You are shifting your attention from whatever the thoughts are about to the actual function and process of thinking itself. For example, if a thought arises in your mind such as "Tony is a really nice person," do not contemplate Tony or ask yourself which of Tony's qualities have prompted your musings. Instead, ask yourself: "What is the nature of that thought? What sort of reality do thoughts about Tony have?"

———

That strong emotions affect us adversely is generally accepted and understood. What is not so well understood is how discursive thoughts also have a similar effect on our everyday thinking about incidents, remarks, and encounters. If we can acquire insight into the multifarious workings of our mind, we will gradually recognize that, in spite of the apparently intractable reality of these thoughts, they are in fact elusive, insubstantial, and ephemeral by nature. When we view our thoughts in this way, we will be a little more at ease with ourselves during meditation. As Rangjung Dorje says in his *Prayer of Mahamudra*:

> *All phenomena are the illusory display of the mind.*
> *Mind is devoid of "mind"—empty of any entity.*

Empty and yet unceasing, it manifests as anything whatsoever.
Realizing this completely, may we cut its basis and root.

Through engaging in this meditative way of thinking—which is most emphatically to be distinguished from ordinary, everyday thinking—you will gradually experience your mind as luminous, but not something that can be identified as this or that, with any defining characteristics. The view you have to come to appreciate through doing this practice is that the mind is not a self-existing entity, yet it is fully and vividly manifest. This proliferation of discursive thoughts is something that we must learn to utilize in our spiritual practice. It is these discursive thoughts that fan the flames of our emotions, which in turn cause all manner of unnecessary but constant worry and anxiety. Mahamudra teaches the skill of how to utilize our deluded thoughts effectively as part of the generation of the meditative state.

Introducing the Nature of the Mind in a State of Movement

The Mahamudra scriptures provide a useful analogy for recognizing the nature of the mind by comparing the way the mind operates to the function of our eyes. Our eyes are equipped with the faculty of perceiving everything present in their visual field, but they are not able to perceive themselves. Likewise, our ordinary, untrained mind perceives everything that is internal and external to itself but remains completely unaware of itself. With the meditation practices that follow, it is possible to develop the capacity to realize the self-illuminating, translucent, perspicacious nature of our own mind through the development of self-cognizing awareness.

With diligent practice of these analyses, you will soon come to recognize that everything you experience is simply the play of the mind. Any difference you see in terms of your experiences is purely a fabrication of your eminently imaginative mind. As such, these discursive thoughts should not be regarded as insurmountable obstacles to meditation. In reality, as we become better acquainted with them, we will be able to perceive the thoughts themselves as expressions of our true nature, which will then allow us to feel less at the mercy of the flurry of mental activities generated by thoughts and emotions. Far from concealing or obscuring the nature of the mind, these thoughts will actually reveal that nature. As Gyalwa Gotsangpa stated: "When a thought arises in the mind, do not view it as a bad thing. If you recognize that the nature of thoughts is emptiness, the thought is realized as the authentic state itself." The following five exercises are traditionally employed to introduce the meditator to the nature of the mind while it is in a state of movement.

MEDITATION 1
Using Mental Images

Begin by contemplating the four preliminaries and four immeasurables and then practicing tranquillity meditation. Try to rest your mind with the help of breathing techniques, if necessary. From that state of tranquillity, give rise to a mental image while keeping your eyes closed, and focus your mind on that object. Although you may imagine any object you wish, from an inanimate object such as a building to an animate object such as a human being, it might be best to think of something that does not arouse strong emotions or generate agitation—perhaps something like an old, nondescript building or a landscape. When you have successfully established this image in your mind, try to ascertain the difference between the previous state of tranquillity and the mind that is now engaged with the image that is present—either vividly or vaguely—in your mind's eye.

Try to discover whether there is in fact any difference between these three things: the mental image, the aspect of the mind that produced the mental image, and the aspect of the mind that has become aware of the mental image. While inquiring into the difference between these things, be quite clear that you are looking to determine the *nature* of these experiences. There will be an obvious difference between them in that in one instance the mind is tranquil and in the other the mind is engaged in focusing on a mental image. However, the real question is whether there is any difference in the *nature* of the mind that is engaged in focusing on a mental object and the *nature* of the mind that is not so engaged and merely rests in tranquillity. Practice this exercise repeatedly until you genuinely reach the conclusion that there is actually no difference between the tranquil state of mind and the nontranquil state of mind. As Tilopa stated in one of his dohas (spiritual songs):

> Like mist and clouds that arise in the sky
> Without proceeding toward any destination or settling anywhere,
> The discursive thoughts that arise in the mind
> Flow like waves through the realized state.

MEDITATION 2
Using Opposing Emotional States

This time the object of focus is the emotions, and here you analyze opposing emotions. The previous exercise related to the discursive thoughts, while this one employs the conflicting emotions as the tool of meditation. This is a radical idea, for meditation is usually about ridding ourselves of the conflicting emotions. In fact, the very notion that these emotions can be put to use in meditation is likely to perplex people who see meditation simply as a method to settle the mind or transport them to a transcendental realm. In the Mahamudra tradition, however, utilizing the conflicting emotions rather than employing methods to dispose of them is an indispensable part of the practice. It is crucial, therefore, not to separate the discursive thoughts from the cognitive and affective aspects of the mind. Our thoughts and emotions are inextricably linked and very hard to separate in the normal course of life. Just thinking about someone or something will invariably arouse emotions. When external situations elicit strong emotional reactions in us in normal daily life, we do not have the sensibility to notice them, and our ability to deal effectively with them is disempowered. In this meditation exercise we are creating an artificial environment, where we visualize situations that have the potential to evoke strong emotions. That gives us the luxury of dealing with these strong emotions without falling under the influence of our habitual patterns.

Begin by contemplating the four preliminaries and the four

immeasurables and engaging in tranquillity meditation as before. Then think of somebody you love, somebody the mere thought of whom evokes joy, and hold this image in your mind. Try to kindle the love and joy that you feel in all of its richness, to the greatest possible extent. After some time, think about the quintessential opposite of that in your affections: someone you despise and scorn intensely. Try to intensify this feeling to the same degree as the love and joy. Then go back to looking at the mind responsible for producing these two radically different mental states, the mind that is stirred up by two opposing emotional responses. When you have managed that, ask yourself: What is the difference between the mind that is loving and the mind that has the capacity to hate? Then ask: Is there any difference at all between these two mental states from the point of view of the mind itself?

Conclude this exercise by looking at the mind that was tranquil at the beginning of the session and the emotions that were experienced subsequently. Although we have two radically different mental states here, one brimming with love and tenderness and the other with a noxious feeling of hate, in reality it is the same mind that is the author and architect. Ordinarily, we hardly ever think about how our mind alters reality; instead we think about how so-called reality affects us. It is always the object of beauty or the object of hatred that is responsible for eliciting whatever emotion we experience. Through exercises of this kind, we will come to recognize how often this assumption is not true. It is the same mind that responds to things in one way in a certain instance and in another way in another instance. The point of these exercises is to try to develop a friendlier attitude toward ourselves and toward our negative emotions, as the following parable suggests.

———

A man went to see a psychiatrist because every night he was visited by a twelve-foot dragon with three heads. He told the psychiatrist that he was a nervous wreck—he could not sleep, was on the verge of total collapse, and had even thought of suicide. The psychiatrist said, "I think

I can help you, but I have to warn you that it will not be cheap or quick to find a cure. It will probably take around two years and cost you three thousand dollars." The man was completely stunned and replied, "Oh, forget it! I'll just go home and try to make friends with it!"

MEDITATION 3
Using Disturbing Thoughts

This is a most unusual meditation exercise, one that requires you to produce a proliferation of thoughts, including good thoughts, bad thoughts, and neutral thoughts. Begin as before by contemplating the four preliminaries and four immeasurables and remaining in the state of tranquillity for a time. Then begin the practice of insight meditation and give rise to as many thoughts as possible and try to scatter the mind in all directions. Then try to determine the difference between the calmness of the stable mind of the meditative state and the mind that is now scattered and highly active. Analyze whether there is any real difference between the agitated state of mind brought on by discursive thoughts, which we find extremely hard to deal with in meditation, and the tranquil state of mind you experienced before you began the exercise. Gradually you will come to realize that whether it is discursive thoughts or tranquillity that is present in your mind, the nature of the mind remains unchanged and impervious to changing mental states. Through "Mahamudra without acceptance and rejection" we can develop a higher perspective that directly recognizes how we continuously manipulate and distort reality with our biased concepts and judgements. Gampopa made this statement in relation to disturbing thoughts:

"Many of the problems in meditation are created by thinking that thoughts are harmful and detrimental to meditation and thus need to be abandoned. Many meditators have strayed by thinking that they have to overcome their disturbing thoughts and, because it is virtually impossible to uproot discursive thoughts, they thereby cause enormous hardships for themselves."

MEDITATION 4
Using the Five Poisons

This exercise is even more unusual than the previous ones. Meditators always seem to complain about how much thinking they do in meditation. In my experience, both new and seasoned meditators complain about how difficult it is to subdue their thoughts in meditation and how this proliferation of thoughts destroys their concentration and robs them of the ability to be mindful. From the Mahamudra perspective, this is not a healthy attitude to take toward meditation practice, for we should not think of discursive thoughts as the enemy. In this exercise, we do the opposite—we try to think as much as we want, about anything that we can, without suppressing anything.

Begin this exercise with the usual preliminaries, immeasurables, and tranquillity meditation. In this exercise, you will utilize the so-called five poisons, or the five conflicting emotions—desire, pride, jealousy, ignorance/indifference, and hatred—as part of insight meditation. As a classic saying of the Kagyu oral tradition expounds:

> Transcending awareness and emotion
> May be merged evenly.
> The former consists of the five buddhas
> And the five transcending awarenesses.[3]

Visualize someone for whom you feel strong attraction and sexual desire and intensify this feeling of lust to a great degree. Then simply look into that experience of lust. Follow this by visualizing a person you find repulsive and who has all the attributes of a disagreeable person, and then intensify this revulsion to a similar point. Then look into that experience. Do the same with the other conflicting emotions of pride, jealousy, ignorance/indifference, and hatred. Maitripa alludes to the usefulness of emotions in these lines:

> You need manure to grow vegetation,
> Lotus flowers blossom in the mud.
> If you abandon your conflicting emotions,
> You will never attain wisdom.

This exercise allows you to refrain from judging whatever conflicting emotions surge in your mind and threaten to disrupt it. If you simply become aware of them, they become self-liberated, without the need to take steps to renounce anything. This notion of self-liberation is the key to the insight meditation of the Mahamudra tradition.

MEDITATION 5
Recognizing That the Mind Is the Creator of All Experiences

Begin as before with the preliminaries, immeasurables, and tranquillity meditation. In this exercise you will contemplate the different kinds of thoughts and emotions, such as pleasure and pain, happiness and unhappiness, friends who give you joy and enemies who for whatever reason cause you distress, and so forth. Ask yourself: "Who is responsible for all these thoughts and emotions? Was it God who produced them? If it was God, what kind of being is it that afflicts pain on us or rewards us with health, wealth, and happiness?"

If you continue to question in this way, you will come to suspect that all these things are created by your own mind. As Saraha says in one of his songs:

> Mind is the creator of all things.
> Within mind are reflected both the delusions of samsara and the
> enlightenment of nirvana.

———

I would like to assure you that all these exercises, including this one using God, are based on standard, authoritative manuals on Mahamudra meditation in the Kagyu tradition. This is the traditional way of examining the mind. Mind (not God or a supreme being) is the designer—or perhaps the author—of the whole gamut of human experience, at both the internal and external levels. It is responsible for everything we experience in our world: for our bondage in the state of ignorance and our freedom and liberation in the state of enlightenment. It is solely our mind that determines these things; no one and nothing else has the power to determine our ultimate fate in this way. As a tantric text known as *Vajrapanjara* states:

> *Since the beginningless state of existence,*
> *External reality has been perceived as such.*
> *But all things are the manifestations of the mind,*
> *Because everything is the projection of the mind.*[4]

The measure of success in all of these Mahamudra exercises is *not* the extent to which discursive thoughts or conflicting emotions arise in our minds but whether we have been able to use these discursive thoughts and conflicting emotions as part of our insight meditation. As I have reiterated throughout these chapters, Mahamudra meditation does not teach us to discard or transform our discursive thoughts and conflicting emotions and undesirable feelings; it shows us a simple and direct way to self-liberate them. Put another way, they will simply subside by themselves if they are not interfered with. As such, the notion of abandonment and the utilization of antidotes so predominant in most methods of spiritual cultivation are not necessary in this context at all. Insight in Mahamudra practice is above all about seeing into the nature of our mind, which includes the nature of the discursive thoughts and conflicting emotions.

For these reasons, the Mahamudra cycle of teachings instructs us in no uncertain terms that there is no need to abandon discursive thoughts and conflicting emotions. The confusion and perplexity that assails us does not come from the disturbing thoughts themselves, as we are so prone to assume, but from the fact that we do not have any insight into their empty and luminous nature.

Introducing the Nature of the Mind through Sensory Impressions

The notion of union or duality is of paramount importance in Mahamudra literature, which is replete with this concept: the union of bliss and emptiness, the union of luminosity and emptiness, the union of the phenomenal world and emptiness, and so on. In the following exercise, we are trying to realize the union of phenomena and the mind.

In our normal perception of the physical world and our own subjective experience as human beings, we think of the physical and mental domains as separate and independent realities. As we pay more and more attention to what we perceive through our sense organs and sense consciousnesses, we realize that the things we perceive do not have a completely independent existence in their own right. *What* we perceive through our senses is contingent on *how* those things are perceived with the sensory apparatuses that we are endowed with. The initial raw sensory data is sorted and processed through different stages of cognitive assimilation.

According to Buddhism, even seeing a tree is not just a case of simple perception. To see a tree as a tree requires that we already know, for example, that it is not a rock, that it is not made of water, and that it can catch fire. There already exists a large store of information that we draw from and conceptual pre-understanding in relation to our simple perception of a tree. This being so, we can understand that there is no material world out there that exists independently of the human mind. It is the human mind that perceives the world as we do and that gives it the shape and form that we collectively agree to.

MEDITATION 1
Recognizing That the Mind and the Sense Impressions of Phenomena Are Intertwined

As with the other exercises, this practice begins by contemplating the four preliminaries and immeasurables for a brief period, quickly followed by tranquillity meditation. From the state of tranquillity, focus your eyes on a particular object and see if there is any separation between these three things: the mind that is aware and conscious, the mind that cognizes the sense impressions of an object, and the object itself. The basic point of this exercise is to become acquainted with how we actually perceive things through the senses. When we become more observant, we will be more acquainted with how the process of sense experience unfolds, thereby revealing its true nature, which is the same as ultimate reality.

Settle your attention on a visual or auditory object and simply focus on the act of seeing or hearing, without analyzing the object. Then do the same phenomenological exercise with all the other senses and sense objects as well. If you persist with this simple exercise in sensory observation, you will see that physical objects are not as separate as you may have thought from the sense impressions and your mental awareness of them.

MEDITATION 2
Recognizing the Inseparability of Body and Consciousness

Now do a similar exercise with regard to the body and consciousness. After contemplating the preliminaries and immeasurables and settling the mind in tranquillity, observe the body and the mind and be attentive to their relationship. Pay attention to your bodily sensations—pleasant or unpleasant, comfortable or uncomfortable, relaxed or nervous, energized or exhausted—and try to determine how they are experienced from a purely phenomenological point of view. While observing the bodily sensations, try to look at *what* is experiencing all these sensations. Ask yourself: "Are they experienced by consciousness through the body, or is it the body that experiences these things and the consciousness that recognizes the experience?" The purpose of this practice is to understand that our normal dualistic way of perceiving the body/mind complex is gravely mistaken. In pure experience, there is no separation between the body and mind. Here too, no precise boundary can be drawn to show where purely physical sensation begins or ends and where the mental apprehension and conceptual understandings of them begin or end.

———

These exercises will help us to form a deeper and much-needed understanding that we experience everything through the terms and conditions set by the mind. There is no way for us to step outside our mental awareness to observe our mind from a detached distance and see the relationship between the mind and nonmental things in a neutral fashion. Through these insight meditation exercises, we will conclude in time that even our experiences of nonmental things are dictated by the structures of the mind itself.

Realizing That the Nature
of the Mind Is Emptiness

As stated earlier, the mind has three aspects: its essence is emptiness, its nature is luminosity, and its characteristic is unceasing mental activity with varied forms of thought and emotion. Gaining insight into and developing understanding of the nature of the mind in relation to all three of these aspects is vital. First, though, we have to appreciate the fact that the mind is not a mental substance. Quite the contrary, the nature of the mind must be understood as empty. Even though mind sees shapes, colors, and so forth, it is itself devoid of any such characteristics. Therefore, mind itself is not a thing in itself, because it has no tangible shape, form, or color.

MEDITATION 1
Realizing That the Mind Is Not
Something That Can Be Found

Begin with the preliminaries, immeasurables, and tranquillity meditation. In the state of tranquillity, give rise to the thought of a mental image and try to determine whether in reality it has any shape, color, and so forth. Then ask yourself these questions: "Where is this thought occurring? When this thought arises, where does it come from, where does it dwell, and where does it dissipate to?" This can be expanded upon, as, for instance, when thoughts arise during meditation, we always complain that our mind is disturbed by them. Instead of reacting like this, ask yourself: "Where is that thought that is so disturbing?" Whenever you have a thought about this or that, simply try to locate it. You will soon discover that the more you try to seize or pinpoint a thought, the harder it becomes to find. The experience of not actually being able to find or locate thoughts is the main purpose of this exercise. It shows us in a direct, personal way something of the character of the mind.

MEDITATION 2
Recognizing That Failure to Understand the Nature of the Mind Is the Root of All Delusions

After practicing the four preliminaries, four immeasurables, and tranquillity meditation for a brief period, engage in the following mental exercises. In the state of tranquillity, first investigate your conceptual mind by asking: "Am I my thoughts?" Then examine your thoughts by asking yourself: "Am I my aspirations, my memory, my dreams? Am I the conscious mental events and states that I am aware of, or am I the subconscious mental events and states that go on beyond my awareness?"

Move on to your emotional states and ask: "Am I my emotions and feelings?" Make further inquiries: "Am I the one who has positive feelings and emotions, or am I the one who has negative feelings and emotions? Which one is the real me?" Go back and forth between the person who has positive feelings and emotions and the person who has negative feelings and emotions and ask yourself: "Which one is me? Am I the same person in both aspects, or am I less real in one aspect and more real in the other?" When examining your thoughts, feelings, and emotions, ask yourself this question: "Is it the same me who is having positive and negative thoughts, feelings, and emotions, or is one aspect of myself more real than the other? Does either of them reveal the true me?"

Next, think of all your physical components and ask: "Am I my body?" Investigate yourself in terms of your body by asking yourself: "Am I my body, or am I only a part of my body, such as the heart or brain? Am I the same as my brain, or am I the same as my whole body? If part of my body were chopped off, would I still be me? If I had a heart transplant, lung transplant, and all kinds of implants, at what point would I cease to be myself? If I no longer had my original heart, lungs, and liver, would I still be me?" Although the idea of a brain transplant is far-fetched, ask: "If I had a brain transplant, would I still be me, or would I be the brain that I inherited?"

Continue to perform these exercises in a systematic fashion in order to repudiate the root cause of your delusions, which is the fixation on a concept of an unchanging self or ego. This so-called self at the center of this fixation is not so easily found, however. Realizing this is the point of the exercise. We take our "self" extremely seriously. We are very protective, defensive, and even aggressive about affairs that concern our own well-being, but this self is a rather elusive entity. Through asking, "Where is this self? What is this self?" in a deep and probing fashion, you will gradually understand the nature of this self in a very personal way.

Through these exercises, you will come to discern that neither the mind nor the concept of the self can be regarded as an entity with any kind of enduring existence. When you realize that the essence of the mind is empty and devoid of any enduring quality or empirical characteristics, you have penetrated the nature of the mind itself. From developing this understanding of the mind, you will develop the further understanding that even the nature of physical things is empty of enduring essence.

Establishing Emptiness as Spontaneously Arisen

The emphasis in this practice is the characteristic of the mind. After you have recognized that the nature of the mind is emptiness, you need to counterbalance that realization by becoming acquainted with the mind's characteristic—the unceasing display of our thoughts and emotions. Although the nature of the mind is empty, this does not mean that there are no thoughts and emotions in the mind or that these thoughts and emotions are completely unreal. Thoughts and emotions continually manifest as the dynamic energy of the nature of the mind.

In Buddhism generally, and in Mahamudra in particular, the mind is not viewed as a passive receptacle that simply stores information relayed to it through our senses. On the contrary, mind is seen as an active, creative force that invents its own reality. This creative energy of the mind also arises from the nature of the mind, which is emptiness. The emptiness of the mind and the creative play of thoughts and emotions are not only inseparable, they also have the same nature.

MEDITATION 1
The Conjunction of Mind, Sensory Organ, and Sensory Object

This contemplation can be practiced in either formal meditation or postmeditation situations. In formal meditation, begin with the four preliminaries, the four immeasurables, and tranquillity meditation, then focus your attention on a sensory object—a visual or auditory object is preferable—and simply pay attention to what has spontaneously presented itself. Do not attend to it in a detailed fashion or force yourself in any way; just gently rest your attention on that object. The instruction is simply to focus your mind on whatever sight or sound has naturally arrested your attention and just hold your attention on it.

Whatever the object of attention at hand, whether it is an unwashed plate, patterns on the carpet, or a sound, do not judge whether it is beautiful or repulsive. Do not try to catalog the details of its appearance or type—for example, that a certain song is performed by so-and-so in such-and-such a style; just pay attention to what is there. This is known as the conjunction of mind, sensory organ, and sensory object. The point of this exercise is to try to combine the three without any elaboration from your conceptual mind. When you perceive sense objects in this way, you do not experience your senses arising from causes and conditions but as spontaneously arisen. Nor do they present themselves as things with any independent substance or existence. They are simply there spontaneously, which is why this exercise is based on the union of mind, the spontaneously arisen sense consciousnesses, and spontaneously arisen appearance.

MEDITATION 2
The Nonduality of Mental States and Appearance

After engaging in the preliminaries, immeasurables, and tranquillity meditation, allow your awareness to settle on any mental state—a thought, emotion, or feeling—and simply hold your attention on it without any kind of judgment or evaluation.

Whether the thought, emotion, or feeling that arises is a good or a bad one is not relevant. Just try to be with whatever appears in the mind.

If you pay attention in this way, you will see that when a thought occurs, it occurs spontaneously; you do not perceive the causes and conditions of that thought. If you pay attention to emotions, you will see that they too arise spontaneously; you do not perceive their preceding causes and conditions. If you pay attention to feelings, the same apparent lack of preceding causes and conditions is discernible. In fact, anything that is apprehended with our mind's eye is always spontaneously arisen and never presents itself as having enduring essence or independent existence, or any other conceptual overlay subsequently applied to our sense experiences. While essential for our ability to function appropriately in everyday life, these conceptual overlays are a hindrance to meditation.

———

The term *spontaneously arisen* is used to orient us to the way we should view our mental activities and our experiences of the phenomenal world. Instead of thinking about our mental activities as a product only of causes and conditions, we should think of them as manifestations of the creative energy of the mind. Even though the notion of causality is crucial to Buddhist teachings, Buddhism only accepts this on the conventional level, not the ultimate one. As an analogy, consider the way clouds form in space. We understand conceptually that they have gathered through the process of moisture dissipating into the air as a result of rising ocean temperatures. Our immediate experience of these clouds does not include an actual perception of such events, however; the clouds simply appear to have arisen suddenly. In the same way, mental events also appear to have arisen spontaneously in our immediate experience.

There is nothing substantial in our mental states or in the appearances apprehended by our senses, yet they appear. This is known as the nonduality of mental states and appearance, which spontaneously arises from the conjunction of our mind, senses, and phenomenal appearances. The way phenomena manifest is traditionally compared to clouds in the sky or to a rainbow. While rainbows make a visible appearance, they do not appear as if they were something substantial or a product of causes and conditions. They appear spontaneously and then just as suddenly vanish again. In just the same way, our sensory impressions and inner mental states appear and vanish spontaneously. This is known in the vocabulary of the Mahamudra tradition as the play of the mind.

Realizing That Spontaneously Arisen Emptiness Is Self-Liberation

From beginningless time, there has been an objective material world and a subjective consciousness. From beginningless time also, the nature of both has been engulfed in the reality of emptiness. These three have always coexisted in harmony, and this harmonious coexistence is a spontaneously established fact. Another way of expressing this is to say that everything exists in a state of equality because everything is imbued with the same reality of emptiness. This truth demonstrates that there is nothing that needs to be discarded or abandoned and nothing that needs to be cultivated or added onto. Everything exists in perfection in the reality that is emptiness.

All negativities become self-liberated, because if we remain in the state of equanimity in emptiness, we will not swing back and forth between hope and fear. There is no fear of being corrupted by emotional conflict (thus leading to harm), nor any hope of attaining liberation from that harm. Contemplating things in this way, we will gain insight into the primordial purity of all that we experience, both in relation to the mind and in relation to the external world. This is the essence of insight in the Mahamudra tradition. It is not sufficient to have fleeting glimpses of the nature of the mind, or some understanding of the union of emptiness and awareness or the union of emptiness and the phenomenal world. We have to have an adequate understanding of the harmonious coexistence of all three. This must become direct experience, because only a direct, unmediated experience of nondual emptiness goes beyond verbalization of that reality. Remaining in this nondifferentiated, authentic state that defies conceptual comprehension is how we realize our true nature. The correct gnosis of insight meditation is attained only then, through realizing what the Mahamudra texts call unbiased wisdom. This wisdom is said to be unbiased because of its nondualistic nature, which is empty in the same way that space is open and unobstructed.

MEDITATION
Self-Liberation of Spontaneously Arisen Mental Appearances

After again engaging in the preliminaries, immeasurables, and tranquillity meditation, pay attention to your thoughts, emotions, and feelings and watch them as they arise, persist, and dissolve in the mind. When myriad thoughts, feelings, and emotions arise, pay attention to where they have come from. When they persist, try to establish where they are. After they dissolve, pay attention to the fact that mental clarity is present in the mind even when no thoughts, feelings, or emotions are to be found. It is very important to notice this mental sharpness, for this is the luminous aspect of the mind.

Do not be concerned if this recognition lasts for only a split second, because the real point of the exercise is to actually have some kind of recognition of the occurrence but not its duration. This is the experience of self-liberation; all discursive thoughts and conflicting emotions have become self-liberated into the natural state of awareness and emptiness. You should not attempt to contrive, improve, or manufacture a higher state of mind, because this self-liberation of your ordinary empirical experiences will self-liberate into mental clarity when awareness is maintained.

The main point of these meditative exercises is that after the distorted thoughts, misguided feelings, and turbulent emotions dissolve, you recognize the mental acuity and alertness that arises from the nature of the mind itself. It is not a state of mental blankness that is indistinct and vague, or a withdrawal into dark subterranean levels of absorption that remain separated from our true condition. If you really notice and understand this with a degree of authenticity and certainty, that recognition constitutes the self-liberation of the spontaneously arisen mental appearances. They are liberated by an awareness that does not entertain any thoughts of hope and fear nor of any fixation in relation to what is being experienced. As a result, whatever arises in the mind will no longer leave any karmic imprints or reinforce negative habits of mind and action. In the vocabulary of the Mahamudra tradition, this is known as the inseparability of luminosity and emptiness.

MEDITATIVE EXPERIENCE AND REALIZATION

As you progress with your practice of insight meditation, certain meditative experiences and realizations are bound to arise. Both the experiences and realizations correspond to various levels of attainment, but they should not be treated as indications of the same kind of meditative acuity or progress. There is a significant difference between meditative experiences and realizations, as we have discussed. Most meditative experiences are still contaminated by conceptualization to some degree, while meditative realizations are not. Meditative experiences are also unstable and impermanent by nature, while meditative realizations are not. Meditative experiences without realizations are incapable of revealing the true wisdom of insight meditation, because the experiences fail to show the essential unity of the experiencer and the experiences themselves. When you realize that there is no distinction between the meditator and the act of meditation, and that ultimately everything is a fabrication of the mind, meditation realization has occurred. The main cause of misperceptions regarding meditation experience is that, after the loss of the initial fervor, we may forget to focus on the essence of meditation and its purpose and instead place more and more emphasis on the underlying meditative experience itself.

All types of positive meditative experiences can be subsumed under three different types of occurrence: bliss, clarity, and mental spaciousness. These meditative experiences will still be contaminated by the conflicting emotions and conceptual distortions at the beginning of insight meditation. Gradually, however, we begin to have an experience of physical and mental well-being, which is less perverted by delusions and unsavory mental states. We can eventually reach the point where we experience a sense of well-being regardless of what is happening to our body or our mind. We will even cease to be afflicted by emotional conflicts resulting from events experienced in the external world, because our mind will be able to remain open, resilient, and clear, whatever the condition, handsome and unhandsome, in the words of Stanley Cavell.[5]

Bliss

It is not uncommon for the meditator to have some fluctuating and strange experiences in relation to the experience of bliss. You may start to think you have attained a high level of spiritual realization and are completely free of conflicting emotions, giving rise to an unreasonable level of magnificence and magnanimity—you may be catapulted into great heights of rapture. Conversely, much to your surprise and chagrin, you may just as likely experience a state of extreme excitement, where your emotional conflicts, conflicting emotions, and agitations seem to have increased. You may also experience a lethargic lack of interest in meditation at certain times and have a compulsion to dance and sing or shout at others. At other times you may sincerely despair that the two obstacles of agitation and stupor have manifoldly increased. However, all the waxing and waning occurrences are various aspects of the same experience, which is commonly known as the experience of bliss.

Clarity

Your sense perceptions will become more acute as part of the meditative experience of clarity. You may occasionally experience the hallucination that things are surrounded by a halo of light—seeing small circles of light bouncing off objects, or objects covered with rainbow colors. Even with your eyes closed, you may still be able to picture things very sharply. The same acuteness of perception applies to all the other senses as well, while your mind remains extremely lucid and awake. You will be less likely to suffer from mental fatigue or stupor and so on. As a result of all this, an enormous confidence will develop in your ability to grasp and understand things.

Mental Spaciousness

In this meditative experience, one has developed the ability to rest the mind in whatever condition it is in. At this level, gross and confusing conceptual activities have subsided and you will gradually learn to deal with the more subtle forms of conceptual formation, which have so far eluded detection. If you refrain from evaluating or judging these experiences, genuine realization can and will occur. As a result of that realization—which by nature is stable and transformative—you will realize the three kayas (three aspects of Buddha's being) within the mind itself. The unceasing activity of the mind is transformed into the *nirmanakaya*; mental clarity manifests as the *sambhogakaya*; and the mind being empty of essence is revealed as the *dharmakaya*. The nature of the mind is primordially pure. When you realize this, you realize the complete purity of the dharmakaya.

OBSTACLES TO INSIGHT MEDITATION

As the aim of these practices is to engage in analysis rather than simply to stabilize the mind and remain in a state of contemplation, the danger of being swept away by discursive thoughts is greater. Mahamudra literature describes the following kinds of obstacles that can occur in insight meditation.

The Five Wrong Views

Apart from engaging in the insight meditation exercises themselves, it is important as an adjunct to strengthen our practice by abandoning wrong views. The five wrong views explained below should be understood purely from a Mahamudra point of view. It is important to meditate on each wrong view at various points in your practice and to try to gain a proper appreciation of each one.

THE WRONG VIEW OF VIRTUE AND VICE

This wrong view entails regarding the three poisons (excessive desire, aversion, and ignorance) as something that you should abandon and the virtuous qualities (generosity, patience, and so forth) as something that you should cultivate. Approaching things this way will only lead to the development of aversion toward the so-called poisons and attachment to the so-called sublime qualities of virtue. From the Mahamudra point of view, this will simply reinforce the mind's inveterate tendency to discriminate dualistically. That is why the Mahamudra teachings encourage us to employ the three poisons as an integral aspect of the path. The Mahamudra view is that, ultimately speaking, the poisons and the qualities of wisdom have the same nature, which is emptiness. Therefore, your mind should not be disturbed by thoughts of things you must renounce and things you must develop, because thinking in this manner is a subtle form of mental agitation.

THE WRONG VIEW OF THE NOTION OF TIME

You should never project your spiritual goals into the distant future, thinking, "If I do this or that practice, I may be able to become enlightened later on in life." From the Mahamudra point of view, the past, present, and future are understood as united in the same reality. As such, you must remain fully in the present, instead of regarding the past, present, and future as discontinuous. As they form a complete whole in reality, we should always think of realizing Mahamudra in the present moment of now.

THE WRONG VIEW OF ORDINARY CONSCIOUSNESS AND WISDOM CONSCIOUSNESS

In many religious systems, including some Buddhist schools of thought, it is said that ordinary consciousness is deluded and thus incapable of leading to spiritual realization. From this perspective, our spiritual goal can be attained only by gradually transcending this ordinary state of consciousness and making use of a transcendental state of consciousness in its place. The Mahamudra viewpoint, however, does not support this duality of an empirical consciousness on the one hand that is deluded and in need of abandonment, and a transcendental consciousness on the other hand that is pure and uncorrupted and, when cultivated, brings the promise of enlightenment. Instead, deluded consciousness and undeluded consciousness are said to have the same nature. In chapter 4, when we spoke of the deluded and undeluded states of mind, we were discussing our *experience* of these aspects of mind, which must be understood from the relative point of view. Here we are talking about how the mind exists in reality, not how we experience it. We need to acknowledge that we have a long way to go before we can experience the level of nonduality discussed here in relation to Mahamudra realization. Even so, it is important to understand, at least on a conceptual level, that our ordinary consciousness and the extraordinary consciousness of an enlightened being are one and the same mind from the ultimate point of view for having the same nature. We should not speak of ordinary and transcendental forms of consciousness but instead realize that it is one and the same consciousness that is both deluded and capable of becoming awakened.

The mind by nature is cognizant of things, empty of inherent existence or enduring essence, and yet still in a dynamic process. As such, it encompasses both the demeaning state of samsara and the edifying state of nirvana. Realizing the nature of this mind, we will become completely free, capable of things well beyond what we were able to do in the past. In this way, the deluded and undeluded consciousnesses, or the empirical and transcendental consciousnesses, should be recognized as having the same nature.

THE WRONG VIEW OF HUMAN NATURE

This wrong view refers to the perception that the nature of human beings and the nature of enlightened beings is somehow different. Human beings have both the capacity and the potential to become enlightened. The condition of human beings is likened to that of a poor family living in a dilapidated house with a lump of gold beneath its foundations, who have no inkling of the wealth that lies below. Such people will assume they must toil to make a living and be thoroughly dependent on others, all because they have not been able to access the wealth already there. In the same way, all the qualities of enlightenment are already present in every one of us. However, these qualities will only remain a potential until we look inside and actualize that potential.

THE WRONG VIEW OF INSIGHT

This wrong view involves thinking that insight comes purely from learning, rather than from discovering something within our own lived experience. Many people mistakenly assume that the more they sharpen their intellect, the more they will understand spiritual matters. While learning is an integral part of the spiritual path, insight will never be gained from learning alone. Wangchuk Dorje is very emphatic on the incompleteness of rational understanding of spiritual matters in his *Ocean of Certainty*. It would be wrong to become overly dependent on your reasoning skills, level of learning, or even whether you are of dull or sharp intellect. Nor should you be held back due to traumatic and upsetting experiences, or think you will succeed only if you are especially diligent. Insight will not necessarily arise through any of these means. Insight arises from practice, from the right frame of mind, and from receiving proper instructions. Unless the mind has been trained and made supple and workable through the practice of tranquillity and insight meditation, no amount of activity or learning will lead to a direct insight into the nature of the mind.

The Three Sidetracks

One of the many challenges that we face on the Mahamudra path of insight meditation are the sidetracks that can occur when we try to deepen and refine our understanding of emptiness. Three major digressions are elucidated in the Mahamudra meditation texts. You should contemplate these three and avoid falling victim to them in your meditation practice.

MISUNDERSTANDING EMPTINESS TO MEAN THAT NOTHING MATTERS

When contemplating the nature of emptiness, you may be led to think: "It essentially does not matter what I do, because, after all, everything is empty." You may begin to believe that doing something harmful is not essentially harmful, because from the ultimate point of view nothing has any substantiality. You may further assume that because everything is merely an expression of emptiness, it is unnecessary to practice any kind of restraint in your actions and behavior, thereby becoming indifferent to the karmic consequences of your actions. This is a dangerous departure from a proper understanding of emptiness. It is important to realize that emptiness does not imply a complete absence of significance in anything that we think or do, or that there is no reality whatsoever to the concepts of what is acceptable or unacceptable, appropriate or inappropriate, and so on. Therefore one must do one's best not to fall into apathetic nihilism or cynical smugness. Emptiness simply means that nothing has any enduring essence, which is not the same as saying you should no longer discriminate between what is beneficial and what is harmful in the context of your private actions and public interactions.

MISUSING EMPTINESS AS AN OBJECT OF MEDITATION

Many meditators think that contemplating emptiness in meditation will purify their karmic accumulations. Others use reasoning to improve their understanding of emptiness. There are, in fact, many methods prescribed in Buddhist texts for employing reasoning to bring about a conceptual understanding of emptiness. In Tantra, there are also mantras of emptiness uttered at the beginning of visualization practice, where one imagines emptiness and then a deity arising from that emptiness. From the Mahamudra point of view, while these methods are eminently beneficial within their respective contexts, they should not be allowed to become diversions from the practice of insight meditation. These methods cannot lead to a direct realization of emptiness, because they all rely on emptiness as the object of contemplation. In Mahamudra, emptiness cannot be seen as the object of meditation as such, because relating to it in this way can bring only a conceptual understanding of ultimate reality. Emptiness is something that has to be experienced directly, because it is beyond the duality of perceiver and perceived.

MISUSING EMPTINESS AS AN ANTIDOTE FOR DISTURBING THOUGHTS

Some meditators become frightened and anxious when afflicted with disturbing thoughts and conflicting emotions in meditation, because they think such events will subvert the possibility of attaining liberation. Often they will employ meditation on emptiness as an antidote to remove their disturbing thoughts and emotions. By thinking of these thoughts as empty by nature, they hope to make them disappear. In Mahamudra, emptiness is not to be used as an antidote in this way— emptiness is to be regarded as part of the disturbing thoughts and conflicting emotions. As emptiness and the thoughts and emotions are not separate, you should allow whatever experiences you have to arise in the mind. This is how those thoughts and emotions become self-liberated. Trying to suppress or eliminate them through the use of antidotes—such as meditation on emptiness—will only subtly reinforce these thoughts and emotions and will never lead to the ultimate goal of enlightenment. Allowing thoughts and emotions to run their course is not the same as submitting to their insidious powers without mindfulness and awareness.

• • •

In summary, the basic thrust of insight meditation is to allow us to establish a firm grasp of how the mind works in the context of its essence, its nature, and its characteristic. Without this insight into the nature of the mind, we will remain in our deluded state, experiencing only the manifest content of consciousness and remaining totally oblivious of the mind's luminous bliss and essential insubstantiality.

Through not having this insight into the mind's luminous bliss and essentially empty nature, we have become trapped in our distorted ways of thinking, which in turn have given rise to conflicting emotions and have attached all manner of mental fixation to them. By engaging in a detailed series of insight meditation exercises, such as the ones here— we can gain a deeper insight into our own mind. As a result, we can develop an appreciation for, as well as some experience of, the luminous bliss and insubstantiality of the mind. We cannot gain this insight into our mind without engaging in the practice of insight meditation.

People often say that Buddhism does not have a monopoly on meditation practice. This is true to an extent. There is the meditation of prayer, the meditation of concentration, and the meditation of contemplation, and these do cross religious boundaries. Many different techniques applied to these types of meditation are practiced throughout the world's religious traditions. However, none of these traditions has an equivalent to insight meditation as it is presented in the exoteric and esoteric traditions of Buddhism or as it is described in the Mahamudra teachings. From its earliest days in India until now, Buddhists have asserted that insight meditation is a purely Buddhist form of meditation practice. It is this technique alone that has given us the key to attaining liberation from samsara, or the insight into the true nature of our own being that constitutes enlightenment. To assert this is not a form of religious chauvinism, because the fact that many Christians meditate to realize Christ consciousness in increasing numbers will not, or at least should not, be taken as a sign of superiority. In order to practice this Buddhist type of meditation, it is essential to make use of Buddhist concepts, doctrines, and views. Correct views are vital in that they guide our analytic practice and lead us deftly through the obstacles and conceptual confusions that will otherwise limit our capacity to have a direct realization of the nature of the mind.

PART FOUR

FRUITION MAHAMUDRA

10

THE FOUR YOGAS
OF MAHAMUDRA

W<small>E HAVE DISCUSSED SELF–LIBERATION OF DISCURSIVE THOUGHTS</small>
and conflicting emotions as the approach of the Mahamudra cycle of
teachings. It will come as no surprise, then, to learn that, in general, we
need not be overly concerned with the concept of a path or a spiritual
journey in Mahamudra, because Mahamudra *is* the state of reality itself.
As such, it can only be conceived of as unchanging and undifferentiated. Since it is unchanging, we cannot ultimately speak about it in relation to time. It follows that we cannot use the concept of a spiritual
journey, for that involves the notion of progress over time. While this is
undeniably true in the ultimate sense, we still need to understand path
Mahamudra from the point of view of our individual experience
within the context of conventional truth.

Anyone making the effort to experience and apprehend this reality
will go through various edifying stages of spiritual fulfillment and con-
summation. In that sense, each of the four yogas of Mahamudra should
be understood as a spontaneous dawning of spiritual fulfillment. We
need to reconcile the concept of spontaneity and stages here if this is to
be intelligible. They can be reconciled if *spontaneous* is not taken to
mean some kind of instinctive reaction or something newly created
without any casual preconditions whatsoever. The spontaneity alluded

to here arises from our own authentic state: the ground Mahamudra, or nature of the mind. As we have said throughout, that nature is inherently pure and uncorrupted from the very beginning. It is the self-liberation of our discursive thoughts and emotional conflicts that allows us to recognize that authentic state within the very thoughts and emotions themselves. When that occurs, our spiritual goal, the ground Mahamudra, manifests spontaneously. This always takes place in the now, in the present moment.

The ground Mahamudra is present in every moment of experience, and realization dawns from that state. Whether that dawning is a full or partial one depends upon the personal character traits and spiritual potential of the individual practitioner, which is why it is possible to talk about fruition Mahamudra in the graduated sense of the four yogas. They attest to the fact that it is important to try to have a total perspective on our spiritual life, with the past, present, and future brought into some kind of harmony. In the end, however, these yogas are only guidelines for the deepening of our meditative experiences. They do not represent the kind of structured path we need to fixate upon as a linear reality with clearly marked lines of delineation. The four yogas are:

1. The yoga of one-pointedness
2. The yoga of nonconceptuality
3. The yoga of one flavor
4. The yoga of nonmeditation

As we saw in the previous chapter, there is a difference between meditative experiences and meditative realization—the former being temporary by nature, the latter being permanent and capable of transforming our conscious experience. As we progress through the four yogas of spiritual fulfillment, our meditative experiences become more and more refined. This is another way of saying that our meditative experiences gradually become converted to meditative realizations.

Each of the four yogas has a level of meditative experience and meditative realization and we generally cannot progress from one yoga to the next before attaining the appropriate realization for that stage. Many meditators have fallen into the trap of mistaking meditative experiences for realizations, and it is important to be alert to this danger. The great Kagyu master Je Gyare distinguished between intellectual knowledge, meditative experience, and realization in these words:

Intellectual comprehension arises from analysis and examination.
Meditative experiences are the dawning of bliss, clarity, and
nonconceptuality.
Recognizing the mind's abiding nature is realization.

In the yoga of one-pointedness, we may have a very tranquil and lucid experience of meditation, but while that experience remains unstable and difficult to sustain for any real length of time, it relates to meditative experience rather than to realization. It is only when that experience of lucidity arises naturally that it can be regarded as a meditative realization.

The yoga of nonconceptuality relates to our experience of the nature of the mind itself. Here we realize that the nature of the mind is unborn and unoriginated because it is not an entity of any kind. This understanding of the nature of the mind is initially a meditative experience rather than a realization because it is elicited by what we have heard and read. When we are able to directly experience the nature of the mind for ourselves, it becomes a meditative realization.

The yoga of one flavor relates to comprehending that neither the body nor the mind nor the material world has any enduring essence. This comprehension is also initially a meditative experience rather than a realization, because it still retains a subtle duality. A realization at this level arises with the recognition that even though the things of the world are independent and distinguishable from one other, they nonetheless all have the same reality. It is said that when the things in the world are seen as reflections rather than as having some kind of enduring essence, we have attained the meditative realization of this yoga.

Finally, the meditative experience of the yoga of nonmeditation is attained when we can genuinely reflect upon the possibility that the meditation and the meditator are one and the same. This reflection still has an element of duality about it, however, because the mind is actively engaged in seeing itself in this way. Meditative realization is attained only when the mind recognizes that meditation and the meditator are nondual from their own side.

As we go through these different stages, therefore, we should be constantly aware of the changes that occur between experiences and realizations in each yoga. Lama Shang emphasizes the importance of the distinction between meditative experience and realization thus:

If direct realization has not dawned in the meditator,
No matter how fine one's meditative experiences are,
It is like chopping down a tree without cutting the root.
Psychological problems and suffering will only increase later on.
The dawning of realization is the quintessential thing.
It does not dawn through hoping for it,
Nor through skill in analytical reasoning;
It is not perceived through great learning.
It is only realized in those with prior cultivation.

ONE-POINTEDNESS

The yoga of one-pointedness relates directly to our meditative experience of mental lucidity and tranquillity. It arises with the ability to allow our mind to rest in a state of one-pointed concentration, where our mental focus is no longer fragmented and jumping from one thought to the next. As a result of this ability to focus the mind, we experience a sense of well-being and mental clarity and an absence of mental agitation. Like all the yogas, the yoga of one-pointedness is traditionally divided into three stages.

Sustaining Concentration for a Short Time

At the initial stage of the first yoga, we allow the mind to rest of its own accord, naturally and without contrivance, and without trying to condition it to be tranquil. As we gain the ability to maintain this state of one-pointedness, our gross mental agitations begin to subside and we experience bliss (a sense of well-being), mental lucidity, and mental spaciousness (a reduction in mental agitation). At this point, we simply apply mindfulness and awareness during meditation in order to sustain these experiences.

These experiences may manifest after we have been meditating for only a short time, or they may fail to arise at all. We might suffer a lack of confidence at this point, and all kinds of doubts and uncertainties might surface. We are advised to simply keep trying and to develop confidence that our meditative experiences are glimpses of what could be attained through persistent practice. Alternatively, there may be a tendency to want to remain in this state of tranquillity—some people even develop a craving for such pleasant experiences. This is not something we should encourage in ourselves. It is important to simply continue trying to remain in a state of one-pointedness, even when mental agitation arises.

Sustaining Concentration for a Longer Period

As the second stage of the yoga of one-pointedness dawns, meditative experiences will occasionally assert themselves even when we are not meditating. When we are engaged in formal meditation practice, the experiences of bliss, clarity, and mental spaciousness become more extensive because of our greater powers of concentration. From this stage onward, any experiences we have in meditation are reflected in our everyday life. We are generally more relaxed and less inclined to react to things violently, impulsively, and mindlessly. The effects also carry over to our sleep; we will generally be less prone even to harmful dreams.

Spontaneously Developing One-Pointed Concentration

At this level, meditation and postmeditation have become fully integrated, as we are able to maintain the experiences we have during meditation throughout the day. The experience of bliss, clarity, and mental spaciousness becomes an everyday occurrence, and we begin to see their intimate relationship to the nature of reality, or emptiness. This level also signals the realization that all we experience, perceive, and conceptualize has no distinct reality independent of our mind. The mind is the key, because the mind makes everything possible. Real confidence emerges through this insight into the nature of the mind and the reality of things. We know what we are doing, and we begin to feel an aversion for our old way of life and old way of perceiving things. Things we previously regarded as precious and indispensable are recognized as less essential, while things we never had much regard for assume greater importance. The essence of this yoga is characterized as the nonduality of bliss and emptiness. As the famous Kagyu hierarch Je Shang expounded:

> When the one-pointed stage dawns,
> One realizes the intrinsic nature of one's mind
> To be an unceasing stream of clarity and emptiness,

Devoid of any center and circumference,
Like the expanse of space,
Settled in serenity and lucidity.
This is absorptive equipoise
On the first stage of yoga.[1]

NONCONCEPTUALITY

When we are able to maintain the one-pointed state of mental equipoise, without craving it or becoming fixated on it, we transcend the need to deliberately apply mindfulness. Accompanying this ability is the realization that whether our mind is in a state of tranquillity or agitation, both are expressions of the nature of the mind. We simultaneously realize that, as far as their nature is concerned, discursive thoughts do not originate anywhere, do not abide anywhere, and do not cease to exist. In other words, the nature of discursive thought is revealed to be the same as the nature of the mind itself. Our experience of the world is irrevocably altered by this realization, because our mind is free of the limitations previously imposed by our confused and erroneous thinking.

The nature of the mind, which is self-aware and luminous, has become manifest as a result of shedding these various layers of conceptual confusion. This self-cognizing awareness is said to be "nakedly" present because it is freed from conceptual pollutants. We now find the confidence that we are in charge of our own mind and no longer feel susceptible or vulnerable to our impulses, passions, conflicting emotions, and various mental aberrations.

In contrast to the previous yoga, our meditative experiences are no longer fickle and fluctuating. Even if there are fluctuations in the perception of our meditative experiences—seeing some experiences as good, wholesome, and comforting and others as bad, unwholesome, and threatening—we no longer react to them in an extremely emotional way, feeling joy at positive meditative experiences or despair at negative ones. As our minds are now freed of erroneous ways of thinking about self and the world and we no longer see the world as having any enduring essence, thereby standing as the objective other pitted against the subjective self, our conceptual categories about them dissolve by themselves. This gives rise to the realization of the authentic aspect of

Buddha's being, the dharmakaya, which is the same as the nature of the mind. About the dawning of the yoga of nonconceptuality, Je Shang had this to say:

> When the [yoga of nonconceptuality] dawns,
> The meditator will realize the essential nature of mind.
> This is an unceasing awareness of pure simplicity.
> When such a mind is absorbed in dharmakāya,
> Which is free from any view of absolute arising or dissolving,
> Acceptance or abandonment,
> There arises the meditative equipoise
> On the second stage of the [yoga of nonconceptuality].[2]

Ultimate Reality and the Phenomenal World Are Coemergent

This yoga dawns when we realize that the ultimate reality of emptiness and the phenomenal world are coemergent—that the nature of the phenomenal world is itself emptiness. At this point we may still occasionally lapse into old habits and react to things in our usual ways. For example, if someone does something offensive, we become outraged and unforgivingly indignant; if someone does something appealing or endearing, we respond with affection and appreciation. At times we may also still be lured by various sense impressions through the irresistible power of habit, responding to the sight of something beautiful or the sound of something pleasant, or conversely to something ugly and repulsive, instead of maintaining the higher perspective we have developed in our spiritual practice.

The Nature of the Mind Is the Basis of All Experience

This second stage of the yoga of nonconceptuality is a more subtle experience. We still have some clinging to the idea that nothing has enduring essence, that everything is contingent and so on, up to this point. Then we start to realize that the very mind we experience—in Mahamudra terminology, the ordinary mind—is the very basis of all our experiences. It is only now that the discursive thoughts and emotional conflicts are fully and properly seen as lacking enduring essence.

When we are able to do this, we are no longer vulnerable to the effects of our emotions. It is said, however, that even though we now have greater control over our emotional upheavals, we may still have a subtle attachment to the physical world, because we have yet to develop a proper understanding of the relationship between the phenomenal world and emptiness. There will therefore remain some discrepancy between our experiences in meditation and everyday life situations, which means that the insight developed during meditation can still be upset by what we encounter in the everyday world.

Things as They Are

The last stage of this yoga is realized once we have gained a genuine understanding of emptiness. To do this, we first realize how our perception of the external world is conditioned by our mind, and then realize that the mind is also devoid of enduring essence. The mind is more like space than like an entity of any kind. At this point, we truly come to see things as they are—devoid of enduring substance—and the phenomenal world and emptiness are realized as undifferentiable.

On this level, we find we can maintain a state of meditation throughout the day without interruption. However, we still have less control over our mind when sleeping, and subtle forms of mental agitation may arise as a result of not maintaining mental clarity during sleep. It is important to understand the significance of mindfulness and of really maintaining it at this point, because the more we become mindful and aware, the more we notice the last vestiges of the subtle conflicting emotions and conceptual distortions that need to be purified.

The fundamental difference between the yoga of one-pointedness and the yoga of nonconceptuality is that in the former we have not fully understood the implications of the nature of discursive thoughts and conflicting emotions. At the level of the second yoga, we not only realize discursive thoughts and conflicting emotions to be empty of essence, but we also realize that we do not eradicate them from our minds because realizing their true nature is sufficient for liberation to occur. Once the true nature of the conceptual categories is realized, we have understood that the nature of thoughts is the same as the nature of the mind, and the ultimate nature of both is wisdom.

ONE FLAVOR

The yoga of one flavor (or one taste) arises when all dualistic concepts and all opposing things begin to have the same flavor, the flavor of emptiness. Whether we speak of the phenomenal world and emptiness, relative truth and absolute truth, samsara and nirvana, bondage and liberation, or suffering and happiness, they can all exist in relationship because they exist within the realm of emptiness.

The yoga of nonconceptuality arose with the dismantling of erroneous beliefs and conceptual confusions and the resultant understanding and appreciation of emptiness and the reality of things. However, at that level, an adequate understanding of the phenomenal world and how it relates to reality is still absent. At the level of one flavor, we no longer need to concern ourselves with the eradication of conflicting emotions and the cultivation of wisdom, because whatever arises in the mind is now perceived differently. This ability is not the result of manufacturing our perception through techniques of any kind; it is developed spontaneously through practice. No technique could ever bring about this kind of insight. This self-cognizing awareness, which has arisen spontaneously, is able to perceive all things in a state of equanimity. Opposites are no longer perceived to be in conflict but are recognized as being in complementary relationship.

Emptiness and What Is Perceived Are Inseparable

The first stage of the yoga of one flavor is attained when we are able to perceive things directly, so that the things perceived and the ultimate reality of emptiness are experienced as inseparable. The basic point here is that emptiness is not perceived as superior to the phenomenal world, and the phenomenal world is not perceived as subservient to reality. They are perceived as complementary, as having the same nature. There is a distinct sense of unity in this experience of our body-mind (which is the link between ourselves and the phenomenal world) and the phenomenal world itself. It is not a case of us being here and the external world being out there, separate from ourselves. The self, the world, and the mind are experienced as a state of total unity.

At this initial stage of the yoga of one flavor, there is still an element of conceptual understanding involved, for the mind is not yet totally free of conceptual proliferation or defilement, nor are we fully free of the influences that come through our sensory impressions in everyday life. There may be some fluctuation and lack of total sincerity regarding our meditation practice as well. It should be emphasized that we may well encounter certain obstacles at this point, for, having developed an understanding of the complementary nature of dualistic concepts, we may be tempted to think that the efficacy of karma is of no real significance, which could develop into a blithe disregard for the feelings of others. We should be wary of this possibility and take the necessary measures to avoid it, such as doing the mind training practices of *lojong* meditation, or engaging in the practice of the Four Immeasurables. At this point, our realization and our manifestation of that realization may not be immediately evident to others. This is because the subtle conflicting emotions that remain obstruct the full dawning of our enlightened qualities. Je Shang counsels us not to be discouraged at this:

> *Misery may not completely disappear*
> *Immediately upon realizing the truth of nonduality.*
> *Who can deny that someone has attained the path of insight,*
> *Even though he has yet to realize the complete qualities?*
> *The early morning sun can neither melt frozen water*
> *Nor heat the ground and stones at once.*
> *Yet, who can deny the existence of the sun?[3]*

Perceiver and Perceived Are Interdependent

The second stage of the yoga of one flavor dawns when we fully eliminate the notion that the perceiver and the perceived are independent of each other. This dualistic fixation on the perceiver and the perceived is the cause of much of our distress, confusion, and ignorance. Buttressed by this added insight, we will experience fewer lapses and fewer obstacles in everyday life. We may still not be beyond occasionally yielding to distraction, but will have little trouble bringing our mind back as we have the ability to directly perceive things in a state of unity, rather than in terms of the duality of subject and object. As such, the yoga of one flavor marks the realization that because everything that exists within the realm of samsara and nirvana has its origin in emptiness, it exists in a state of equanimity. Now that the material world and the mind are not experienced as totally distinct but are seen as having the same nature, we are able to understand the real significance of emptiness. Je Shang comments:

> *When the one flavor stage dawns,*
> *One will cognize the characteristics of mind;*
> *One will realize that the diverse things of saṃsāra and nirvāṇa*
> *Arise from the mind's nondiscriminatory dharmakāya.*
> *Appearance and absence of appearance,*
> *Stability and absence of stability,*
> *Emptiness and absence of emptiness,*
> *Clarity and absence of clarity*
> *Are all of one flavor in the luminous dharmakāya.[4]*

Nondual Wisdom

When we attain this third stage of the yoga of one flavor, we acquire nondual wisdom and begin to perceive the world as magicians perceive their own creations. Even with this attainment of nondual wisdom, there are still very subtle obstacles that need to be overcome, such as becoming distracted in everyday life. The essence of this yoga, however, is viewing things to be in a state of equanimity. We do not regard certain qualities as worthy of cultivation and others as requiring abandonment but appreciate the complementary nature of that which appears to be in total opposition. At this level, the importance of the phenomenal world—which was not emphasized enough in the yoga of nonconceptuality—is brought back into focus.

The fundamental difference between the yoga of nonconceptuality and the yoga of one flavor is that in the former we had not yet developed the ability to regard whatever arises in the mind as complementary to our meditation and spiritual growth. There was also a subtle fixation on the concept of emptiness. As a result of insight into nonduality, the yoga of one flavor is sometimes referred to as the path of effortlessness. Nonetheless, if we compare this to the final yoga of nonmeditation, a subtle element of effort is still involved in one flavor. The only real obstacle to be aware of here is feeling meditation and nonmeditation to be the same and consequently believing that there is no longer a need for formal meditation practice. It is crucial to persist with the practice of meditation at this point. Nonetheless, at the level of the yoga of one flavor, we have developed the ability to use the phenomenal world itself (including our emotional conflicts and so forth) as manure for the cultivation of wisdom. In this way, whatever we perceive about the phenomenal world becomes an extension of our meditation, which will come as a welcome relief. As the great Indian mahasiddha Savaripa claimed:

> *A realized mind does not conceive the duality of meditation and*
> > *meditator;*
> *Just as space does not conceive space,*
> *So emptiness does not meditate on emptiness.*
> *Just as water and milk blend naturally,*
> *So nondual awareness and diverse cognitions blend harmoniously*
> *Into the one flavor of the unceasing stream of bliss.*[5]

NONMEDITATION

The yoga of nonmeditation is characterized by a sense of well-being irrespective of what we are experiencing. Even when we are not practicing meditation, we remain continuously in a meditative state. There is no need to apply mindfulness or concern ourselves with distractions of any kind, because whatever happens to us internally or externally, we are in a continuous state of meditation.

At this level there is also a shift in the experience of luminosity. There are two types of luminosity of the mind: a temporal type and an innate type. The temporal type of luminosity can be cultivated over time through meditation practice and is termed son luminosity. The innate type of luminosity is identified as mother luminosity. As we give rise to the different levels of the yogas, these two types of luminosity begin to merge until they become indivisible, just like the ocean and its waves. It is the merging of these two types of luminosity that brings about the actualization of the authentic aspect of Buddha's being.

Those who have attained the yoga of nonmeditation should be understood as unique and superior to ordinary human beings. Whatever they do or think is always beneficial for both themselves and others. If they are alone, they do not suffer from loneliness, and if they are in company, their very presence brings joy and peace to others. Such people can, if they wish, shed all inhibitions, because they are no longer bound by any conventional conceptual categories. They are completely confident about expressing themselves in a sincere manner and are unafraid of others' judgments. Despite the elevated state this yoga represents, it can still be divided into three discernible stages.

Being in a Meditative State Regardless of Circumstances

Initially we develop the ability to be in a meditative state regardless of our circumstances or states of mind. Obstacles in the form of conflicting emotions or everyday life situations cease to have any impact. There is no longer the need for deliberate mindfulness, because even the subtlest conflicting emotions that may have been lurking in our unconscious have become purified. That unconscious has now been fully transformed into primordial wisdom. At this point, nothing is hidden; there is not even an element of opacity. The mind has become completely translucent. Again, Je Shang eloquently comments:

> When the nonmeditation stage of yoga dawns,
> The essence of awareness detaches itself
> From any inbred supports.
> The yogin will find nothing to meditate on,
> Because the unreality of the meditator has been exposed.
> It is proclaimed that the potential of enlightenment
> Is contained in every mind.
> Adorned with the three Aspects of Buddha's Being
> And the five modes of wisdom,
> One will discover this by oneself.[6]

Spontaneously Establishing the Indivisibility of Samsara and Nirvana in Emptiness

The second stage of this yoga is attained through establishing oneself in the indivisible state of samsara and nirvana, which is spontaneously established in emptiness. Whether one is awake or asleep, one's mind is impervious to defilement, no matter what one's actions. The meditative state is maintained even during sleep. Not only is it impossible to leave negative karmic imprints at this level of spiritual fulfillment; one does not leave any positive karmic imprints either, because every action one carries out from this point forward will be completely unsullied.

Transforming Ordinary Consciousness into Wisdom Consciousness

The third stage of the yoga of nonmeditation is attained when ordinary empirical consciousness is fully transformed into wisdom consciousness. When this state is attained, the full-fledged wisdom consciousness and emptiness have become totally integrated and actualized. Upon attainment of this last stage of nonmeditation, one has become a fully enlightened one, a buddha. There are no remaining conflicting emotions to be purified, no practices to be pursued, and no techniques to be applied. One's state of being at this point is completely unadulterated, unsullied, authentic, and uncontrived. One has successfully developed the ability to benefit oneself through the actualization of the authentic state of Buddha's being, the dharmakaya, and the ability to benefit others through the actualization of the physical aspect of Buddha's being, the nirmanakaya. These two abilities enable a fully enlightened being to work for the benefit of all sentient beings indefinitely. Lama Shang, an enigmatic early Kagyu master expresses it this way:

> In the yoga of nonmeditation
> Meditation and postmeditation
> Are both aspects of the Dharmakaya.
> I don't have the mouth for a lot of talk.
> I don't have the mouth for swallowing dry tsampa.
> Do not wrap up your own head.

At this last stage of the yoga of nonmeditation, there is absolutely no difference between meditative and postmeditative states. The fully enlightened being is always in a state of meditation. The term *nonmeditation* simply means there is nothing to be meditated upon. At this point, the practices of tranquillity and insight meditation have culminated in full enlightenment due to the fusion between wisdom and the reality of things.

The actualization of the dharmakaya is the product of insight meditation because that practice enables us to cut through the conceptual web created by our erroneous ways of thinking. The actualization of the nirmanakaya is accomplished due to the mastery of tranquillity meditation. It is only through this full, authentic expression of the nirmanakaya that one attains the ability to work for the benefit of others.

In this way, fully enlightened beings, without wavering from their own true condition or authentic state, engage in various physical expressions oriented toward helping and benefiting others. There is no time limit to how long these buddha activities will continue, nor is there a fixed standard as to how an enlightened being should engage in these beneficial acts. Buddhas use a variety of techniques and manifestations depending upon the attitudes and dispositions of the sentient beings with whom they come into contact.

The Mahamudra tradition regards the realization of this optimal state of physical and mental potential to be possible within this very life. Once we have progressed through the four yogas of Mahamudra, we will realize buddhahood, the fruition of the spiritual path. Ultimate reality—which is Mahamudra—must be distinguished from the words and labels employed to describe it. As far as the true condition of things is concerned, nothing can be identified as this or that for the simple reason that reality is not an entity. This does not mean that traces of that reality cannot be intimated through the use of words and labels. The role of language is like a finger pointing to the moon. While the finger can never be the moon itself, without its guidance we may never know that the moon is in the sky at all. In a similar way, only through employing relative techniques can we realize enlightenment. Ultimately, it is the sharpening of our intellect that leads to acquiring intuitive wisdom.

Mahamudra itself is atemporal because it is uncaused, devoid of conceptualization, and all-pervasive. Because it is not an entity and is uncaused, it does not change and has no fluctuation. Since it is devoid of conceptualization, it is free of the evaluative concepts of good and bad. It is all-pervasive because it encompasses the realms of both samsara and nirvana. This reality is not brought into being by the buddhas, nor can it be tarnished by the delusions of sentient beings. It is devoid of all the characteristics of "thinghood." In brief, it is the existential condition of all things. On the objective side, Mahamudra is identical with emptiness. On the subjective side, Mahamudra is identical with unadulterated wisdom. This unity of emptiness and wisdom is what is referred to as the Great Seal.

If Mahamudra seems too remote from everyday experience and not something an ordinary person could attempt to understand, remind yourself that this unadulterated wisdom is only to be found within the stream of your own ordinary consciousness. It exists within the very consciousness that becomes agitated and confused and performs cognitive acts. To realize unsullied wisdom is therefore not to realize something other than the nature of your own consciousness, for there is nothing that can be attained that is extrinsic to your own mind. In other words, the realization of Mahamudra has nothing to do with acquiring a new kind of consciousness. The very mind that you possess is no different from the mind of an enlightened being. Whether you realize Mahamudra or do not is determined simply by how much you understand your own consciousness. When you are completely ignorant of the workings of your mind, that is known as samsara. Gaining insight into the nature of your mind is known as nirvana. The mind that is unconditioned and left in its own natural state is Mahamudra, because this is the same mind as the luminous bliss of an enlightened being.

11

ON THE
SPIRITUAL JOURNEY

I BEGAN THIS BOOK BY EMPHASIZING THE IMPORTANCE OF developing a correct view. If we lack a clear conception of our goal, we will just fumble along, dabbling in all kinds of contradictory pursuits and finding it difficult to follow through with anything. Only by developing a correct view can we steer ourselves in an authentic direction on the spiritual path. In order to embark on this path that leads to the luminous bliss of spiritual realization, we must gain some understanding of ultimate reality and our true condition.

In approaching the spiritual path, we need some understanding of what the journey involves. Many different spiritual experiences may arise in the course of our journey. To make sense of them, it is important for us to grasp where our experiences originate and have some appreciation for the inconsistencies in these subjective occurrences. Some experiences may appear to be enlightened when they are deluded, and others may appear to be deluded but actually portend enlightenment.

An important method for developing our discernment is to fathom the spiritual path in terms of deluded mind and enlightened mind. We need to understand deluded states of mind as something we need to overcome and enlightened states of mind as something we need to cultivate. Only then can we confidently steer a course through the myriad subjective revelations that can and do unfold on the spiritual journey.

At the same time, we should engage in our spiritual pursuits—and indeed in whatever we do—with a sense of caring, love, and compassion as well as a sense of joy. If not, our healthy emotions will atrophy, and we will be forever trapped in our conflicting emotions, which will filter down to influence our spiritual experience and practice. Therefore, in spiritual practice, love, compassion, and joy have to be experienced in an unperturbed way through equanimity.

In the Mahamudra tradition, the notion of self-liberation is paramount. Through self-liberating our conflicting emotions and discursive thoughts by allowing them to simply arise and dissipate without any grasping or fixation, we transcend any spiritual requirement to renounce, purify, or transform them. This is the unique skillful means of path Mahamudra that inexorably leads to spiritual realization.

Thus the journey we take in Mahamudra is one that fundamentally involves returning to our true home, our original dwelling place. We can see, then, that ground Mahamudra and fruition Mahamudra are identical, because when fruition Mahamudra is realized, so too is ground Mahamudra; and when ground Mahamudra is realized, it is instantly apparent that this *is* fruition Mahamudra. In other words, to realize our authentic state of being is to realize the fruition of the Great Seal of all-encompassing reality.

Although the spiritual journey is a homecoming of sorts, it is still indispensable to proceed on the path in the first place. We cannot say that since our authentic state is the enlightened mind of luminous bliss, we need not embark on any kind of spiritual journey. We cannot afford to think we are already there. Although our original state of being is the same as that of the buddhas, we are not buddhas yet. We are deluded sentient beings, and our minds are layered with defilements and obscurations. In fact, due to the density of our obscurations, we are not even in a condition to catch the occasional glimpse of our original condition. There should be no doubt that we categorically need to engage in some kind of spiritual practice, one that is genuine and effective and can be systematically utilized to illuminate the darkness of our ignorance.

The Mahamudra meditation of tranquillity and insight meditation is one of the most effective ways to achieve this end. If we follow this path with genuine interest and invest the necessary time and energy, we will quickly feel the effects of these practices. To really devote ourselves to this practice, it is essential to fully integrate ground, path, and fruition Mahamudra. This way, we will eventually *be* Mahamudra. The luminous bliss of Mahamudra is what represents our own true nature. We could even say that in our own true nature we *are* Mahamudra.

Appendix

PRECIOUS SUN

Padma Karpo's Spiritual Advice

This human body that you possess is not owned by you.
It is borrowed, and you will not possess it for an indefinite period.
While you have the opportunity to do something worthwhile,
Don't you think you should make use of it?
Please turn your mind within and reflect on this.

Wholesome thoughts are only intermittent
Like illuminations caused by lightning in the dark of a stormy
    night.
On the rare occasions that you momentarily come to your
    senses,
Don't you think you should put some effort into doing something
    about it?
Please turn your mind within and reflect on this.

All conditioned things are impermanent and subject to change.
If you take a closer look at conditioned phenomena,
You will find that they have no enduring essence.
Don't you think it is mistaken to be obsessed with notions of
    acquisition?
Please turn your mind within and reflect on this.

The appearance of the phenomenal world is similar to your dream
    experiences:
When unexamined it may give some temporary pleasure to your
    deluded mind;
If you analyze it, you will see that there is no substance to be found
    in it.
Don't you think you should use critical analysis to discover this?
Please turn your mind within and reflect on this.

If you look closely at your normal activities,
You will discover that they do not deserve the trust you accord
    them.
You are not the agent in power but the victim of your projections.
Don't you think you should look closely into that?
Please turn your mind within and reflect on this.

When you are wealthy, friends and relatives gather around you like
    clouds,
But when you become poor, they scatter in all directions.
They are really such superficial company.
Don't you think you should look into yourself and ask why you need
    them?
Please turn your mind within and reflect on this.

You may have built a mansion and be living in luxury,
But still you are not free from suffering.
The temporary pleasures you may get can never be a substitute for
    lasting happiness.
Don't you think you should look at your attachment and do
    something about it?
Please turn your mind within and reflect on this.

When you are a child, you while away your time in mindless
    activities;
As an adult, you while away your time in activities on a larger
    scale.
You spend all your time trapped by conflicts through attraction and
    aversion.

Don't you think you should look at your emotions and do something
   about them?
Please turn your mind within and reflect on this.

When old age creeps up on you unawares, taking you by surprise like
   a thief,
Your mental faculties and physical strength can only deteriorate.
The suffering of old age is only accentuated if there is no spiritual
   focus.
Shouldn't you think about your life?
Please turn your mind within and reflect on this.

When you depart from this world, you do not know your destination,
And the fear and terror of the bardo are great;
When you are lying on your deathbed, you will have a mass of regrets.
Shouldn't you look back before it is too late?
Please turn your mind within and reflect on this.

This life is so fragile that you can never be certain that you will not
   die before dusk:
Any kind of adverse circumstance can terminate your life.
There is no cause to be confident in your perpetuity.
Shouldn't you be more cautious about the outcome of your projects?
Please turn your mind within and reflect on this.

Though you are known as a living being in the morning,
You can instantly become a corpse in the afternoon.
Tomorrow only your name will remain.
Shouldn't you have fewer expectations about life?
Please turn your mind within and reflect on this.

When the time of death approaches, you will leave your relatives and
   friends behind,
And you cannot take with you the wealth you have accumulated.
You have to depart from this world alone.
Don't you imagine that you will be screaming in terror if you have
   no spiritual focus?
Please turn your mind within and reflect on this.

Each moment that passes means you are that much closer to death.
Your life force is like a dewdrop on the grass and can vanish at any
     time.
The constancy of the breath is like a weak rope.
Shouldn't you realize that this tenuous connection can be lost at any
     time?
Please turn your mind within and reflect on this.

In your unreflective moments, you mistake what is trivial for what is
     significant.
Having obtained a human body as precious as a priceless jewel,
You discard it as if it were worthless.
Isn't this like casting your most cherished things to the wind?
Please turn your mind within and reflect on this.

You obtained this body through merit, not through accident.
If you use it wisely, it will take you to your real destination.
Not doing that is like wasting a valuable vehicle.
Shouldn't you do something about this?
Please turn your mind within and reflect on this.

When you hear flattery from others, your mood lifts;
You spend days and nights engaging in or listening to meaningless
     gossip.
There is an appropriate cause and effect of every action.
Shouldn't you become more conscious about what you do?
Please turn your mind within and reflect on this.

When you are alone, you think about what entertainment you can get;
When you are with others, you hope that they will entertain you or
     you them.
This will cause some to suffer and others to have their already inflated
     ego expand.
Isn't it a mistake to do that?
Please turn your mind within and reflect on this.

As a human being you want to compete with those who are superior
     to you
And tread upon those weaker than you.

Those you think are your equal leave you stricken with envy.
Isn't interacting like this the source of all your misery?
Please turn your mind within and reflect on this.

You want to have a good life, but you always do the wrong thing to
    get it
And look for the causes of suffering to create a contented life.
You have become a slave to your impulses.
Isn't this an indication that your mind has not been tamed?
Please turn your mind within and reflect on this.

Everything that your superiors do is seen as a series of mistakes or
    transgressions,
While you abuse your inferiors instead of protecting them.
You verbally ridicule those you consider your equals.
Can't you see that your body, speech, and mind are abusive?
Please turn your mind within and reflect on this.

When you work with others and do the job well, you want to take
    the credit;
When the work is not done well and people complain, you blame
    others.
You get completely lost in secretive tactics.
Isn't your approach underhanded?
Please turn your mind within and reflect on this.

Even when you spend time listening, contemplating, and meditating
    on the teachings
You only do it to prop yourself up in the eyes of others.
When you behave with morality, it is only to obtain other people's
    respect.
Don't you think it would be better to do something that will benefit
    yourself?
Please turn your mind within and reflect on this.

When engaged in study and learning, you get overwhelmed by
    laziness;
When you make a slight effort to meditate, your mind is overcome by
    distractions.

All of a sudden you want to become a spiritual teacher to others.
Aren't your efforts overrated?
Please turn your mind within and reflect on this.

Not realizing what a sham you have become, others shower you with
    humility and respect,
While inside yourself you have become a mad person.
You are insane with the power and riches that you have gathered.
Isn't this kind of power the product of self-deception and lies?
Please turn your mind within and reflect on this.

If you behave in this fashion and do not practice the Dharma
    properly
Both you and your teacher will end up like a bunch of hooligans
    because of your negative karma.
Material wealth accumulated through spiritual means is not easy to
    digest.
Won't you have to pay for it sooner or later?
Please turn your mind within and reflect on this.

In this day and age it is very important for you to come to some
    resolve;
You have to put your trust in others, whether they are of high or low
    status.
Just pursuing your own personal security will never be enough.
Isn't failing to bring about fulfillment in your life a loss?
Please turn your mind within and reflect on this.

Life is short, but there is so much to learn;
I advise you to extract the essential points,
Then retire alone to meditate on them.
Shouldn't you do something like this?
Please turn your mind within and reflect.

In most countries the forces of nonspirituality prevail;
You must pursue your spiritual practice through your own initiative.
Do not pay attention to what others say, but continue with your
    practice.

If you have practiced well during your life, you will live well;
When the time to die comes, you will die well and have no regrets.

Everything you experience about the world is contingent upon your
    mind.
If you employ mindfulness consistently to tame your mind,
Then even if the whole world turns against you
It will not be able to harm
So much as the tip of a hair upon your body.

When you analyze samsara and nirvana with the use of discriminating
    wisdom,
You will find that there is nothing to be discovered.
This is known as the Great Insight.
This is not something you realize because somebody else has said it.
You realize it because it is the natural condition of your being.

In the heart of the land of the Snowy Mountains, I, Padma Karpo, have
written this text to remind myself and to encourage others to continue
with their practice. I pray that the teachings of the Buddha will flourish for a very long time.

Notes

_____

1. WHAT IS MAHAMUDRA?

1. From Herbert V. Guenther, trans., *The Life and Teaching of Naropa* (Boston: Shambhala Publications, 1963), 234–35.

2. Quoted in *Buddhist Texts through the Ages*, translated and edited by Edward Conze, I. B. Horner, David Snellgrove, and Arthur Waley (Boston: Shambhala Publications, 1990), 238.

3. Quoted in Takpo Tashi Namgyal, *Mahamudra: The Quintessence of Mind and Meditation*, translated by Lobsang P. Lhalungpa (Boston: Shambhala Publications, 1986), 317.

4. See *Buddhist Masters of Enchantment: The Lives and Legends of the Mahasiddhas* by *Abhayadatta*, trans. Keith Dowman (Rochester, Vt.: Inner Traditions International, 1998); *Masters of Mahamudra: Songs and Histories of the Eighty-Four Buddhist Siddha*, by Keith Dowman (Albany, N.Y., SUNY Press, 1985); *Krsnacarya*, by David Templeman (Dharamsala: Library of Tibetan Works and Archives, 1989); *The Seven Instruction Lineages of Jo Nang Taranatha*, by David Templeman (Dharamsala: Library of Tibetan Works and Archives, 1983); *Buddha's Lions: Abhayadatta's Lives of the Eighty-Four Siddhas*, trans. James B. Robinson (Berkeley, Calif.: Dharma Publishing, 1983).

5. Jonang Taranatha, *History of Buddhism in India*, translated by Alaka Chottapadhyaya and Lama Chimpa (Delhi: Motilal Banarsidass, 1980).

6. Namgyal, *Mahamudra*, 101.

7. Quoted in David Jackson, *Enlightenment by a Single Means* (Vienna: Austrian Academy of Science, 1994), 14.

8. From *The Rain of Wisdom: The Essence of the Ocean of True Meaning*, translated by Chögyam Trungpa and the Nalanda Translation Committee (Boston: Shambhala Publications, 1988), 83.
9. Quoted in Jamgön Kongtrül, *Cloudless Sky: The Mahamudra Path of the Tibetan Buddhist Kagyu School* (Boston: Shambhala Publications, 1992), 7.
10. Namgyal, *Mahamudra*, 193.

2. THE IMPORTANCE OF CORRECT VIEW

1. In Mahayana texts, *prajna* is generally translated as "wisdom," as in "compassion (*karuna*) and wisdom (*prajna*)." However, later textual sources distinguish between two types of wisdom, namely prajna and *jnana*. Prajna is a mediated understanding of things ultimate, and jnana is a direct realization of ultimate reality, such as emptiness.
2. Kongtrül, *Cloudless Sky*, 5.
3. *Tripitaka* means "three baskets," all of which represent different types of Buddhist teachings. The *sutra-pitaka* represents the Buddha's discourses, the *abhidharma-pitaka* contains Buddhist psychology and metaphysics, and the *vinaya-pitaka* consists of the Buddha's instructions on monastic rules and regulations. There are many different versions of the Buddhist canon—there is the Pali version, the Sanskrit version, the Chinese version, the Tibetan version, the Japanese version, and so on. There is actually a fair amount of consistency among these versions, which could be said to collectively constitute the Buddhist canon. The Kangyur is the Tibetan version of the Buddhist Tripitaka.

3. THE SPIRITUAL PATH

1. This path is called *tharlam* in Tibetan, meaning "path of liberation."
2. Ira Progoff, trans., *The Cloud of Unknowing* (New York: Delta, 1989).
3. Garma C. C. Chang, trans., *The Hundred Thousand Songs of Milarepa* (Boston: Shambhala Publications, 1989), 74–75.
4. Saint John of the Cross, *Dark Night of the Soul*, translated by Mirabai Starr (New York: Riverhead Books, 2002).
5. Chang, *Songs of Milarepa*, 449–50.

5. THE FOUR PRELIMINARIES

1. From Longchenpa's autocommentary to his root text *Kindly Bent to Ease Us*.

6. THE FOUR IMMEASURABLES

1. It is worth reiterating that Buddhism is a nontheistic religion rather than an atheistic one, for while it may refute different arguments that attempt to prove the existence of God, Buddhism neither denies nor affirms the existence of God in its own doctrines. Thus the word *god* or *godlike* does not have the same theological meaning in Buddhist literature as it has in Western discourse.

2. Daniel Goleman, *Emotional Intelligence: Why It Can Matter More Than IQ* (New York: Bantam, 1997).

3. Peter Harvey, *The Selfless Mind: Personality, Consciousness and Nirvana in Early Buddhism* (London: Curzon Press, 1995).

7. BUDDHA-NATURE

1. His Holiness the Dalai Lama, *Self and Buddha-Nature.*

2. Kongtrül, *Cloudless Sky,* 23.

3. Chokyi Nyima Rinpoche, *Song of Karmapa: The Aspiration of the Mahamudra of True Meaning by Lord Rangjung Dorje,* translated by Erik Pema Kunsang (Boudhanath: Rangjung Yeshe Publications, 1992), 70.

8. TRANQUILLITY MEDITATION

1. Namgyal, *Mahamudra,* 174.

2. Ibid.

9. INSIGHT MEDITATION

1. Quoted in Namgyal, *Mahamudra,* 245.

2. Ibid., 317.

3. Quoted in Namgyal, *Mahamudra,* 340.

4. Ibid., 195.

5. Stanley Cavell, "Conditions Handsome and Unhandsome: The Constitution of Emersonian Perfectionism," in *Carcus Lectures,* vol. 19 (1988) (Chicago: University of Chicago Press, 1991).

10. THE FOUR YOGAS OF MAHAMUDRA

1. Quoted in Namgyal, *Mahamudra,* 359.

2. Ibid., 361.

3. Ibid., 407.

4. Ibid., 360.

5. Ibid., 394.

6. Ibid., 361.

Glossary

AFFLICTED CONSCIOUSNESS (*mana-vijnana*) The seventh of the eight levels of consciousness, this level retains the sense of a self or "I" and generates the conflicting emotions by reacting to the empirical world with excessive desire, aversion, and indifference. It gives rise to conceptual categories and likes and dislikes, and it discriminates between things as desirable and undesirable on the basis of previous images and judgments stored in the basic consciousness. It also leaves imprints within the basic consciousness.

ARYADEVA (ca. third century) The principal disciple of Nagarjuna, credited with founding the Madhyamaka school of Mahayana Buddhism. His works are mainly commentaries on the writings of Nagarjuna.

ASANGA (ca. fourth century) One of the founders of the Yogachara school and brother of Vasubandhu. According to tradition, he received his teaching directly from the future Buddha Maitreya.

AWARENESS (*samahita*) Literally, "aware-ing," or the process of being aware. Awareness is something that manifests spontaneously because it is a natural quality of mind; however, because of our ignorance and delusions, we have to learn to retrieve this through the practice of mindfulness.

BASIC CONSCIOUSNESS (*alaya-vijnana*) The eighth of the eight levels of consciousness. This is the neutral, unconscious, and impartial ground that serves as the repository of karmic traces and dispositions. The transformation of this basic consciousness into wisdom consciousness is what constitutes enlightenment.

BLISS (*sukha*) The experience that arises when the mind is stable and can maintain awareness with openness and receptivity.

BODHICHITTA, Skt.   See enlightened heart.

BODHISATTVA, Skt.   Literally, "awakened being," one who is traversing the spiritual path via the cultivation of wisdom and compassion (as encapsulated in the six transcendental actions and bodhichitta) and dedicating his or her actions to the welfare of other beings.

BUDDHA-NATURE (*tathagatagarbha*)   Our in-dwelling spiritual nature that is defined as the middle way between the notion of an empirical self and a psychic substance such as a soul. Our buddha-nature is not something that we have as part of our psychological makeup; it is something that we are in our very being, our innate primordial nature. In the Mahamudra tradition, this is seen not as the cause of enlightenment but as enlightenment itself.

CHANDRAKIRTI (ca. 600–650)   Founder of the Prasangika-Madhyamaka school, whose main impetus was to reestablish the teachings of Nagarjuna.

COMPASSION (*karuna*)   The wish that other beings may be free of suffering and the cause of suffering. This is an active form of responding to the suffering of others with the intention to alleviate that suffering without becoming immersed in their despair. Compassion is one of the principal antidotes to self-obsession in Mahayana Buddhism.

CONCEPTUAL PROLIFERATION (*prapanca*)   The proliferation of discursive thoughts, characterized by an inability to relinquish a thought without creating a commentary on it.

CONFLICTING EMOTIONS (*klesha*)   The emotional properties that dull the mind and cause one to misapprehend the true nature of existence. They form the basis of all unwholesome actions and thus bind us to samsaric existence. The principal defiling emotions are excessive anger, overwhelming desire, inflated pride, jealousy, and ignorance.

CORRECT VIEW (*drsti*)   A view that leads one to liberation. Correct views that lead to a genuine and authentic understanding of our human condition lead to transcendental knowledge.

DELUDED MIND (Tib. *namshe*)   Our ordinary samsaric state of mind from moment to moment, which is a state of confusion driven by conflicting emotions.

DEPENDENT ORIGINATION (*pratityasamutpada*)   The fact that things have no inherently existing, self-sufficient being of their own and simply come into existence due to causes and conditions.

DHARMA, Skt.   The core principle of Buddhism, usually referring to the ultimate truth underlying existence. Also used to describe the Buddha's teachings.

DISCURSIVE THOUGHTS (*vikalpa*)   The tendency to dwell on the past, anticipate the future, and discriminate between the types of thoughts and emotions that we experience based on the mental categories of good and bad. This tendency is based upon the fixation of binary concepts at a fundamental level of thought.

DOHA, Skt.   A spontaneous form of spiritual song made popular by the mahasiddhas of northern India in the eighth to twelfth centuries and made famous in Tibet by the ascetic yogi Milarepa.

DUSUM KHYENPA (1110–1193) The first Karmapa, originator of the Karma Kagyu tradition and one of the key disciples of Gampopa.

EMPIRICAL CONSCIOUSNESS (*vijnana*) The sixth of the eight levels of consciousness, which cognizes and classifies the objects perceived through the five sense consciousnesses.

EMPTINESS (*shunyata*) The central notion of Mahayana Buddhism, the understanding that both individuals and phenomena are devoid of any independent, lasting substance and are therefore only mere appearances. This concept should not be taken to mean that nothing exists at all, but rather that everything exists in the same manner as a dream, because it has no inherent existence. Emptiness carries and permeates all phenomena and makes them possible.

ENLIGHTENED HEART (*bodhichitta*) There are two aspects to enlightened heart: ultimate and relative. Ultimate enlightened heart refers to the nature of the mind itself, and relative enlightened heart refers to the cultivation and generation of compassion.

ENLIGHTENMENT (*bodhi*) Equated with the annihilation of the ego and awakening to the nature of how things really are; the nowness of emptiness. Without this experience there would be no Buddhism.

EQUANIMITY (*upeksha*) A spacious state of mind that is free from attraction, aversion, and indifference.

ESSENTIAL INSTRUCTIONS (*upadesha*) The inner expression of the teachings by enlightened masters that are practical instructions on how to cultivate ourselves on the spiritual path, especially in relation to meditation practices.

FOUR IMMEASURABLES (*brahmaviharas*) Literally, "abodes of Brahma," they are immeasurable love, immeasurable compassion, immeasurable joy, and immeasurable equanimity. The four immeasurables constitute a meditation practice of arousing positive states of mind to generate compassion and wisdom and radiate them in all directions.

FOUR YOGAS OF MAHAMUDRA The stages of realization within fruition Mahamudra, each representing the fruition of a certain level of meditation practice. They are the yoga of one-pointedness, the yoga of nonconceptuality, the yoga of one flavor, and the yoga of nonmeditation.

FRUITION MAHAMUDRA The culmination of the spiritual path of the four yogas in the mystical teachings of Mahamudra, whereby the ground Mahamudra spontaneously manifests and is realized as the nature of the mind.

GAMPOPA (1079–1153) One of the founding fathers of the Kagyu school, Gampopa began his spiritual career as a Kadampa monk before meeting Milarepa and receiving the transmission of the Mahamudra teachings from him. After the death of Milarepa, Gampopa founded the Kagyu monastic tradition.

GELUG One of the four great schools of Tibetan Buddhism, known as the reform tradition and emphasizing intellectual study and analysis.

GNOSIS/WISDOM (*jnana*) The innate primordial awareness that naturally manifests as the result of the cultivation of transcendental knowledge.

GROUND MAHAMUDRA The ground is pure from the beginning, is atemporal, and transcends all dualistic concepts of being and nonbeing, samsara and nirvana, permanence and impermanence. This term is used interchangeably with ground of being.

GROUND OF BEING (*alaya*) Synonymous with ground Mahamudra, buddha-nature, and the nature of the mind. It is the innate primordial ground that has been pure right from the beginning and gives rise to the actual possibility of enlightenment. As such, it is more fundamental to our nature than our basic consciousness.

HINAYANA, Skt. Literally, "Small Vehicle," a pejorative term that was employed by Mahayana adherents to refer to the early Buddhist schools of India and continues to be used by Tibetan scholastics. It was originally intended for the doctrines of a now defunct sect of early Buddhism. The criticisms that are implied by this designation do not apply to the Theravada school, the only surviving tradition of early Buddhism.

IGNORANCE (*avidya*) A lack of awareness whereby we go about our business in a mindless and inattentive fashion without being fully conscious of what we are doing, thinking, and feeling.

IMPERMANENCE (*anitya*) The fundamental property of every conditioned thing is its transitory nature. This fact is the basis of life because existence would not be possible otherwise.

INSIGHT MEDITATION (*vipashyana*) The way to cultivate wisdom consciousness by gaining genuine insight into how our mind substantializes everything by attributing fictitious characteristics and attributes. The techniques of insight meditation reveal how all of our experiences are based upon distorted ways of thinking that misperceive and mistrust everything.

INTERESTED HUMILITY (Tib. *mögu*) Often translated as "devotion" in Western Buddhist texts, interested humility is what makes us a proper vessel for the Dharma. It comes from recognizing the impoverishment of a life without spiritual practice and from an eagerness to continue learning without becoming complacent or self-important.

KAGYU SCHOOL Literally, "Oral Transmission Lineage," one of the four principal schools of Tibetan Buddhism (along with the Nyingma, Sakya, and Gelug), the central teaching of which is Mahamudra. These teachings were transmitted from the Indian mahasiddhas Tilopa and Naropa to the Tibetan mahasiddha Marpa, who taught them to Milarepa, who taught them to Gampopa, the founder of the monastic tradition of the Kagyu.

KANGYUR, Tib. The Tibetan version of the Indian Buddhist canon (Tripitaka), containing both sutric and tantric teachings.

KARMA, Skt. Universal law of cause and effect whereby our own actions determine our predispositions, personal tendencies, habitual patterns, and to a large extent the kinds of experiences we have in our lives. Unwholesome karma will plunge us into demeaning states of existence, and wholesome karma can transport us to elevated states of existence. These karmic imprints reside in our basic consciousness.

KARMAPA, Skt. and Tib. Roughly translated as "Man of Buddha Activity." Said to be the embodiment of compassion, the Karmapa is the spiritual authority of the Karma Kagyu school. His is the oldest tulku lineage of Tibetan Buddhism. There have been seventeen incarnations of the Karmapa to date, beginning with Dusum Khyenpa.

LIBERATION (*moksha*) The removal of the ignorance caused by mental defilement and the consequent freedom from samsaric bondage.

LOVING-KINDNESS (Skt. *maitri*; Pali. *metta*) A sympathetic response to the existential condition of beings, defined as the wish for others to be happy. Loving-kindness constitutes a love that is pure and uncompromised by conflicting emotions and is regarded in Mahayana Buddhism as one of the principal antidotes to self-obsession.

LUMINOSITY (*prabhasvara*) The inherent clarity of the nature of the mind, or the cognizant aspect of empty consciousness, which is synonymous with gnosis/wisdom.

MADHYAMAKA, Skt. The Middle Way school of Mahayana Buddhism, founded by Nagarjuna and Aryadeva, emphasizing the doctrine of emptiness. The middle way describes the position taken by its adherents in relation to the existence or nonexistence of things. Madhyamaka philosophy uses elaborate reasoning to prove that things do not have any enduring essence.

MAHAMUDRA, Skt. Literally, "Great Seal" or "Great Symbol," meaning that the totality of existence is encompassed within the seal of ultimate reality or emptiness, which is not different from the nature of the mind itself. A special teaching transmitted mainly by the Kagyu school.

MAHASIDDHA Skt. Literally, "great saint," the designation given to the spiritual adepts of the eighth to twelfth century Indian tantric movement. Regarded as enlightened beings, they often manifested supernatural abilities as evidence of their yogic attainments.

MAHAYANA, Skt. Literally, "Great Vehicle," the altruistic movement of Buddhism that began around the first century CE and incorporates the ideal of the bodhisattva and a conception of enlightenment that transcends both samsara and nirvana.

MAITRIPA (1010–1087) An important figure in both Mahayana and Vajrayana Buddhism. Maitripa and Asanga's important work on buddha-nature, the *Uttaratantrashastra*, became widely followed in Tibet. He also transmitted the esoteric aspect of buddha-nature, embodied in the Mahamudra teachings. He was brought to his own enlightenment through Mahamudra under Savaripa and became an important guru of Marpa.

MARPA (ca. 1012–1097) Renowned yogi from southern Tibet, known as Marpa the Translator. Marpa was a student of the Indian mahasiddha Naropa and brought the Mahamudra teachings to Tibet. Teacher of Milarepa, he is known as one of the four founding fathers of the Kagyu school.

MEDITATION (*dhyana*) This term comprises a variety of methods, all of which are designed to bring one's consciousness to the state of enlightenment or liberation. A mind that is stable, does not easily become distracted, and can remain focused and concentrated is generally said to be a mind in meditation. The two principal types of Buddhist meditation are tranquillity and insight.

MEDITATIVE EXPERIENCE (*vetana*)   Meditative experiences are fickle and tainted by conceptualization; they fail to show the essential unity of the experiencer and experience. They may correspond to various levels of attainment but should not be treated as an indication of progress.

MEDITATIVE REALIZATION (*adhigama*)   Distinct from meditative experience, realization is stable and signifies the overcoming of dualistic concepts of subject and object, experiencer and experience.

MENTAL EVENTS (*caitta*)   The mind, or consciousness, gives rise to mental events that seize on the specific features of our experience. While these mental events are distinguished from mind, they actually occur at the same time as consciousness.

MILAREPA (ca. 1040–1123)   One of Tibet's most renowned spiritual masters and one of the four founding fathers of the Tibetan Kagyu tradition (along with Naropa, Marpa, and Gampopa). Famous for his spiritual songs and for the hardships that he endured at the hands of his relatives and his guru Marpa.

MIND (*chitta*)   An overarching term for the operations of consciousness, which gives rise to mental events.

MINDFULNESS (*smrti*)   The ability to remain in the present moment by preventing the mind from becoming distracted by remembering the past or anticipating the future.

NAGARJUNA (ca. 150–250)   One of the most important philosophers of Buddhism and the founder of the Madhyamaka school. He systematized and deepened the teachings presented in the Prajnaparamita (Perfection of Wisdom) sutras and gave the most comprehensive and methodical presentation of the concept of emptiness.

NAROPA (ca. 1016–1100)   Along with his teacher Tilopa, one of the best-known Indian mahasiddhas and an important holder of the transmission of the Mahamudra teachings. The teacher of Marpa, Naropa was one of the founding fathers of the Tibetan Kagyu school.

NATURE OF THE MIND (*chittata*)   A core concept of the Mahamudra tradition. The mind is said to be empty of essence and this emptiness pervades all of our mental events. The nature of the mind is the actuality of the ground of being, or buddha-nature, as well as the foundation of all our mental functionings and constructs. The Mahamudra tradition does not distinguish between the empirical mind and the nature of the mind during meditation but recognizes the nature of the mind within the nature of thoughts and emotions.

NIRVANA, Skt.   Characterized as the cessation of suffering, nirvana is the goal of spiritual practice in Buddhism. It signifies the departure from cyclic existence and freedom from karma.

NYINGMA   Literally, "School of the Ancients," one of the four principal schools of Buddhism, bringing together the oldest Buddhist traditions of Tibet.

ORDINARY MIND (Tib. *thamal gyi shepa*)   The Mahamudra designation for the mind, indicating that the nature of the mind is not transcendent or difficult to access and can be realized through understanding the mind in its ordinary manifestations.

PATH (*marga*)   The spiritual journey of change and transformation culminating in enlightenment.

PATH MAHAMUDRA   The process of eradicating the adventitious mental defilements as a means of realizing the innate ground Mahamudra.

RECHUNGPA (ca. 1083–1156)   One of Milarepa's two principal disciples, along with Gampopa, Rechungpa remained a yogi all his life. He traveled to India and brought back profound teachings that were absorbed into several Kagyu lineages. Rechungpa founded the Rechung Kagyu lineage.

SAHAJAYANA, Skt.   The mystical vehicle that describes the Mahamudra tradition.

SAKYA   One of the four main schools of Tibetan Buddhism.

SAMSARA, Skt.   The vicious cycle of transmigratory existence, which arises out of ignorance and is characterized by suffering.

SARAHA (eighth century)   One of the eighty-four Indian mahasiddhas and the earliest known exponent of the Mahamudra teachings that came to be preserved in the Kagyu lineage.

SELFLESSNESS/SOULLESSNESS (*anatman*)   The absence of any kind of immutable psychic substance that is unchanging and permanent. This term does not refute an individual self-identity of some kind but maintains that it is only an empirical self that is contingent on ever-changing psychophysical conditions.

SELF-LIBERATION (Tib. *rangdrol*)   A method unique to Mahamudra meditation. As nothing has any intrinsic nature—including our conflicting emotions and discursive thoughts—these defilements do not need to be deliberately eradicated, purified, or transformed. We simply allow them to self-liberate naturally and spontaneously by resting in our own natural state of mind without fixation.

SHAMATHA, Skt.   See tranquillity meditation.

SHANTIDEVA (CA. 695–743)   Author of the Bodhicharyavatara, an exposition of the bodhisattva's path to enlightenment, distinguished by poetic sensitivity and fervor.

SKILLFUL MEANS (*upaya*)   An expression of compassion which relates directly to the first five transcendental actions of Mahayana Buddhism. This term generally conveys the sense that enlightened beings teach the Dharma skillfully depending on the needs and capacities of sentient beings.

SUTRA, Skt.   The Hinayana and Mahayana texts in the Buddhist canon that are directly attributed to Shakyamuni Buddha.

TANTRA, Skt.   Literally, "continuity," a synonym for Vajrayana. This term refers to both the root texts of this vehicle and the systems of meditation they describe.

TATHAGATAGARBHA, Skt.   *Tathagata* means "thus come" or "thus gone," and *garbha* means "essence," thus signifying someone who has gone beyond suffering and arrived at innate wisdom. See also buddha-nature.

TENGYUR, Tib.   Compiled as a supplement to the teachings contained in the Kangyur, the translations in this collection consist of commentarial material from mostly Sanskrit sources. There are also treatises on logic, metaphysics, epistemology, composition, grammar, and literature.

TILOPA (ca. 988–1069) The first lineage holder of the Kagyu tradition and teacher of Naropa. His name derives from the fact that he made his living producing sesame oil.

TRANQUILLITY MEDITATION (*shamatha*) A basic meditation practice common to most schools of Buddhism, the aim of which is to tame and stabilize the mind in order to practice insight meditation.

TRANSCENDENTAL ACTION (*paramita*) Mahayana practices that actualize wisdom and compassion and symbolize going beyond our conventional notion of the self so that our actions and attitudes are performed in a non-egocentric manner.

TRANSCENDENTAL KNOWLEDGE (*prajna*) A central notion of Mahayana Buddhism that refers to the immediate experience of genuine, penetrating, intuitive insight that cannot be conveyed in intellectual terms. This is still a conceptual form of understanding, but it is the precondition for the dawning of wisdom consciousness.

ULTIMATE REALITY (*dharmata*) Synonymous with emptiness, ultimate reality can only be known through direct experience.

VAJRAYANA, Skt. Literally, "Indestructible Vehicle," a synonym for Tantra, the esoteric branch of Buddhism, which arose primarily in northern India during the middle of the first millennium.

VASUBANDHU (ca. 330–400) Outstanding scholar and cofounder of the Yogachara school with his brother Asanga. Originally an exponent of Hinayana doctrines, he was the author of the *Abhidharmakosha* before being converted to the Mahayana by Asanga.

VEHICLE (*yana*) See Hinayana, Mahayana, Vajrayana.

VEIL OF COGNITIVE DISTORTIONS (*jneya-varana*) Distorted ways of thinking that are primarily responsible for the development of our erroneous views.

VEIL OF CONFLICTING EMOTIONS (*klesha-varana*) The belief in me and mine, self and other, which results in the three poisons of attachment, aversion, and indifference.

VEILS (*avarana*) Defilements that obscure our ability to recognize things as they are and consequently keep us living in the illusion of samsara.

VIPASHYANA, Skt. See insight meditation.

WISDOM CONSCIOUSNESS (Tib. *yeshe*) An innate capacity of the mind that gives rise to the generation of genuine, penetrating insight and is realized upon the eradication of deluded consciousness.

YOGACHARA, Skt. Philosophical school of Mahayana Buddhism founded by Maitreyanatha, Asanga, and Vasubandhu. The name stems from the value its adherents placed on yoga, a general way of referring to meditation practice. The central notion of this school is that everything exists as a process of knowing, not as independent objects outside of conscious awareness.

Recommended Reading

BARTH, PETER, with THRANGU RINPOCHE. *Piercing the Autumn Sky: A Guide to Discovering the Natural Freedom of the Mind.* Petaluma, Calif.: Lame Turtle Press, 1993.

BOKAR RINPOCHE. *Opening the Door to Certainty.* San Francisco: ClearPoint Press, 1996.

Buddhist Texts through the Ages. Translated and edited by Edward Conze, I. B. Horner, David Snellgrove, and Arthur Waley. Boston: Shambhala Publications, 1990.

CAVELL, STANLEY. "Conditions Handsome and Unhandsome: The Constitution of Emersonian Perfectionism." *Carcus Lectures*, vol. 19 (1988). Chicago: University of Chicago Press, 1991.

CHANG, GARMA C. C., trans. *The Hundred Thousand Songs of Milarepa.* Boston: Shambhala Publications, 1989.

———. *The Six Yogas of Naropa and the Teachings of Mahamudra.* Ithaca, N.Y.: Snow Lion Publications, 1986.

CHETSANG RINPOCHE. *The Practice of Mahamudra.* Ithaca, N.Y.: Snow Lion Publications, 1999.

THE DALAI LAMA. *The Buddha Nature: Death and Eternal Soul in Buddhism.* Woodside, Calif.: Bluestar Communications, 1997.

DORJE, LAMA SHERAB. *Mahamudra Teachings of the Supreme Siddhas.* Ithaca, N.Y.: Snow Lion Publications, 1995.

DOR-JE, WANG-CH'UG, the ninth Karmapa. *Mahamudra: Eliminating the Darkness of Ignorance.* Translated by Alexander Berzin. Dharamsala: Library of Tibetan Works and Archives, 1978.

DOWMAN, KEITH, trans. *Buddhist Masters of Enchantment: The Lives and Legends of the Mahasiddhas by Abhayadatta*. Rochester, Vt.: Inner Traditions, 1998.

————. *Masters of Mahamudra: Songs and Histories of the Eighty-Four Buddhist Siddhas*. Albany: State University of New York Press, 1985.

GAMPOPA. *The Jewel Ornament of Liberation: The Wish-Fulfilling Gem of the Noble Teachings*. Translated by Khenpo Konchog Gyaltsen Rinpoche. Ithaca, N.Y.: Snow Lion Publications, 1998.

GETHIN, RUPERT. *The Foundations of Buddhism*. Oxford: Oxford University Press, 1998.

GOLEMAN, DANIEL. *Emotional Intelligence: Why It Can Matter More Than IQ*. New York: Bantam, 1997.

GUENTHER, HERBERT V. *Ecstatic Spontaneity: Saraha's Three Cycles of Doha*. Berkeley: Asian Humanities Press, 1993.

————. *The Jewel Ornament of Liberation by sGam.po.pa*. Boulder: Prajna Press, 1981.

————. *The Life and Teaching of Naropa*. Boston: Shambhala Publications, 1995.

GYALTSEN, KONCHOG. *The Garland of Mahamudra Practices*. Ithaca, N.Y.: Snow Lion Publications, 1986.

————. *The Great Kagyu Masters: The Golden Lineage Treasury*. Ithaca, N.Y.: Snow Lion Publications, 1986.

GYAMTSO, TSULTRIM. *Buddha Nature*. Ithaca, N.Y.: Snow Lion Publications, 2000.

GYATRUL RINPOCHE. *Naked Awareness: Practical Instructions on the Union of Mahamudra and Dzogchen*. Ithaca, N.Y.: Snow Lion, 2000.

HARVEY, PETER. *An Introduction to Buddhism: Teachings, History and Practices*. Cambridge, U.K.: Cambridge University Press, 1990.

————. *The Selfless Mind: Personality, Consciousness and Nirvana in Early Buddhism*. London: Curzon Press, 1995.

JACKSON, DAVID. *Enlightenment by a Single Means*. Wien: Der Osterreichischen Akademie Der Wissenschaften, 1994.

KING, SALLIE B. *Buddha Nature*. Albany: State University of New York Press, 1991.

KONGTRÜL, JAMGÖN. *Cloudless Sky: The Mahamudra Path of the Tibetan Buddhist Kagyu School*. Boston: Shambhala Publications, 1992.

————. *Timeless Rapture: Inspired Verses of the Shangpa Masters*. Translated by Ngawang Zangpo. Ithaca, N.Y.: Snow Lion, 2003.

KUNGA RINPOCHE and BRIAN CUTILLO, trans. *Drinking the Mountain Stream: Songs of Tibet's Most Beloved Saint, Milarepa*. Boston: Wisdom Publications, 1996.

KYABGON, TRALEG. *The Essence of Buddhism: An Introduction to Its Philosophy and Practice*. Boston: Shambhala Publications, 2001.

LHALUNGPA, LOBSANG P. *The Life of Milarepa*. New York: Dutton, 1977.

The Life of Marpa the Translator. Translated by the Nalanda Translation Committee. Boston: Shambhala Publications, 1986.

MAR-PA CHOS-BYI BLO-GROS. *The Life of Mahasiddha Tilopa*. Translated by Toricelli and Sangye T. Naga. Dharamsala: Library of Tibetan Works and Archives, 1995.

NAMGYAL, TAKPO TASHI. *Mahamudra: The Quintessence of Mind and Meditation*. Translated by Lobsang P. Lhalungpa. Boston: Shambhala Publications, 1986.

NORBU, PADMA KARPO NGAWANG. *The Practice of Co-Emergent Mahamudra*. Translated by Anzan Hoshin Sensei. Ottawa: Great Matters Publications, 1991.

PROGOFF, IRA, trans. *The Cloud of Unknowing*. Delta, 1989.

The Rain of Wisdom: The Essence of the Ocean of True Meaning. Translated by Chögyam Trungpa and the Nalanda Translation Committee. Boston: Shambhala Publications, 1980.

RIGGS, NICOLE. *Like an Illusion: Lives of Shangpa Kagyu Masters*. Fremont, Calif.: Dharma Cloud Publishers, 2002.

ROBINSON, JAMES B. *Buddha's Lions: Abhayadatta's Lives of the Eighty-four Siddhas*. Berkeley: Dharma Publishing, 1987.

RUEGG, DAVID SEYFORT. *Buddha-Nature, Mind and the Problem of Gradualism in a Comparative Perspective: On the Transmission and Reception of Buddhism in India and Tibet*. London: School of Oriental and African Studies, 1989.

SAINT JOHN OF THE CROSS. *Dark Night of the Soul*. Translated by Mirabai Starr. New York: Riverhead Books, 2002.

STEWART, JAMPA MACKENZIE. *The Life of Gampopa: The Incomparable Dharma Lord of Tibet*. Ithaca, N.Y.: Snow Lion Publications, 1995.

TAI SITU RINPOCHE. *Third Karmapa's Mahamudra Prayer*. Ithaca, N.Y.: Snow Lion Publications, 2002.

TAI SITUPA. *Tilopa: Some Glimpses of His Life*. Eskdalemuir, Scotland: Dzalendara Publications, 1998.

TEMPLEMAN, DAVID, trans. and ed. *Krsnacarya*. Dharamsala: Library of Tibetan Works and Archives, 1989.

―――. *The Seven Instruction Lineages of Jo Nang Taranatha*. Dharamsala: Library of Tibetan Works and Archives, 1983.

THRANGU RINPOCHE. *Rechungpa: A Biography of Milarepa's Disciple*. Boulder, Colo.: Namo Buddha Publications, 2002.

―――. *The Life of Tilopa and the Ganges Mahamudra*. Auckland: Zhyisil Chokyi Ghatsal, 2002.

―――. *The Spiritual Biography of Marpa the Translator*. Auckland: Zhyisil Chokyi Ghatsal, 2002.

―――. *The Uttara Tantra: A Treatise on Buddha Nature*. Translated by Ken and Katia Holmes. Delhi: Sri Satguru Publications, 1989.

WILLIAMS, PAUL, and ANTHONY TRIBE. *Buddhist Thought: A Complete Introduction to the Indian Tradition*. London: Routledge, 2000.

Traleg Kyabgon's Centers

TIBET

Thrangu Monastery
Xihangcun Village
Yushu County
Chinghai District
People's Republic of China

AUSTRALIA

E-Vam Institute
673 Lygon Street
North Carlton, Vic. 3054
Tel: (03) 9387 0422
Fax: (03) 9380 8296
E-mail: e_vam@smartchat.net.au
www.evaminstitute.org.au

UNITED STATES

E-Vam Institute
595 Route 217
Hudson, NY 12534
Tel: (518) 672-6333 or
(518) 204-7690
Fax: (212) 787-3128
E-mail: office@evam.org
www.evam.org

Index

About the Author

The ninth Traleg Kyabgon Rinpoche is president and spiritual director of Kagyu E-Vam Buddhist Institute in Melbourne and E-Vam Institute in Upstate New York.

Traleg Kyabgon Rinpoche, who is one of the highest ranking tulkus of the Kagyu lineage, was born in 1955 in Nangchen, eastern Tibet. He was enthroned as Supreme Abbot of Tashi Choling Monastery of Thrangu district at age two by His Holiness Gyalwa Karmapa.* Rinpoche had to flee his native land at the age of four and escaped with his party to Bhutan and from there to Rumtek, the headquarters of His Holiness the sixteenth Gyalwa Karmapa in Sikkim. Rinpoche was educated by His Holiness with the other young *tulku*s in exile until he was nine, when he went to a center near Darjeeling and studied under the guidance of His Eminence Thugsey Rinpoche and was taught exclusively by Khenpo Noryang and Khenpo Sodar for many years.

When Rinpoche was sixteen, His Holiness the Karmapa sent him to study at the Sanskrit University of Varanasi, where he had the opportunity

---

* A short history of both Thrangu Monastery and Traleg Rinpoche can be found in an official book released by the Chinese government, *The Tibetan Monasteries of Gansu and Qinghai Provinces (Gan-Qing Zangchuan fojiao siyuan)*, edited by Pu Wencheng (Xining: Qinghai Peoples' Publishing House, 1990), pp. 304–5.

to study with *khenpo*s and *geshe*s of all four schools of Tibetan Buddhism until he was nineteen. He was subsequently put in charge of the Zangdog Palre (the Glorious Copper-Colored Mountain) Monastery in east Bhutan with many of the old monks from his own Thrangu Monastery, including Khenpo Karthar, currently of Woodstock, New York. After Khenpo Karthar's departure, Rinpoche was placed under the private tutelage of Dregung Khenpo by His Holiness the Karmapa in order to continue his study of Sutra and Tantra. When Rinpoche was twenty-two he returned to Rumtek to be with His Holiness the Karmapa. Rinpoche also received many teachings from prominent Kagyu and Nyingma masters. In 1980, at twenty-five years of age, Rinpoche arrived in Australia and established the Kagyu E-Vam Buddhist Institute two years later. Rinpoche also served for five years as the spiritual head of Kamalashila Institute, one of the main Kagyu centers in Europe.

Traleg Rinpoche was recognized as the ninth incarnation of the Traleg line by His Holiness the sixteenth Gyalwa Karmapa and was accorded the title Kyabgon, a significant distinction retained by only a few lineage holders in the Tibetan tradition.

Rinpoche regularly gives lectures and seminars worldwide on Buddhism and related topics, and has become well known for his erudition, fluency in English, and background in Western psychology and comparative religion. He is especially respected for his skill in working with people of diverse interests, ages, and backgrounds. Rinpoche has both a strict traditional Buddhist education and a comprehensive Western education, holding a degree from La Trobe University; he is currently engaged in academic research for a doctoral dissertation.

Rinpoche inaugurated the annual Buddhist Summer School in 1984 and more recently the biannual Buddhism and Psychotherapy Conference. Both of these programs have developed into major national events in Australia and have hosted many well-known spiritual teachers, Western psychologists, and thinkers. Rinpoche's first book, *The Essence of Buddhism*, has been translated into a number of languages. Rinpoche also publishes a nonsectarian, contemporary, quarterly magazine called *Ordinary Mind: An Australian Buddhist Review*.